WE WILL WAIT

SARAH FISHMAN

WE WILL
WAIT

WIVES OF FRENCH

PRISONERS OF

WAR, 1940 – 1945

Yale University Press   New Haven and London

Designed by Jill Breitbarth.
Set in Sabon type by
Brevis Press, Bethany, Connecticut.
Printed in the United States of America by
BookCrafters, Inc., Chelsea, Michigan.

Library of Congress Cataloging-in-
Publication Data

Fishman, Sarah, 1957–
We will wait : wives of French prisoners of
war, 1940–1945 / Sarah Fishman.
p.   cm.
Includes bibliographical references (p.   ) and
index.
ISBN 0-300-04774-6
1. World War, 1939–1945—Women—
France. 2. Wives—France—History—20th
century. 3. Prisoners of war—France.
4. Prisoners of war—Germany. I. Title.
D810.W7F57   1991
944.081′6′082—dc20   91-4010
                                CIP

The paper in this book meets the guidelines
for permanence and durability of the
Committee on Production Guidelines for
Book Longevity of the Council on Library
Resources.

10 9 8 7 6 5 4 3 2 1

To my father
Erwin Fishman
and the memory
of my mother
Lois Lyman

CONTENTS

I am indebted to many people who generously shared their time, insights, and resources. Two people were so essential to my research that without them it could not have been done. The late Robert Paumier of the Fédération nationale des combattants prisonniers de guerre–Combattants d'Algérie, Tunisie, Maroc (FNCPG-CATM) encouraged me from the start, provided me with names for interviews and questionnaires, and invited me to many private functions of the FNCPG. The tremendous value of the professional suggestions and advice of Dominique Veillon, of the Institut d'histoire du temps présent, was more than equaled by her kindness and hospitality. To both of them I owe my deepest gratitude.

I should like to thank Pierre Doridam, who interviewed me for the FNCPG's monthly journal, *Le P.G.-C.A.T.M.* The interview elicited many letters from former prisoners and prisoners' wives.

I owe a tremendous debt to all the former prisoners' wives and prisoners of war who helped me. Robert and Andrée Aulas in Lyons, Josette Morisson in Le Havre, and Joseph and Madeleine Blaire in Bernaville spent days talking to me about the war years and furnished many valuable contacts, as well as generously opening their homes to me. Jean Vedrine, Jacqueline Deroy, Jeanne Bajeux and Georges Tamburini provided me with contacts for interviews, information about the war years, rare books, and valuable documents.

I should also like to thank the prisoners' wives who collected questionnaires for me: Anne-Marie Borelly, Jeannine Cassiède, Agnès Fargeix, Paulette Landré, Jeanne Lerme, Marcelle Merceron, Marie-Françoise Monoré, Gabrielle Villemagne. Madeleine Blaire, in addition to collecting questionnaires, taped four superb interviews for me. Finally, my thanks to all the former prisoners' wives I interviewed (whose names I have changed to protect their privacy). Every one of them received me graciously and had an important story to tell.

Thanks to Gracie Delépine and Thérèse Muller of the Bibliothèque de documentation internationale contemporaine for their help in locating two essential uncataloged dossiers, and Chantal de Tourtier-Bonazzi, chief archivist of the contemporary section at the Archives nationales, for her excellent advice on locating sources.

It has been a pleasure working with Charles Grench and Susan Laity of Yale University Press. Thanks also to Meighan Pritchard for her meticulous editing.

I have benefited enormously from the guidance of many scholars. My dissertation director, Patrice Higonnet, is largely responsible for whatever understanding I may have developed about French history. My intellectual debt to Stanley Hoffmann and Robert Paxton, who reconceptualized Vichy and opened up a new generation of scholarship, cannot be measured. John Sweets, Charles Maier, Molly Nolan, Roderick Kedward, Roger Austin, Bernard Sinsheimer, John Hart, Karl Ittmann, Jim Jones, Susan Kellogg, Steven Mintz, Robert C. Palmer, and Bailey Stone provided encouragement, support, and intellectual and practical advice. For their friendship, insight, and inspiration, thanks to Kathy Kete, Peter Baldwin, Jennifer Laurendeau, Paula Schwartz, Susan Pedersen, and Miranda Pollard. Claudine Frank kindly contributed her profound understanding of both French and English to the translations.

Generous financial assistance from the University of Houston, the Whiting Foundation, the Center for European Studies at Harvard University, the Krupp Foundation, the Alliance Française de New York, and the Fribourg Foundation made the research and writing of this book possible.

I would like this book to be my tribute to the memory of Robert Paumier, Agnès Fargeix, Eliane Clause, Joseph Blaire, and my mother, Lois Lyman.

I am grateful to everyone in my family, and most of all my husband, Andy Boyd, for unwavering love and support.

In April 1945, on the eve of Germany's defeat, a short story appeared in a journal written by and for the wives of the French prisoners of war in Germany. "The Soup Bowl on the Hearth" told the story of a peasant family during the Napoleonic Wars. The husband, a laborer and the father of three boys, was called to arms one day. His wife comforted him with the thought that perhaps there had been a mistake and he would come home that night. "I'll always keep your soup warm," she promised him. That evening before she served her boys, she filled a bowl of soup for her husband and put it on the hearth to keep it warm. Her husband did not return that night. Every night his wife filled his bowl and left it on the hearth, never doubting he would return. The Russian campaign ended, Napoleon was defeated and exiled, and still her husband did not return. Seven years had passed, during which time he fought in Russia, was taken prisoner in Poland, and then returned to France on foot. Fearful that his family had given up on him, that they might have sold the farm, that his children would not even know his name, that his wife, believing him dead, had married another man, he finally returned to his home and opened the door. Looking past his wife and three sons, he saw "amongst the ashes, the steaming bowl of soup that [had] awaited him for seven years."[1]

When the story appeared, France had been liberated for eight months, the war in Europe was drawing to an end, and hundreds of thousands of prisoners' wives still waited for their husbands' return. The Napoleonic soldier's wife taught them not to give up hope, to be ready at any moment for their husbands to return—to continue waiting for their husbands, even when many of them had already waited five years.

Many firsthand accounts and scholarly monographs describe the experience of being a prisoner of war. But what of the wives of these men? What does it mean to be a prisoner of war wife, to maintain the home alone, to wait for an uncertain return? In the case of France during World War II, the magnitude of the phenomenon of captivity deepens the significance of the experience. Never before had so many prisoners been captured in such a short period. Compared with the 563,000 French prisoners of war during all of World War I, in 1940 an estimated 1.58 million men were held captive in Germany. This figure represented about 4 percent of the French population—a vital 4 percent, as the geographical and occupational distribution of these men, most of them between twenty and forty years of age, matched closely that of the French work force as a whole. Of the prisoners, 57 percent were married and 39 percent had children. Captivity shaped the lives not only of these men but also of their wives and children. French captivity during World War II, more than a military experience, became a "great social phenomenon."[2]

Because the experience touched so many women in France during the war, I address in this book the broader issue of war and social change. When I began my research, I assumed that prisoner of war wives felt empowered by their new responsibilities within their families, by their control over the family's income and property. Prisoners' wives, liberated from their husbands' authority for as many as five years, would gain an independence and autonomy that would alter postwar family relations.

As my research progressed, I dropped those assumptions. What prisoners' wives had to say about the experience led me to a more subtle thesis. Prisoner of war wives indeed took over their families and did what they had to for survival. They worked for pay or ran the family farm or business, raised children, and made important decisions alone. But, rather than evoking a sense of freedom and liberation, the testimonies of prisoners' wives paint a picture of grinding hardship, heavy burdens, and tiring and overwhelming responsibilities. Prisoners' wives survived the crises of war and defeat, received meager support from the government to compensate for the loss of their husbands' income, endured rationing and shortages, shopped, cleaned, raised children—all without the material or emotional support of their husbands. Rather than generating a desire to maintain their wartime independence, the war years fed dreams of an idyllic family life in which the wives could have and raise children and let their husbands take back the heavy responsibilities of earning money and deciding how to spend it. The women's postwar desire to return to prewar patterns represented less a reversal of wartime liberation than an outgrowth of deeply felt needs and longings generated by the war.

The study of prisoners' wives in France during World War II contributes to recent scholarship on war and social change. In particular, it helps to explain a paradox about the impact of twentieth-century wars on society.

On the surface, women seemed to have made significant gains after the war. French women voted for the first time in 1945, and the government decreed equal pay for equal work. Yet French society remained highly conservative. Lack of change in women's legal status reflected the underlying stability of attitudes toward men and women and their appropriate roles. Prisoner of war wives help us understand the paradox of continuity beneath apparent change. Looking at one group in depth provides clues as to how certain groups mitigated the impact of drastic changes by maintaining old ideas and values in a new situation.

The two world wars of the twentieth century clearly differed from any previous wars in scale, drawing in nations across Europe and around the globe, reaching new heights of destructiveness, killing unheard-of numbers of soldiers and civilians. Twentieth-century warfare meant total war, or the mobilization of all national resources in support of the war effort. Describing those areas not directly in the battle zones as "home fronts" implies the new level of involvement by civilian populations.

Such total mobilization naturally led historians to explore the impact of modern wars on the societies involved. Government regulation of economies and control over the labor force to ensure war production in many cases laid the foundations of the welfare state. As demand for production rose and the labor supply dwindled, labor itself gained power and control. With many of the working men siphoned off into the army, new groups were drawn into the labor force. Perhaps the largest and most noticeable group was women.

The first historians to examine the impact of twentieth-century wars on women took their cue from the fact that in the United States, Great Britain, and Germany, women finally won the right to vote after World War I. The connection between the war and feminist victories afterward could be explained by the changes in women's lives during the war. Ever-increasing demand for munitions drew women away from such traditional "female" sectors of industry as textiles into heavy industry, where wages were higher. The expansion of government bureaucracies drew many middle-class women into the paid labor force for the first time.

John Williams, in his study of the World War I home fronts in England, France, and Germany, claims that by 1917 women were "a commonplace sight in almost every job they could physically perform." In his opinion, women thereby gained experience in new fields, a greater sense of independence and self-worth, and a new level of personal freedom. Furthermore, their hard work and contribution to the war effort earned women their nation's gratitude. When the war ended, it was impossible to return to the old ways. Thus Williams describes World War I as a "revolutionary chapter in the story of women's emancipation."[3]

Many other historians, looking at shifts in employment, wages, and union activity for women, have arrived at similar conclusions. Arthur Marwick and Richard Titmus both asserted that World War I created a social revolution in England. For America, less involved in that war, World War II has been the focus of most attention. William Chafe, one of the earliest historians to examine the impact of Word War II on American women, revealed the radical transformation in women's economic status brought about by the war: the female labor force increased 50 percent, the number of married women working outside the home doubled, wages rose, and four times more women were unionized. A quick look at the press, propaganda, and other forms of popular culture suggests that attitudes toward women working had also changed. Chafe concluded that "the war marked a watershed in the history of women at work."[4]

Undoubtedly, the objective situation of women changed during the wars of the twentieth century, and in Europe and the United States certain key feminist victories followed each war. However, extending the view beyond the immediate postwar period reveals conflicting trends. In the United States, for example, after World War II ended and despite working women's strong desire to keep their new jobs, women were fired in massive numbers as the economy shifted back to peacetime production and millions of demobilized soldiers competed for jobs.[5] More puzzling, however, was the seeming about-face in attitudes. The upheaval of war cultivated not a social revolution but the conservative 1950s, the era of the "feminine mystique," a period in which domesticity for women was vigorously promoted.

New scholarship, by looking beyond the objective realities of work and wages, can help explain the paradoxical shift from wartime liberation of women to their postwar domestication. D'Ann Campbell's book, *Women at War with America,* reminds us that attitudes and values can be as important as material factors in understanding how women reacted to the war. She argues that the war experience itself, coming as it did on the heels of the nation's worst depression, set the stage for the "suburban" ideal of the 1950s.

Other recent works have focused on cultural history, exploring the politics of gender as it relates to the politics of war. High literature and popular culture, propaganda, diaries, medical tracts—all reveal the connections between war and sex. Fighting represents the most masculine of activities, with weapons as only the most obvious phallic symbols. Publicity often portrays the enemy in feminine terms and describes battles in the vocabulary of sexual conquest.[6]

War and gender connect in other ways. Wartime separation of men and women raises sexual anxieties to a new pitch. The strong male bonding that occurs among soldiers arouses both homoeroticism and homophobia. Men both idealize women as the ones the war is fought to protect and resent women for sending men off to be killed. In short, war is represented as sexual disorder.[7] In addition to the ambiguous love-hate feelings men at the front have toward women, men fear that the women at home, freed from male control, will be unable to behave or to control their sexual appetites. During both world wars, exaggerated fears of unleashed female sexuality led to assertions of rampant immorality in the absence of the soldiers.[8] From this perspective, the perceived sexual disorder of war leads, not surprisingly, to a postwar reassertion of order and of traditional relations between men and women, which is only part of a wider attempt to "return to normalcy."

Prisoner of war wives deserve to be studied as a group just by virtue of the existence of the group and its numerical significance, a reflection of the extraordinary number of French prisoners of war. The exact number of men captured has never been ascertained with certainty, but estimates range from the Red Cross's number of 1,605,000 to the German figure of 1,929,000. In any case, 1,580,000 were eventually transferred to Germany in 1940, and 940,000 remained in captivity at the end of 1944.[9] Many books have been written about the French prisoners of war, but so far there has been no comprehensive study of their wives. Yet according to Durand's figures, 790,000 prisoners left wives, 616,200 of them with children.[10]

The war continuously impacted on prisoners' wives, in many ways more forcefully than on most other French citizens, with the exception of resisters, Jews, and forced laborers. For up to five years, prisoners' wives lived without their husbands and acted as heads of their households, making decisions about housing and the family budget. Women had to raise their children alone, impose discipline, and decide about educational plans. All of these responsibilities were exclusively the husband's prerogative under France's Civil Code.

French society's views of its prisoners' wives revealed much about general attitudes toward men and women, the fear of disorder evoked by the war, and the exaggerated fear of solitary women's sexuality. Social attitudes toward these women in particular were complex, ambiguous, and contradictory. At times prisoners' wives were praised as hard-working, long-suffering heroines who kept their families together in the husbands' absence. Other sources portrayed them as sexually liberated vamps, untrustworthy, acceding to the least temptations. They were also seen as children, unable to take on their new responsibilities alone, needful of guidance and protection.

In this book, I wish to probe the objective, material conditions of the lives of prisoners' wives, the subjective, cultural interpretation of their experience in Vichy France, and the Vichy regime's treatment of these women. Cultural interpretations and the state's treatment of prisoners' wives illuminate the relation between the politics of war and the politics of gender. I also wish to explore how individual wives experienced the war, the defeat, and their husbands' prolonged absence and eventual return. How did these women survive from day to day, and how did they interpret their experiences? As the war went on, prisoners' wives increasingly acted on their own behalf. For five years, these women underwent profound changes in ways that would lead one to expect postwar changes in gender relations. Yet once the husbands returned, most of these families did not establish more egalitarian relationships but resumed a more traditional, patriarchal family structure.

To answer the question of whether the war changed the status of women in France, I shall briefly outline the situation on the eve of World War II. Women in France lacked all political rights and were legally handicapped and placed under the authority of their husbands. Although positive changes had taken place for women in the economy and in education, other forces worked against them. In the interwar years, fear generated by the economic changes and the demographic transition France had undergone created a sense of crisis that often focused on women.

The war placed prisoners' wives in a separate category from other women. The pain and anxiety of separation for millions of soldiers and their wives and the waiting through the phony war were followed by one of the worst traumas in France's long history. Germany launched its lightning war on its western front on May 10, 1940. Within six weeks, the French army had crumbled, the government had abandoned Paris, refugees clogged the roads, and nearly two million French soldiers had been captured. Faced with the prospect of another total war waged from North Africa or London, new leaders in the town of Vichy decided to accept defeat and negotiated an armistice with Germany. Most people in France breathed a sigh of relief, as did many prisoners' wives once they received notice from their husbands.

Marshall Philippe Pétain, leader of the French government, decided to end the fighting and create the "French State" at Vichy. The shock and humiliation of France's rapid defeat brought men to power who believed that collaboration could bring about, among other things, the repatriation of the one-and-a-half million French POWs in Germany. The Vichy regime's foreign policy brought home many POWs, but it also left both the prisoners and people in France confused, misinformed, and usually disappointed.

Vichy's foreign policy of collaboration related only indirectly to prisoners' wives in France. But the French state at Vichy intended to do more than improve France's international situation. The plans of the men who came to power in 1940 included a conservative national revolution and a restoration of the patriarchal family. Prisoners' wives were therefore doubly important to Vichy, as wives of France's captive sons and as family members that needed protection and support in their husbands' absence. Vichy's ambitious ideological goals contrasted starkly with the reality of its treatment of prisoners' families, which fell far short of its goals. State financial policies actually encouraged married women and mothers to join the labor force, in contradiction to Vichy's ideological pronouncements against women in the work force.

Examining prisoners' wives as objects of state policy lays the groundwork for a more direct examination of their lives. What changes did prisoners' wives experience in their daily lives? How did they cope alone with the difficult conditions created by the war and occupation? Being a prisoner's wife modified all personal relationships, starting, obviously, with the husband-wife relationship and including relations with children, parents, in-laws, neighbors, and friends. Prisoners' wives experienced certain emotional difficulties such as loneliness, anxiety, and depression, owing to the lengthy separation from their husbands and the burden of new responsibilities. Most prisoners' wives did not view wartime responsibility as freedom from their husband's authority. To them the war meant hardship and unhappiness.

Recognizing the difficulties faced by prisoners' wives, two major agencies developed during the war to help these women and their families. The Famille du prisonnier, a semipublic agency created in 1941, concerned itself with the moral and material welfare of prisoners' families. The Commissariat général aux prisonniers de guerre rapatriés, a government agency also created in 1941, aided POW families and helped repatriated POWs readapt to civilian life. Publicly the two agencies worked together toward a common goal. Under the surface, however, there was constant fighting. The size of the potential group of clients raised the stakes in power struggles over controlling policies, raising funds, and distributing aid. In addition, different class attitudes, disagreements over the importance of professional training, and (despite claims of neutrality) politics all contributed to the quarreling. Yet, although almost every possible issue divided the two agencies, no one in either group questioned paternalism toward women. Both wanted not just to help out prisoners' families in temporary distress but to take over in the absence of the head of the household. Overlooking the qualities prisoners' wives demonstrated by surviving, both agencies assumed the women needed not a helping hand but a strong arm.

Prisoner of war wives' creativity manifested itself not only in their ability to survive but also in the formation of their own movement. Their solidarity, one positive result of the war, could have been a catalyst of consciousness-raising. Prisoners' wives initially constituted a group solely by virtue of their husbands' status. Eventually they developed a sense of shared identity that led them to create support groups and networks, formal and informal, throughout France. One group in particular, the Fédération des associations de femmes de prisonniers (FAFP), eventually became a national organization with a huge membership. This federation linked local associations across France, published newspapers, commissioned novels and surveys, and lobbied the government to defend the rights of POW wives. Although the federation represented sisterly solidarity and provided many women with leadership and organizational experience, activity in the federation did not change the women's ideas about their role in society and in the family. Rather, the federation intellectually reinforced traditional family values and roles, helping prisoners' wives to conceive of the experience of being head of a household in ways that did not challenge stereotypes of men and women. The federation and other POW wives' groups did not promote social change, but they did allow prisoners' wives to be active in shaping their lives, rather than remaining passive clients of public agencies and government policy.

Popular literary portrayals of prisoners' wives expressed prevailing social attitudes toward the nature of women, the role of the wife, and sexual morality. Social norms about women alone colored the public's attitude toward prisoners' wives. They also influenced the way prisoners' wives thought about themselves, creating tensions and contradictions as the women tried to reconcile these norms with reality. The women's self-conception as temporary heads of the family, delegates of their absent husbands, ultimately limited the extent to which the new experience changed their relationships with their husbands after the war.

Finally, in the immediate postwar period, what impact did the return of the prisoners of war have on prisoners' families? The men came home changed by their five years of captivity, and the women who met them altered by five years of running their households alone. Social values, espoused by the wives themselves, determined the way these women coped with the changed men who returned. Reunion meant a difficult period of readjustment, but prisoners' wives expected to smooth things over, adapt, accede to their husbands' demands, and put up with their moods and tempers. In addition to these expectations, many women ardently hoped to return to "normal" life, to quit working if possible and resume the traditional role of wife and mother.

Social norms changed only slowly in France, contradicting the illusion of postwar progress. Women benefited from important reforms in 1945, finally gaining the right to vote, for example, and the right to equal pay for equal work. But these reforms resulted less from new attitudes toward women than from the post-liberation rejection of Pétainist Vichy and its paternalist baggage.

After the initial difficulties of readjusting, most prisoners' wives were happy to let their husbands be the head of the family again. In the end, prisoners' wives experienced the war not as a period of exhilarating liberation but as one of tiring hardship, overwhelming responsibility, and painful loneliness, a period most of the women happily put behind them.

Prisoner of war wives were, throughout the Vichy years, special objects of public attention. Relief agencies sprang up to help them, government ministers debated over them, great quantities of literature addressed them, articles and short stories about them appeared in women's magazines, and novels featured them. In addition, prisoners' wives wrote about themselves in letters to newspapers and women's magazines and in essays in periodicals and books. They also wrote their own periodicals, pamphlets, and books.

Supplementing the written sources, personal testimonies fall into two main categories: those that date from the war years, and present-day recollections. A repatriated prisoner of war, Albert Robic, with the backing of two POW wives' organizations, collected a series of testimonies from prisoners' wives in 1943 and published them under the title *Femmes d'absents . . . Témoignages.* In presenting the testimonies, Robic included women from a variety of regions and occupations. He divided the accounts into those by women with and without children. No names were given, although the book includes twenty-seven clearly separate testimonies. Robic did not indicate how he distributed the questionnaires; nor did he include the questionnaire in the book, although the questions can easily be inferred from the responses. Also dating from the war years are hundreds of letters to Marshall Pétain from prisoners' wives, parents, and even children.

Jacqueline Deroy, a former prisoner of war wife, began to collect testimonies in the early 1980s. She made many of her contacts through a religious POW organization to which her husband belongs, the Association nationale pour les rassemblements et pèlerinages des anciens prisonniers de guerre (national association for gatherings and pilgrimages of former prisoners of war). Her recently published book, *Celles qui attendaient . . . témoignent aujourd'hui,* includes fifty-seven accounts by former prisoner of war wives. Like Robic, Deroy included women from a variety of regions. She divided her testimonies into agricultural, artisanal, and urban wives, and she included the entire text of a diary kept during the war by Laure, a prisoner's wife from southwestern France.

I collected my own group of testimonies, seventy-three total. I interviewed twenty-seven prisoners' wives in 1984–85 and sent out thirty-three questionnaires during the same period (see the Appendix). Additionally, in response to an interview published in a POW veterans' journal, *Le P.G.-C.A.T.M.,* thirteen POW wives wrote to me spontaneously; most of them subsequently filled out questionnaires. In my group, sixteen wives lived in Paris and the surrounding area; the rest came from all across France. The sample included twelve agrarian wives, fifteen officers' wives, two Jewish women, and one wife of a Jewish POW. Except when discussing the leaders of national organizations, I have changed all the names to protect privacy.

Unless otherwise indicated, all translations of both written and oral sources are my own.

My contacts came primarily from two networks. Robert Paumier of the FNCPG, a national nonsectarian apolitical POW veterans' group, provided me with forty-seven names. The Fédération des associations de femmes de prisonniers (FAFP), though it no longer exists, was an invaluable informal network. Jean Vedrine, an active member of POW organizations both during and after the war, put me in touch with the former president of the FAFP, who then gave me names and addresses of several former members. I made the rest of my contacts through personal friends.

Although I could not meet the demands of statistical rigor in compiling this information, the sample includes a wide variety of prisoner of war wives, some devout Catholics, some Jewish women, some working-class women, some members of the *haute bourgeoisie.* In general, prisoners' wives, far from being reluctant to talk or write about the war years, were often pleased to have the opportunity to tell their stories, and many of them feel that the suffering they experienced has never been acknowledged. There is no reason to suspect exaggeration. If anything, time has tempered the accounts of difficulties and hardships, as these women are no longer in the midst of the ordeal, or *l'épreuve,* as it was called in the 1940s.

A surprising number of similarities emerge from a close reading of the above sources. Most prisoners' wives would agree on what stood out as essential to the experience of being a prisoner's wife. Given human variety, however, the women differed in their responses to these problems.

A B B R E V I A T I O N S

AN	Archives nationales
BDIC	Bibliothèque de documentation internationale contemporaine
CATM	Combattants d'Algérie, Tunisie, Maroc
CCA	Comité central d'assistance aux prisonniers de guerre (parallels Red Cross in occupied zone)
CEA	Centre d'entr'aide
CGF	Commissariat général à la famille
CGPGR	Commissariat général aux prisonniers de guerre rapatriés et aux familles de prisonniers de guerre; originally the Commissariat général aux reclassement des prisonniers de guerre
DSPG	Direction des services des prisonniers de guerre; section of the Ministère de la guerre
FAFP	Fédération des associations de femmes de prisonniers
FFI	French Forces of the Interior
FNCPG	Fédération nationale des combattants prisonniers de guerre
JOC	Jeunesse ouvrière chrétienne
JOCF	Jeunesse ouvrière chrétienne féminine
LOC	Ligue ouvrière chrétienne
MNPGD	Mouvement national des prisonniers de guerre et déportés
MPF	Mouvement populaire des familles
MSR	Mouvement social révolutionnaire
RNP	Rassemblement national populaire
SDPG	Service diplomatique des prisonniers de guerre, Scapini mission
SN	Secours national
UFAC	Union française des anciens combattants

Women in France before the War

So I finished my studies and got my Bac. After that I spent some time learning to be a secretary, and then I got a job as a secretary at a high school. Then when I got married, I quit my job. At that time, women did not usually work in France. And then I found out that I was pregnant, and I had my little girl.

—Germaine Doucet

What was the impact of World War II on prisoner of war wives in France? To see how their lives were changed by the war, we should start by looking at their lives before the war—but before the war there were no prisoners' wives. The war set them apart. The general mobilization on 1 September 1939 called up all men between the ages of twenty and forty, with few exceptions. From then until the Battle of France there were soldiers' wives. After the battle began, months passed before soldiers' wives discovered whether they were war widows, prisoners' wives, or the lucky ones whose husbands returned home.

The status of women in general sets the stage for the changes prisoners' wives underwent. Women in France before the war were not in a static situation that can be summarized easily. Change was constant, in the direction both of greater freedom for women in some respects and of less freedom in others. Unable to gain political rights, women slowly improved their legal and economic status and expanded their educational opportunities. But the constant sense of crisis—fear of the international decline of France reflected in the diminishing size of its population relative to its neighbors—imbued leaders with a sense that society and the French family in particular were coming apart. Many observers blamed social and family

TABLE 1.1   *Percentage of the Total Labor Force*

Period	Men	Women
Prewar	68.1	31.9
August 1914	61.7	38.3
July 1915	60.2	39.8
July 1916	60.4	39.6
July 1917	59.8	40.2

Source: Arther Fontaine, *French Industry during the War*, 45.

disintegration on World War I and the changes it brought about for women.

The Impact of World War I

Was World War I a turning point for women in France? The "objective" answer to this question aside, people living in France after the Great War were certain that it marked a crucial turning point for women. Likewise, many historians, including John Williams, Arthur Marwick, and Michel Collinet, point to the undeniable increase in female employment during World War I in France (see table 1.1). Restrictions loosened to accommodate working women, and people became more accustomed to seeing young women out alone and working alongside men in previously "male" occupations. Visibly symbolizing change, a new style of dress appeared after the war: corsets, huge hats, and long, restrictive skirts gave way to shorter, lightweight, more practical dresses.

Another phenomenon of the 1920s indicated the liberation of women: the flapper, or *la garçonne*. Contemporaries sensed that a new woman had emerged from the war, a liberated woman, comfortable with her sexuality, a woman who worked outside the home, lived alone, and preferred parties and dancing to starting a family.

Certainly the new woman represented a real social phenomenon, although, several historians argue, not a particularly widespread one. Only major cities had significant numbers of independent, unmarried, working women, and France had few large cities.[1] Statistics also indicate that most women dropped out of the labor force when they married or had children. Thus, the attention paid to the new woman was out of proportion to the actual number of women who fit that category, indicating how shocking her values were to the rest of French society. The new woman symbolized a small step toward more freedom for women rather than a profound change in social attitudes.[2]

Despite certain signs of progress, wartime changes for women in France were limited, as indicated particularly by the failure of the female suffrage movement after World War I. Although the Chamber of Deputies, to its credit, voted 344 to 97 for women's suffrage in 1919, favoring female suffrage did not indicate that the male deputies had repudiated traditional assumptions about the nature of women and their proper role in society. Rather, they believed that women had earned the vote by their contribution to the war effort. As one deputy explained, "The war has fully illuminated the immense value of feminine cooperation in the nation's life!"[3] Many republican men accepted the feminist argument that a moral, sentimental female presence in the electorate would harmonize a calculating, rationalistic all-male political system. Others believed that women should vote because the state increasingly intruded into the female domain of marriage, children, and family life. In other words, supporting female suffrage in 1920 did not indicate a liberated attitude toward women.[4]

Although female suffrage passed in the Chamber, the Senate narrowly defeated the measure in 1922 and blocked its revival throughout the interwar years.[5] Stephen Hause, specialist on the French female suffrage movement, argues that World War I itself, not just the conservatism of the senators, dealt a major blow to the suffrage movement in France. The war destroyed the momentum of a vigorous and growing prewar suffrage campaign that peaked in 1914 but could not recover from the wartime suspension of its activities. Furthermore, female suffrage paled in comparison to such postwar problems as economic recovery, the demobilization of vast numbers of men, and international diplomatic concerns. In addition, the war's huge death toll intensified fears of French depopulation and hardened the general resolve not to give in to feminist pressures for change. Partly to blame themselves, suffragists, certain that women would be rewarded with the vote for contributing to the war effort, failed to campaign adequately after the war.[6]

Thus women had few political rights before World War II.[7] An active suffrage movement developed in France after the turn of the century, but it failed to win the right to vote for women after the war and never regained its pre-1914 vigor. Not only did French women fail to gain political rights, but after the 1922 suffrage defeat few people even raised the issue or forced discussion of female suffrage.[8]

Given the contradictory nature of the evidence, World War I would be best evaluated as one important event in a long, slow series of changes, some regressive, some progressive, in the status of women in France. Improvements for women in France dated from before, during, and after the war, as did setbacks and regressive measures.

The Legal Status of Women and the Napoleonic Codes

The focus of French feminism on female suffrage after the turn of the twentieth century came after a long and divisive controversy among feminists. In the nineteenth century, the reborn feminist movement of the early Third Republic intentionally gave priority to improving women's civil status. Leaders such as Maria Desraismes and Léon Richer believed suffrage would be too controversial, too ambitious, and even dangerous for the fledgling republic. Early feminists feared that women, assumed to be under the sway of the Catholic church, might destroy the Republic if given the right to vote before being weaned from Catholicism.

Nineteenth-century feminists had another important reason to work on improving women's civil status. The law in France holds a uniquely elevated position, and the fundamental laws of France discriminated against women. The Civil Code Napoleon I promulgated in 1804—his attempt to codify ideal Roman law—has remained in effect ever since, despite eight changes in government. The legal tradition of France differs greatly from the common-law traditions basic to England and the United States. Equally important, French legal theory begins with a broad conception of the role of law. Whereas in common-law countries the law serves to settle social conflicts, the law in France defines and orders social relationships.[9] The specific rights, duties, and responsibilities of each person to everyone else, employer and employee, parent and child, husband and wife, are all spelled out in detail.

Napoleon appointed a committee of four legal experts to draft the Civil Code in 1800. Although he rarely intervened personally, Napoleon took an active hand in the sections dealing with family law. According to Lefebvre, Napoleon was "intent on strengthening the authority of the father and the husband in the home."[10] Napoleon believed that paternal power should reflect within the family Napoleon's relationship to France—that of a dictator. He explained: "As the head of the family is absolutely at the disposition of the Government, so is the family absolutely at the disposition of its head." Therefore, the Civil Code (also known as the Napoleonic Code) states that a child "at every age owes honor and respect to his father and mother." The father made all decisions about his children's education, discipline, and career without consulting the mother. Even if the father died, the mother could never be appointed sole legal guardian of her children; she could be only a member of a "family council" (which might include her husband's parents) set up to act as guardian. A father could even send his child under age sixteen to prison for a period of one month (up to six months if the child was between sixteen and twenty-one) without stating his motives or obtaining a court order.[11]

Napoleon's Civil Code fixed women's legal status based upon his belief in "the weakness of women's brains, the instability of their ideas, . . . their need for perpetual resignation." Legally equivalent to children, women could not act as witnesses to any act of the Civil State (marriages, wills). Napoleon maintained not only that women were not equal to men but that they were "nothing more than machines for producing children."[12] From 1804 until a major series of reforms were undertaken in 1965, women in France remained legal minors, and married women became "virtual wards of their husbands."[13]

Under article 231 of the Civil Code, a wife owed obedience to her husband, who in return owed his wife protection. Furthermore, a wife had no control over the administration of common property, which included any property she brought to the marriage. A wife could not give, sell, mortgage, or acquire by sale or gift any property without her husband's written consent. He alone had the right to decide, without consultation, where the family lived and whether his wife could work for pay or enroll in a university. The husband controlled any wages his wife earned.

The Civil Code also endorsed the double standard of morality. For example, a wife's adultery was a civil and criminal offense, both grounds for divorce and punishable by fines and even jail terms. A husband's adultery, not a criminal offense, constituted grounds for divorce only if it took place regularly in the "conjugal residence." The original Civil Code allowed for divorce by mutual consent, largely because it served Napoleon's purposes. Otherwise, the only three grounds for divorce were adultery, cruelty and abuse, and conviction of one of the parties for a serious criminal offense.[14]

After Napoleon's defeat, the restored Bourbon monarchy enacted the

Constitutional Charter of 1814. In a key modification of the Code, it abolished divorce entirely. During the Third Republic, a group of republicans led by Alfred Naquet campaigned to restore divorce, succeeding in 1884.[15] Grounds for divorce, however, were restricted to adultery, cruelty and abuse, or serious criminal conviction.

Given the marital regime in effect under France's Civil Code, the reestablishment of divorce proved to be a favorable change for women, who initiated some 60 percent of all divorce procedures.[16] The Third Republic also saw several other crucial legal modifications favorable to women, in part due to the feminist strategy of working to improve the civil status of women. In 1907 the Married Women's Earnings Law restored to wives control over their own wages. Also in 1907 working women gained the right to vote for and serve on the councils of trade-dispute arbiters (*conseils des prudhommes*). In 1912 the Code removed the prohibition of paternity suits. In 1917, women gained the right to become legal guardians.[17] These reforms may seem minor victories, but they had a significant impact on women's lives. Being able to file a paternity suit and force the father to take responsibility for his child makes a huge difference to an unwed mother. Equally significant for widows was the legal right to act as sole guardians of their children.

Just before World War II, another key modification took place. The law of 18 February 1938 replaced the notion of the marital power of the husband with a somewhat attenuated principle: the husband as the head of the family. The law also set down what had been a temporary measure taken during World War I: a wife could, in the absence or incapacity of her husband, act as head of the family. The 1938 law also gave married women the right to work without their husband's express permission. The husband's consent was assumed unless he publicly, and in the best interest of the household, opposed his wife's working.[18]

Not every early twentieth-century legal change improved women's status. For example, the post–World War I "blue horizon" chamber passed a law in July 1920 forbidding any form of encouragement of birth control or abortion.[19] Although the measure was taken to reverse the decline in France's birth rate, women's ability to control reproduction was also seen as a challenge to patriarchy. Even today, feminists see access to contraception and abortion as critical because women who control their bodies control their destinies, whereas women who cannot will always be dependent upon men. In France, population trends since 1800 attest to widespread knowledge of contraceptive practices; thus, the attempt to restrict such knowledge in 1920 was a setback for women.

In spite of both positive and negative legal changes, the overall civil status of women remained one of inferiority. Married women still had no control over where they lived, their property, or their own children unless husbands were absent or otherwise incapacitated. A wife could be prevented from working for wages or attending a university or any other postsecondary school. Adultery provisions legally encoded the double standard of morality.[20]

The legal description of the status of women does not necessarily describe relations in a typical French family. Undoubtedly, many husbands were not tyrants and made decisions about where to live or where to send their children to school together with their wives. Still, in theory the Civil Code defined and ordered relations within society, and certainly it set limits. In cases where the husband insisted on exercising his prerogatives, the wife had no legal recourse.

Female Employment

None of the reforms before World War II altered the fact that women in France lacked basic political rights and were treated as legal minors; none contradicted the fundamental assumptions about the nature of men, women, and family relations.

During the first third of the twentieth century, women's participation in the labor force changed considerably. Statistics on the number of women in the labor force reveal some curious trends that run counter to prevalent expectations. Both contemporaries in France and later observers believed firmly that ever-increasing numbers of women were joining the labor force and that World War I crowned the triumph of working women. But the sense of rising female employment derived from a "social optical illusion."[21] In fact, the rate of female participation was surprisingly high in France early in the twentieth century and declined until 1965. In table 1.2, one can see the seeming paradox of the decrease in the rate of female participation in the labor force.

The figures testify to a broad economic shift away from a predominantly rural economy—in terms of production, the proportion of the labor force involved in agriculture, and the number of people living in rural areas—and toward an urban, industrial one. Such a shift occurred across Europe

TABLE 1.2   *Rates of Male and Female Labor Force Participation (percentages)*

Year	Males	Females
1906	66.5	36
1911	67	35.5
1926	69	33
1936	64	30.5
1946	66	32
1954	62.5	30
1962	58.5	27.5
1968	55	28

Source: J.-J. Carré, P. Dubois, E. Malinvaud, *French Economic Growth*, 49.

after the Industrial Revolution, but in France the change took place more gradually than in Great Britain or Germany. In 1870, the proportion of France's labor force in agriculture was an extraordinarily high 52 percent; even as late as 1940, 35 percent of France's labor force was still agricultural.[22]

The slow shift away from agriculture had a direct impact on the number of women in the labor force because the French census counted wives who worked on their family farms as employed. Therefore, the high proportion of France's population involved in agriculture explains the high rate of female participation in the labor force in France early in the century: 36 percent in 1906, compared to Great Britain (25 percent in 1900), and the United States (about 19 percent in 1900).[23] The declining rate indicates the changes taking place as farmers and rural workers moved into the industrial and service sectors of the economy.[24]

Compared to other Western countries, France in the early twentieth century also had a surprisingly high rate of female participation in industry owing to the large size of the textile and clothing sectors. Female labor traditionally dominated the textile industry in France, based primarily on domestic piecework. Over the century, however, the number of women in the industrial sector also declined. In 1906 women constituted 34 percent of the total industrial work force, in 1931 they represented 28 percent, and by 1962 the number fell to 23 percent. Not only did the numbers drop, but the remaining women shifted slightly from textiles to different branches of industry such as electronics, paper-processing, and plastics.[25]

TABLE 1.3 *Active Female Population in Thousands*

Year	Agriculture	Industry	Tertiary	Total
1896	2,749	1,817	1,725	6,291
1906	3,329	2,019	2,079	7,427
1926	3,389	1,981	2,293	7,663
1936	2,917	1,583	2,510	7,010
1946	3,263	1,639	2,849	7,751
1962	1,272	1,754	3,463	6,489

Source: Françoise Guélaud-Leridon, *Le Travail des femmes en France*, 14.

Another trend compensated for the decrease of female employment in industry: the rise of the tertiary, or service, sector of the economy and the growing percentage of clerical, administrative, and sales positions held by women. In 1906 women represented 17 percent of the labor force in the tertiary sector; by 1950 that number had risen to 39 percent.[26] This development began before and continued after World War II (see table 1.3). The twentieth-century French economy has seen a "pink collar" revolution.

What impact did the two world wars have on economic trends for women? Because World War I killed many young men and World War II uprooted an equivalent number, both wars encouraged the shift from a rural to an industrial economy—a development bemoaned by many observers in France as the "rural exodus." World War I drew large numbers of women into the labor force and altered female patterns of employment. Working-class women left the textile industry and entered heavy industry and munitions, where jobs were better paid. Bureaucracies multiplied because of increased state economic intervention, creating new clerical and administrative job opportunities for middle-class women. But most of these women in the service sector were young and unmarried. Few women, either bourgeois or working class, reached top levels of management or held anything higher than the least skilled jobs with the fewest responsibilities. In the shift from wartime to peacetime production after World War I, many women lost their jobs or were encouraged with bonuses to quit in order to make way for the returning soldiers. Thus, the dramatic increase in women in the labor force during World War I proved less important in the long run than the war's contribution to the long-term economic trends of urbanization, industrialization, and the growth of the service sector.[27]

Slowly, however, women's economic status was changing. Because more and more families left the farm for the city and because women who worked in the home were not counted as active, unlike women who worked on their family farms, the overall rate of female participation declined. Eventually, economic trends created more opportunities for women, and the rate of female participation began to rise again after the mid-1960s.[28]

The Education of Women

By 1940, dramatic changes in the primary and secondary education of girls and in higher education for women had also taken place. The Third Republic's Ferry Laws of 1881–82 made public schools free and secular; school attendance became compulsory for all children ages six to thirteen. The education of girls had always fallen behind that of boys as a state priority, and before the 1880s most girls who attended went to church-run schools staffed by nuns. Jules Ferry and Camille Sée hoped to break the Catholic church's hold on girls and women in France by educating girls to be good republicans. Thus, in addition to opening more public primary schools to accommodate girls, the Third Republic opened state secondary schools for girls and normal schools for young women in order to train lay female schoolteachers and replace nuns.

The education of girls was not undertaken to encourage them to pursue professional careers. Rather, Ferry explained that his new schools would provide "republican companions for republican men" and thereby "guarantee the unity of the French family."[29] Anticlericalism, not feminism, motivated these important reforms. Ferry and Sée hoped to win over Catholic girls, whom they assumed to be future mothers. Still, the significance of reforms in female education is reflected in the fact that female illiteracy, 25 percent in 1880, disappeared by the eve of World War I.[30]

The competition between the church and anticlerical republicans led to another positive change for girls. Initially, public secondary schools for girls offered courses in morals, needlework, and music instead of Greek, Latin, and philosophy. Without Latin, girls could not take the baccalauréat, which served both as diploma and as entrance requirement for all universities in France. To lure back girls lost to public secondary schools, Catholic secondary schools began to offer Latin. In response, some public secondary schools also began offering Latin to girls. Inevitably, once they had the necessary training, girls began to show up at the baccalauréat examinations.[31] Still, in 1905 only 26 women received the baccalauréat out of a total of 6,159 (0.4 percent); in 1920 the number rose to 1,326 out of 10,516 (12.6 percent). In 1924 the lycée curriculum for girls and boys officially became identical. In 1940, the number of women who received the baccalauréat was 9,292 (33.5 percent).[32]

Once girls trained for and passed the baccalauréat examination, they began enrolling in universities. Thus, the number of female university students expanded from 583, or 2 percent of the total in 1900, to 4,903, or 10 percent of the total in 1920. By the eve of World War II, not only did women receive one-third of the baccalauréat degrees, they made up 32 percent of university students.[33]

But the improvement in female education and the increasing number of women attending institutions of higher education had little impact on the number of women in top-level management and the professions. In the civil service, for example, only two office directors were women between 1918 and 1939. Although more and more women attended law school, only one-third of the women in law school were called to the bar, and in 1929 there were only one hundred women at the Paris bar. Similarly, the few women in medicine were usually directed toward specialties in obstetrics, gynecology, or pediatrics. By World War II, the one profession women had truly broken into was teaching. At the elementary and secondary school levels, teaching had become an acceptable profession for women.[34]

Although the number of women pursuing secondary and higher education grew steadily throughout the early century, only a few girls stayed in school past the compulsory age of thirteen. Most girls' exposure to formal education stopped at the primary schools. Linda Clark's analysis of primary school textbooks for girls reveals the extent to which both Catholic and public schools prescribed the idea of a distinct female personality that uniquely suited women to the domestic roles of wife and mother.[35]

Domesticity for Women

The domestic ideology, usually associated with the Victorian era of bourgeois cultural ascendancy in Europe and the United States, is based on the assumption that men and women are different by nature. Men are physically stronger, rational, independent, autonomous, and aggressive. Women, in contrast, are weak, yielding, emotional, intuitive rather than rational, and needful of protection. The nature of each sex therefore suits it to a task. Man's nature leads him to run public affairs and the state and to support a family by working. Woman's nature dictates that she bear, raise, and ensure the moral education of children and maintain her natural sphere of activity—the domestic sphere. The complementary natures of men and women find their perfect match and fulfill their potential within the family.

Although the domestic ideology became much more explicit and highly developed with the flowering of bourgeois culture in the nineteenth century, the nineteenth-century middle class had no monopoly on it. First, the notion of separate spheres and its underlying gender determinism has a long history in Western culture, extending back through the Middle Ages and even to the Roman Empire. Second, in France the norms reinforcing a traditional family structure intensified well into the twentieth century. The first real challenge took place in the 1960s.

The continued strength of the domestic ideology in France on the eve of World War II reflects certain peculiarities of French history, including the stability of its largely rural society, the intense anxiety about depopulation, and the absence of any sizable groups in France disputing domesticity for women. These peculiarities rendered social norms, despite deep political and religious divisions in French society, more universally accepted there than in perhaps any other Western society.

To a large extent, concerns about French population trends reinforced ideas about women's natural domestic role in twentieth-century France. In the late nineteenth century, France, along with other European nations, experienced an intensification of nationalism. Unlike other Western nations, however, France had already undergone the "demographic transition" to a low birth rate—a transition experienced by the rest of Europe only in the twentieth century. Thus, the desire for national assertion grew as the birth rate fell, throwing into question France's ability to keep up with competitor nations. Fear of national decline was first expressed in the 1850s, when national census data revealed that the birth rate was falling more rapidly than the death rate, and reached a hysterical peak after France's humiliating defeat in the Franco-Prussian War of 1870.[36]

The eventual establishment, after the 1870 defeat, of a liberal republic did not weaken either nationalism, the fear of depopulation, or norms of domesticity for women. Third Republic anticlericalism did not challenge church doctrine on women and the family, which championed domesticity for women based on the teachings of Saint Paul and the early Fathers. The church viewed women as powerful transmitters of Catholic religious, social, and political values to future generations. Anticlerical republicans did not question the notion of women as moral educators. Instead, they hoped to spread republicanism, rather than Catholicism, through mothers. The role of the mother would not change, only the ideas she was to transmit.[37]

Neither was the idea of domesticity for women unique to Catholics and republicans. Ultimately, neither the socialists nor the feminists chose to attack patriarchy. Historians attribute the break between the socialists and feminists in France to Pierre-Joseph Proudhon's towering influence over French socialism before World War I, which far outweighed that of Marx. Proudhon's social conservatism and sexism are legendary. He proved mathematically women's moral, intellectual, and physical inferiority to men, concluding that women belonged in the home. As a result, socialists and syndicalists, rather than defending the right of women to work outside the home, used the image of the working-class woman as a symbol of bourgeois exploitation. They maintained that women who worked outside the home drove men's wages down. Rather than demanding equal pay for equal work to remedy this situation, working-class leaders demanded a family wage for men that would free women from the need to work outside and allow them to stay at home. The mother in the home became a "sentinel of the autonomy and identity of the working class."[38]

Recent research, however, reveals the untapped potential for cooperation between socialists and radical feminists in the nineteenth century. In contrast to Proudhon, the utopian socialists provided a counter tradition strongly committed to the elevation of women's status.[39] The 1879 founding congress of Jules Guesde's French Workers' Party passed a resolution calling for complete equality of the sexes in both public and private life. But Charles Sowerwine details the feminists' decline within the socialist movement, which he links to the internecine battles fought as socialists struggled to unify.[40] The fragile bridge between feminism and socialism collapsed in the 1890s as the socialists opted for a centralized party designed to win elections. The new strategy excluded radical women both because women could not vote and out of fear of alienating potential male electoral support. By the 1890s, even Guesde opposed working for women's rights as diversionary.[41]

By 1900 not only had all remnants of women's militancy disappeared but the socialists had embraced traditional domestic rhetoric, telling women that "their place was in the working man's home, where they could fulfill their 'natural duties' to him and to *his* children." Socialists labeled feminist demands for equal civil rights and suffrage bourgeois reformism, secondary to the struggle for the emancipation of the working class.[42] The unified Socialist party also stressed family values and the special nature of women to dispel the opposition's charge that socialism promoted free love and would destroy French family life. The splintering of the Socialist party and creation of a Communist party in 1920 did not bring a new awareness of feminist issues to the left wing. The Communist party's strict Marxism dictated an economic determinism that allowed for little interest in feminist issues.

Early in the twentieth century similar opportunities for cooperation between feminists and syndicalists also briefly arose. The Confédération général du travail (CGT) stepped into the gap created after the socialists edged women out. From 1907 to the eve of the war, the CGT proclaimed both women's right to work outside the home and the right to equal pay for equal work. World War I intervened, however, cutting short the CGT's attempt to bring female workers into its unions. Wartime conditions heightened working men's resentment of working women, blamed for lowering wages, diluting skilled labor, and freeing men for the war front.[43] After the war, the CGT reversed its position, declaring that female employment lowered male wages and demanding a family wage for men. Only in 1935 did the CGT again acknowledge that women should have the right to work outside the home. Even then, left-wing militants did not publicly attack the ideology of female domesticity.[44]

One final group that could have challenged traditional family values before the war, the feminists, also opted not to in France. The early republican feminist movement of Léon Richer and Maria Desraismes, which focused its efforts on civil rights for women, based feminist claims on the idea of equivalence. Men and women played different but equivalent roles in society.[45] Karen Offen labels their brand of feminism "familial" feminism, an ideology that "predicated a biologically differentiated, family centered vision of male-female complementarity: 'equality in difference' was the favored phrase."[46] Although twentieth-century feminists adopted more daring tactics and ambitious goals, they still demanded political equality and suffrage on the basis of women's positions as mothers and wives. What Offen calls the "individualist" feminism of Madeleine Pelletier, who demanded equal opportunity regardless of sex, never developed a significant following in France until after World War II.

Pelletier, the exception that proves the rule, symbolized the various challenges to social values about women and family life. She trained as a doctor, never married, and flirted with socialism and feminism before becoming disillusioned with both. Feminism she found to be profoundly bourgeois and disinterested in the plight of working-class women; yet socialism was indifferent to sexual oppression. Pelletier also believed, with the neo-Malthusians, that women would control their destinies only when they controlled their own bodies. Pelletier thus was one of the few who dared to question the very foundations of her society.[47]

Few dissenting voices in France questioned, much less rejected, the prevalent view of inherent gender differences that justified different roles for men and women in society and the family. Few thinkers wondered if woman's destiny could be anything other than marriage and motherhood. Aside from Pelletier, some of the prewar neo-Malthusians, and Simone de Beauvoir after the war, such questioning awaited the revived feminist movement of the late 1960s.

Perception of Change, Persistence of Assumptions

In spite of the continued strength of the domestic ideology, many twentieth-century alarmists declared that the French family was falling apart. I have already shown that despite interwar perceptions of radical change centered on two "threats"—the new woman and female employment—a closer examination of social realities reveals the absence of change. In both cases, the disproportion of the reaction represented a pattern typical of French discourse.

France is a nation of vigorous intellectual debate. Many of the political, religious, and cultural divisions spawned by the Revolution of 1789 continued (and continue) to inspire debates well into the twentieth century. Conflicts dating from the Revolution—republicans versus monarchists, Catholics versus anticlericals—laid the groundwork for new disputes: legitimists versus Orléanists and Bonapartistes, Dreyfusards versus anti-Dreyfusards, and so on.

One area of intense controversy overlooked until recently centered on what in the nineteenth century was termed "the woman question": a series of debates about the position of women in society, female suffrage, legal reform, the education of women, female employment, divorce, and the birth rate. Attention to women's history reveals the centrality of gender issues to French political discourse; major political debates raged over all of these issues from the late nineteenth century on. Interestingly, as with the new woman and the problem of female employment, the debates often focused on false issues. Certain shared fundamental beliefs, rarely even mentioned because they were so widely accepted as true, circumscribed the differences between the schools of thought on women's issues.

Divorce

This is not to suggest there were no real differences of opinion. For example, divorce was always a highly emotional topic. The Naquet Law of 1884 was restrictive enough that tempers cooled until 1900, when a group of deputies tried to introduce divorce by mutual consent. A full-scale national debate, a "war of words," erupted.[48] Liberal republicans disagreed fundamentally with Catholic conservatives. Republicans considered divorce necessary to guarantee an essential freedom and to liberate the family from church control. They preferred to see marriage not as a sacred engagement but as a legal bond joining two partners. Catholics and conservatives believed marriage should be indissoluble and insisted on the sacred nature of the bond. The durability of the family, the basis of all other institutions, was essential to social stability. Weakening the family via divorce weakened the strength of the nation; limiting paternal authority destroyed all authority. Feminist writers took an intermediate position, fearing that easy divorce could ruin women economically and morally and leave them vulnerable to the male desire for youth and variety.[49] Feminists preferred to improve the position of women within marriage, through reform of the Civil Code, rather than making it easier to end a marriage.

Notwithstanding the disputes among those who favored divorce by mutual consent, those who wanted restricted divorce, and those who opposed any form of divorce, virtually all parties to the debates shared certain basic assumptions. Joseph Caillaux, a leading twentieth-century republican politician, for example, favored divorce and had divorced his wife, Berthe Gueydan, in order to marry his mistress, Henriette. In 1914 Caillaux found himself embroiled in a scandal when Henriette committed a murder. When called upon to testify about his divorce from Berthe, Caillaux explained, "Between a man to whom everyone grants authority, vigor, and power, and you [Berthe] in whom those qualities are overdeveloped as well, it was impossible that things would last." In comparison, his second wife, Henriette, was a real woman, "with a character and a nature to which I could attach myself."[50] Caillaux may not have believed in the sanctity of marriage, but he believed firmly in the natural differences between men and women and their proper roles in the family. These shared assumptions ran so deeply through French society that they limited how far most people were willing to go in challenging the traditional family structure.

The reinstitution of divorce in 1884 only provided another issue onto which the deeper fears and anxieties raised by the specter of depopulation in France could be projected. The issue of divorce continued to disturb conservatives, who triumphed temporarily when the Vichy regime introduced new restrictions on divorce in 1941.

Pronatalism

From about 1870 on, debates raged over what to do about France's declining birth rate.[51] Jacques Bertillon, a doctor, demographer, and founder of the Alliance nationale pour l'accroissement de la population française, claimed that France's birth rate had declined because of laws limiting men's control over their property and patrimony. He assumed that men alone decided about having children; therefore, reform of tax and inheritance laws, by encouraging men to have large families, would reverse the decline. On the other side, such feminists as Léon Richer, Hubertine Auclert, and Maria Martin reminded Bertillon and others that having children was above all a woman's decision. The miserable legal and moral situation of women and children had more to do with the declining birth rate than did tax laws. Feminists therefore insisted that their efforts to improve the legal situation of women and children would improve the status of motherhood, strengthen the family, and thereby reverse the population decline.[52]

In addition to disagreements over which parent decides to have children, those concerned about France's population decline also divided over whether the state should concentrate on raising the birth rate (referred to as pronatalism) or on strengthening the family (familialism). Pronatalists Bertillon and Fernand Boverat represented the thinking of many doctors, demographers, and others of scientific orientation who felt that state policy needed to focus on the population problem by encouraging births, stopping birth control and abortion, protecting all children—even those born out of wedlock—and redistributing the costs of raising children. Familialists tended to be Catholic and stressed that the state should reinforce the family, end divorce, and strengthen paternal power but should never condone pre- or extramarital sex by protecting illegitimate children. Familialists felt that reinforcing the traditional family would naturally lead to large families and increase the birth rate. The two schools differed over whether the state should focus its efforts strictly on the birth rate or strictly on the family. Originally, both groups coexisted in the Alliance nationale, but the debate became bitter enough to provoke an organizational split.[53] The dispute, however, represented a difference in focus, not a fundamental disagreement about the need to reverse France's population decline or about the nature of the family. The domestic ideology set a boundary that few were willing to cross.

Shared assumptions notwithstanding, women's issues raised before the turn of the century continued to inspire debates up to and after World War I. War changed the debates. The 1.4 million men killed, the continuing decline of the birth rate, the diplomatic isolation France increasingly felt in dealing with Germany—all gave force to those pushing for drastic measures to strengthen the family and rebuild the population. But pronatalist discussions took a new turn, largely because almost all observers—conservatives, Catholics, republicans, feminists—believed that the Great War had caused a revolution in the status of women.

Although in reality the war had done little to change either social values or women's legal, political, or economic situation, many people perceived drastic changes in women's status. A whole series of evils were attributed to working women based on the assumption that they had definitively won the right to work outside the home and that ever-growing numbers of them were doing so. Employment gave women money and exposed them daily to the opposite sex, feeding their female taste for luxury and flirtatious narcissism. Working wives scorned housework as tedious, avoided pregnancy, and left children to fend for themselves. Miserable husbands became alcoholics; neglected children became juvenile delinquents. World War I thus transformed the rhetoric. Before the war the declining birth rate was widely interpreted as a "crisis of male virility";[54] afterward many saw it as a "crisis of female egoism" supposedly unleashed by the new freedom and independence women had attained during the war.

The Family Code

Although conservatives, republicans, feminists, pronatalists, and Catholics may have disagreed about causes and cures, nearly everyone agreed by the 1930s that France faced a population crisis. From the mid-1930s on, as Germany violated the Treaty of Versailles and grew ever more powerful, the often immobilized Third Republic finally took action. After years of lobbying and debate, the Republic passed an extensive Family Code in July 1939, little over a month before World War II broke out.

The Family Code, more than a collection of measures to reverse the declining birth rate, had a grand design, outlined at length in the report by Prime Minister Daladier that preceded the code.[55] He explained that France's very well-being, its extensive riches and technological progress, had ironically caused the size of its population to decline. Hoping to conserve their happy situation, French people were having fewer children, causing France, which had the largest population in Europe in 1800, to fall to the fifth rank. The consequences of falling behind its neighbors included the "aggravation of external danger." Population decline meant fewer men to serve in the army, fewer people to share the burden of military and social spending, labor shortages, abandoned farms, even colonial contraction; a feeble population also dealt a blow to France's intellectual and artistic prestige.[56]

Daladier explained that although remedying the situation went beyond the question of money, still, "It became clear to us that the public authorities would fail in their mission if they did not concern themselves with supporting large families from a material point of view."[57] Daladier also clarified that the code was not a welfare measure to help only poor or working-class families; rather, the code's provisions were universalist, funded by contributions of all working people in order to redistribute the costs of child rearing between childless families and families with children, especially those with three or more children. Daladier justified redistributing these costs thus: "Children constitute the most important part of our national patrimony; it is therefore fair that each individual share in the cost of raising them."[58]

The code's key provision extended family allowances. Rather than innovating, the Third Republic adopted and universalized a system already widespread in industry and commerce.[59] A family allowance was a sum of money per child added to a worker's salary, set at a certain percentage of the average monthly salary in each department. If both parents were employed, the allowance was added to the father's salary. Both employers and employees paid contributions into a regional fund, the *Caisse des allocations familiales,* which distributed the benefits. The Family Code extended the benefit of family allowances from salaried workers to all French families, including farmers, the self-employed, and members of the liberal professions. In addition, families received allowances only after the birth of a second child. The allowances went from 10 percent of the average departmental monthly salary for the second child to 20 percent for the third child and up.[60]

Although regular income supplements began only with the second child, a one-time "first birth bonus" (*prime à la première naissance*) encouraged newly married couples to have their first child quickly. The child had to be legitimate and born alive within two years of the marriage. Unlike family allowances, the birth bonus was usually paid to the mother, who received half after delivery and half six months later if the child was still alive and in her care.

In order to promote traditional roles, another provision of the code encouraged mothers to stay at home with their children—the "mother at home" allowance (*de la mère au foyer*). Ten percent of the average departmental salary was paid to families with at least one child who received only one salary and lived in towns of two thousand people or more. If the family had only one child, the allowance ceased at age five; if there were several children, it continued until the youngest turned fifteen. Although the single salary could in theory be earned by the father or the mother, the "mother at home" allowance was clearly intended to compensate families for the loss of the wife's salary.

Contemporary wisdom held that the move of families from the countryside into the cities harmed France's traditional social equilibrium and lowered the birth rate.[61] The Family Code thus included two provisions intended to halt the rural exodus. Newly married couples could apply for loans of up to twenty thousand francs to establish a farm. Second, the 1939 Family Code amended the Civil Code's equal-inheritance law to compensate children who stayed and worked on the farm by allowing fathers to leave them a larger share of the inheritance.

In addition to financial rewards, the Family Code included a lengthy chapter on the "moral" protection of the family. The host of "moral protection" measures included the protection of maternity, which meant the repression of abortion as well as the establishment of maternity homes in each department where single women could live during their pregnancy and keep their condition secret.[62] The new Family Code also completely revised adoption law, shifting the focus away from protecting the rights of legitimate children toward protecting all children and promoting the integration of adoptive families.

The Family Code included a chapter on "protection of the race," an ominous-sounding phrase that merely meant repressing vice and other social evils such as pornography and alcoholism.[63] The Republic naturally turned to schools for help in constituting a healthier race. Revised curricula included "lessons in demography" that taught children about "the mission life has reserved for them."

The Family Code of 1939 was extensive and ambitious; it included both pronatalist and familialist provisions. Its universal benefits required no means test, only having the requisite number of children. Because having children was defined as a national duty, the entire nation took responsibility for maintaining its children. The code reinforced paternal power by paying family allowances to the father and encouraging women with children to stay at home. It also took years to hammer out, and by the time it passed, in July 1939, it was far too late to have any impact on the relative strength of France's population compared to that of its enemy, Germany.[64]

The Trauma
of Separation

The crisis of 1939–40 only initiated a series of traumas for the women who endured the exodus and defeat and capture of their husbands. Once the armistice had been signed, the new state followed policies that also had profound repercussions on prisoners' wives but that equally fell beyond their control. During the occupation, from 1941 to 1943, prisoners' wives managed to achieve some stability in their lives, but in 1944 renewed fighting in France initiated the final year of trauma. Thus the war determined the rhythm of the women's lives—trauma, stability, and renewed trauma—beginning with the general mobilization of 1 September 1939.

The Crisis of War and Defeat

All of France sustained a series of shocks from September 1939 through June 1940, each one worse than the previous: the outbreak of another war with Germany only twenty-one years after the end of the Great War, the blitzkrieg that began in May 1940, and the quick defeat of the formidable French army. Not only was the army defeated but the government collapsed and the very fabric of society seemed to be coming apart. The traumas of war and defeat for the nation precipitated millions of personal crises. Interviews forty years later reveal that this period stands out in individual memories. Other years blend together, but key dates and events of the period from the autumn of 1939 through the summer of 1940 are engraved in the memories of the people who lived through it with remarkable accuracy.

From Hitler's announcement of German rearmament in 1935 on, tensions in Europe mounted. But only after Hitler violated the Munich agreement of September 1938 did Great Britain and France abandon the policy of appeasement and offer guarantees of "all support in their power" to Poland, Rumania, and Greece.[1] After signing the Nazi-Soviet Pact, Hitler quickly provoked a war with Poland, which began on 1 September 1939. That same day, France ordered a general mobilization, and on 3 September, Great Britain and France declared war on Germany.

Although the expectation of imminent war had been widespread, the actual outbreak of war came as a shock to France. For women whose husbands were mobilized (all men between the ages of twenty and forty with fewer than four children), the crisis signaled the start of a personal ordeal. Fernande Damart remembered the day her husband was called up vividly because it was her birthday and her husband had given her flowers. "I threw that bouquet down and said, 'Yeah, sure, some birthday!'"[2]

The declaration of war was followed by a long period of inactivity known as the "phony war." Aside from occasional sorties, little actual fighting took place owing to the defensive strategy of France's and England's military and political leaders. The allies passed up their opportunity to attack Germany while it was fighting in Poland based on several, ultimately mistaken, assumptions: that it would be a long war of attrition, that the Maginot line was inviolable, and that an attack against the German Siegfried line would be too risky. Hence, military leaders relied entirely on a strategy of defense, sure that the German armies would be unable to break through the Maginot line supported by continuous forces from the Ardennes Forest to the North Sea. Unfortunately, the phony war diminished the morale of the French soldiers at the front, who were left in a constant state of bored attention and uncertainty.[3]

The phony war at least allowed husbands to return home for brief visits. Most POW wives recall vividly the few days their husbands spent with them during this period. In some cases, couples actually married during the leave. Josette Garnier and her husband postponed their original wedding date, 16 September 1939, because of the mobilization. While her fiancé was home on his first leave, they decided to marry during his next visit. They spent a few days together after the marriage in late April 1940 but did not see each other again for five years.[4] The Doucets, married four months before Raymond's mobilization, were expecting a baby on 15 May 1940. Luckily the baby arrived early, on 26 April. By 15 May Raymond would not have been able to come home, as the phony war had ended. As it was, he visited on 27 April and spent three days with his wife and daughter. His return home did not occur until five years later—to the day.[5]

The phony war ended abruptly with the German attack of Belgium and Holland on 10 May 1940. French and British troops rushed into Belgium to reinforce the collapsing Dutch and Belgian armies, hoping also to keep the bulk of the fighting off French soil. Meanwhile Hitler concentrated his attack on France in an unexpected area: the Ardennes Forest, assumed by French strategists to be impregnable. German tanks quickly passed through the Ardennes and crossed the Meuse River. In five days Germany accomplished what it had been unable to do in the four years of fighting of World War I. By 15 May three key cities, Monthermé, Dinant, and Sedan, had fallen, and the Germans succeeded in breaking a ninety-kilometer gap through the Allied front. The French high command, ineffectively trying to reestablish a continuous front rather than assembling forces capable of withstanding Germany's concentrated attacks, sent small "packets" of troops, which Germany easily defeated.

The Allies' last attempt to close the gap failed on 26 May, allowing the Germans to complete a three-pronged attack, demolish the remaining armies, and capture record numbers of prisoners of war. One wing of German troops swiveled around to the north, trapping the armies in Flanders and pushing them to the North Sea coast at Dunkirk. German tanks unexpectedly halted for a critical period, allowing the British to rescue some 330,000 troops, 130,000 of them French, from the German trap. Still, the Germans took 50,000 prisoners at Dunkirk. From there the Germans continued west and south to take control of the Atlantic coast. Another wing of German tanks moved back east, capturing the armies at the Maginot line from the rear. In part because the French high command delayed in pulling troops out, some 400,000 prisoners were taken.[6] The third wing of German troops moved southeast to join up with Italian forces.[7]

Already, Germany had rounded up a remarkably large number of prisoners of war. Clearly it was an integral part of their strategy. On 4 June, two weeks before France's defeat, Göring declared, in opposition to those demanding the conscription of German women to meet the labor needs of the war economy, that Germany would soon have enough POWs to meet its manpower needs.[8] Germany had every interest in rounding up as many POWs as possible to feed its own war machine, but French strategic ineptitude practically delivered hundreds of thousands of soldiers up to Germany. The troops who rushed into Belgium were trapped; the small packets sent to the Meuse were quickly captured; the German army circled around behind the Maginot line and simply rounded up the remaining soldiers there.

As the German armies advanced, retreating French armies were joined by hundreds of thousands of refugees, first from Belgium and Holland and then from the north and east of France. Panic struck when the government decided to leave Paris on 10 June, and some two million Parisians left the city, hoping to cross the Loire and escape the German armies. The French expression for this period, "the exodus," highlights the cataclysmic nature to them of June 1940.[9]

Several of my witnesses left during the exodus. Authorities had ordered the evacuation of frontier regions in the northeast, but the orders were "incomprehensible." Entire towns packed up and left while neighboring towns stayed put. Elisabeth Doremus, who lived in a small village in the north, left with her two children following the evacuation orders and because "we were still mentally influenced by stories about the 14–18 war." When she found German troops already ahead of her, she turned around and went home. "The Germans were everywhere, so there was no point in going any farther."[10] For those who left, the exodus proved to be extremely slow because of clogged roads and gasoline shortages, dangerous because of strafing, and ultimately futile. Once the fighting had ended, returning home proved just as slow and difficult, and those who had come from the "forbidden zone" in the northeast of France were not allowed to return there.

Less than six weeks after it had begun, the Battle of France ended. On 17 June, Marshall Pétain, who had just taken over as prime minister, announced that he had asked Germany for armistice conditions and that "the fighting must stop."[11] The armistice was not valid until 25 June, a week later, but Pétain's message left the French soldiers in a quandary. Should they continue to fight until an armistice had been signed, as some regiments did, or should they stop resisting, in which case the Germans took them prisoner? Once again, French ineptitude played into German hands: Germany captured nearly one million French soldiers in the week between Pétain's speech and the signing of the armistice.[12]

After such a crushing blow as the Battle of France, it might seem that France had little choice but to admit defeat and sign an armistice with Germany. Pétain led a pro-armistice group of deputies, including Pierre Laval and Adrien Marquet, who believed that an armistice was France's best choice. Not everyone agreed. Paul Reynaud, prime minister when the German attack began, wanted to make a military stand in June, but he resigned in the midst of the governmental crisis that month.[13]

At least two other options were considered and rejected. The French government could have gone to North Africa and carried on the fight from there, or it could have formed a government in exile in London, as did other European countries.[14] Some French political leaders preferred either of those two options, and twenty-six deputies left on 21 June for North Africa aboard the *Massilia*. Even a military leader, General Charles de Gaulle, disobeyed his commanders, Maxime Weygand and Pétain, and left for London. On 18 June, the day after Pétain's announcement, de Gaulle addressed France over the BBC, insisting that the war was not over and calling on those who agreed to join him in London and carry on the fight. But the armistice was not merely the result of the internal scheming of a defeatist faction of Pétain, Laval, and others within the government.[15] The majority of the French people greeted Pétain's announcement with a tremendous sense of relief.

After the Armistice

Although the Battle of France was brief, the shock and trauma of the debacle cannot be overestimated. Fear of chaos, the possibility of a second Paris Commune, exaggerated stories of the horrors of German occupation during World War I—all won Pétain gratitude from most of the French for having "saved us from the abyss."[16]

The armistice that became valid on 25 June 1940 was harsh. Germany occupied nearly two-thirds of France. A line of demarcation divided the occupied zone from the so-called free zone, establishing a virtual frontier that was extremely difficult to cross; even mail was limited to three hundred letters a day. All war material had to be turned over to Germany; the French army was limited to 100,000; and captured French soldiers remained prisoners of war, with the Geneva Convention of 1929 serving as framework, until a peace treaty was concluded. France paid Germany occupation costs of 20 million marks a day, which, under the exaggerated exchange rate set by Germany at twenty francs per mark, amounted to 400 million francs a day. In perhaps the most shocking provision of the armistice, France agreed to turn over to Germany all German nationals who had sought asylum in France after the Nazi takeover.[17]

Pétain took over the government in June 1940 as prime minister of the Third Republic. He and his followers had no intention of continuing to work within a system they detested. Shortly after the armistice had been signed, a domestic revolution took place. To Vichy leaders, the Third Republic, based on false assumptions, represented the culmination of all the evils first perpetrated by the 1789 revolutionaries: egalitarianism, liberalism, and anticlericalism. The defeat only proved what they already knew: a republic was incapable of leading France. Therefore, after the National Assembly voted on 10 July to give full powers to Pétain, he set in motion a counterrevolution formally destroying the Republic. His four constitutional acts established a new government, called simply the French State (*l'Etat français*), in theory headquartered only temporarily in Vichy. Pétain himself became the head of the state; initially in 1940 and again after 1942, Pierre Laval was the head of the government.

As some 92,000 men had been killed and 1,800,000 prisoners of war captured, soldiers' wives did not share in the general feelings of relief.[18] For them, the real nightmare began after the armistice. The French Army had collapsed so quickly and so many soldiers were captured that it took Germany months to ascertain the number of casualties, to identify those killed in action or taken prisoner, and finally to notify the families in France.

Soldiers' wives thus waited for months to find out whether their husbands were alive or dead. "The hardest thing for me," explained Hélène forty years later, "was the period from June to November of 40 when I had no news. All my friends had already heard and they said, 'Can't you see that it's hopeless.' "[19] Hélène Noiret returned to her farm after the exodus "discouraged, without news of my husband, two months pregnant. My parents who lived through the 1914–18 war comforted me and helped me understand that everything has an end and that I should stay on the farm."[20] Simone de Beauvoir described Paris at the end of June 1940 as she anxiously awaited news of Sartre: "It's the same old story everywhere, in the Métro, on doorsteps, with women exchanging virtually identical lines: 'Any news?' 'No, he must be a prisoner.' 'When will the lists come out?' and so on."[21]

Some men managed to send messages from their temporary camps in France (*Frontstalags*) to their families as early as July. Most wives did not receive notification until August, some waited through the fall of 1940, and notices were still being sent as late as January 1941. Notification usually took the form of a card printed by the Red Cross on which the prisoner of war crossed out the lines that did not apply, usually leaving the seventh line to read, "I am a prisoner and in good health." No further communication was permitted on this card.

Even such sparse news produced a sense of relief. Beauvoir writes in her journal after finally receiving a note from Sartre, "This note is of unbelievable importance, yet its content is nil. All the same, I breathe a little easier now."[22] Geneviève Jamon wrote her father on 26 July 1940, "Paul is a prisoner! The telegram which arrived this morning just confirmed officially what for 26 days I had wanted to believe. . . . If Paul could only know the alleviation of our anguish and the magnificent burst of confidence that now carries us into the future!"[23]

The initial relief quickly gave way to new uncertainty. Marthe Jolliet, after receiving the news that her husband was a POW, responded, "What joy, and what sadness too, when will we see each other again?"[24] Most wives seemed to think their husbands would be home shortly. Laure wrote in her diary on 3 August 1940, "You are a prisoner. It's true, but I cannot make a drama out of it since you are alive. ALIVE. That's all that counts!" Two days later, she wrote, "I hope to see you soon. They are talking about captivity furloughs! I am burning with impatience to see you again."[25]

The status of the French prisoners of war could not be separated from the course of the war in a global sense, but the French government encouraged the belief that the war was over and the prisoners would soon be home. Georges Scapini, French ambassador in charge of the POWs, told prisoners' families in January 1941 "to have confidence in a better future near at hand." In the fall of 1941, widespread rumors that a peace treaty was about to be signed prompted the government to issue a public denial.[26]

Most prisoners' wives did not understand that Germany, still at war, had no intention of releasing a potentially hostile fighting force and planned to use POW labor to mitigate severe labor shortages.[27] In other words, POWs would be released only after Germany's defeat. In 1985, one wife, when asked whether she realized her husband's return would follow the end of the war, responded, "But the war was over in '40!"[28] The majority of wives had no idea how long their husbands would remain captive. For those who did not connect their husband's fate with the course of the war, the return could come at any time. Michelle Dupuy recalled that every year at Christmas she thought, "He will be here for the next one."[29] Germaine Doucet recounted that one of her fellow POW wives read tarot cards to predict the future. In the fall of 1940 she informed Doucet, "I read the cards. Without a doubt, he will be home with the first roses of spring."[30] Most government leaders at Vichy shared and encouraged the sentiment that for France, the war was over and the prisoners would soon be liberated.[31]

Some prisoner of war wives, less naïve or more mindful of the larger context of the war, expected from the start a long captivity. Marie-Hélène Corbel, a politically aware Communist sympathizer, knew her husband's fate depended on the war. Still, she found the waiting to be tortuous: "When would the war ever end, when? And how, and in what way?"[32] Only one of the POW wives I interviewed, highly educated and married to a historian, had read the armistice. "First of all, the armistice conditions specified that the prisoners would not be liberated until after the signing of a peace treaty. And I understood that England was there and would never surrender. So I had an idea that it was going to be long."[33]

She was correct: the armistice clearly stated that the 1.5 million POWs eventually transferred to Germany would remain there as prisoners until the conclusion of a peace treaty. But one of the very justifications for maintaining a French state under these harsh conditions was the belief that Vichy would be able to negotiate the early release of the POWs. Many leaders at Vichy believed in 1940 that a peace treaty would quickly follow England's imminent collapse. Therefore, the greater part of Vichy's effort on behalf of the prisoners of war went initially into negotiating with Germany for their release. Once it became clear that Germany would not liberate all the prisoners, Vichy policy toward the prisoners shifted. Negotiations focused on obtaining the release of certain groups of POWs. At home, the state's attention turned toward protecting families in the absence of these prisoners.

The Vichy Regime, the Prisoners of War, and Their Families

My attention falls first on the destiny of the prisoners. I am thinking of them . . . because they fought to the extreme limit of their strength. . . . I want their mothers, their wives, their sons to know that my thoughts never leave them, that they too are my children.
—Philippe Pétain

The prisoner of war issue weighed heavily on France. The national economy suffered from the reduced labor force. The absence of so many men created a psychological ripple effect among their immediate families, their friends and neighbors, and their communities. Everyone had a POW in the family or knew someone who did. Politically, the prisoners were central to the French state at Vichy. To a large extent they justified Vichy's very existence and were a constant factor in relations between France and Germany. Leaders at Vichy considered the liberation of the prisoners essential. "The very fabric of France depends on it," Laval proclaimed in 1940.[1] In nearly every speech, Pétain referred to the prisoners in Germany, who would be the vanguard of the national revolution.[2]

The armistice specified that the French prisoners of war would remain in German hands. Political and military leaders at Vichy who accepted the armistice in 1940 differed about how to interpret it, however. A few high-ranking military officers, unhappy about the armistice, accepted it out of military duty and loyalty to Pétain.[3] Other prominent leaders accepted it wholeheartedly but felt Franco-German relations should be governed by a strict interpretation of the armistice and nothing more. General Weygand claimed after the war that he interpreted the armistice, which he favored, as a strict cease-fire that would allow France to rebuild and eventually to take revenge on Germany.[4]

Laval, who became the head of the new French state at Vichy, considered the armistice only the first step in reestablishing normal relations between France and Germany. He interpreted the armistice as only the prelude to reaching a quick peace settlement with Germany. To him the French fleet (which the armistice left intact and under French control), France's colonial empire, and the threat of joining the Allies put France in a good position to bargain with Germany. He believed that Germany would defeat England quickly. Accepting the armistice and then negotiating would allow France to recover from the initial trauma of the defeat, to restore and maintain order, to improve conditions in France, and to bring the prisoners of war home.[5]

With Laval were such men as Admiral François Darlan and General Charles Huntziger, both of whom felt France should continue to negotiate with Germany.[6] By anticipating German demands—for example, collaborating with Germany against the British in Syria—France would be able to win favorable concessions. Because the policy of collaboration had Pétain's support, the Vichy regime, rather than strictly following the armistice, attempted to negotiate with the Germans as partners and not as belligerent nations. In trying to gain favorable treatment from the Germans—benefits that would legitimate the Vichy government to the French people—Vichy often became caught up in a game it could only lose. Negotiations over the prisoners of war illustrate France's collaboration strategy as well as its dangers.

France, Germany, and the Prisoners of War

As specified in the Geneva Convention, a neutral country, the United States, was appointed to protect France's prisoners of war and to serve as an intermediary between the belligerent nations. However, the Vichy government accepted a German proposal, substituting itself for the United States as protector of its own prisoners. Under a protocol signed with Germany in November 1940, Vichy established a mission in Berlin, the Service diplomatique des prisonniers de guerre (SDPG), and appointed Georges Scapini ambassador.[7]

Why did the French government go along with this arrangement, which Germany proposed in its own best interests? France, which Germany had defeated and occupied and which had no German prisoners to use as a counterweight, replaced the United States, an independent, powerful nation over which Germany had no hold. After the war, Scapini argued that, had France refused to act as protecting power, it would have been abandoning its own prisoners. Germany in retaliation might have treated the prisoners more harshly. Scapini also claimed that the United States would not have obtained better results than he had. At least as protecting power, the French government maintained direct contact with the prisoners, supplying them directly with food, clothing, and medicine. Scapini had no scruples about bypassing the Geneva Convention: "It is childish to speak of rights during wartime when war itself is the denial of all rights, for which it substitutes the single element of force."[8]

Scapini did not conclude from this perspective that the imbalance in force between Germany and France worked against his effort to negotiate as equals with the Germans. Rather, he believed that by working alongside the rules, placing the prisoners within the framework of more friendly Franco-German relations, and demonstrating to Germany mutual interests, he would be able to obtain concessions. In 1940, he attempted to persuade the Germans that their best interests would be served by freeing the French prisoners, which would produce in France a climate favorable to collaboration. The Germans were not convinced. Along the same lines, he suggested replacing the prisoners of war with voluntary French laborers as a demonstration of the two nations' mutual interests. At that point, Germany had no desire to release a potentially hostile force, and the labor of the prisoners themselves satisfied German needs.[9]

The problem of POW labor in war industries illustrated the dangers inherent in Scapini's approach. Article 31 of the Geneva Convention prohibited the use of POWs in war industries—a prohibition widely ignored by Germany. Early in 1942, Scapini and General Hermann Reinecke met after seven French prisoners of war protested the violation. Reinecke pointed out that "the convention had largely been supervened, especially since the German government had granted conditions of treatment and liberations that were not foreseen by the approved convention. Moreover, the orientation of French policy and the negotiations underway gave much larger perspectives to our relations in terms of our common work for a reconstruction of Europe."[10]

The French negotiator backed down and agreed to explain to the prisoners why Article 31 no longer applied. Durand aptly points out that from the perspective of the prisoners, held in Germany as enemy soldiers, Franco-German relations often left them bewildered. Prisoners of war are captured enemy soldiers whose duty is to escape or, barring that, to resist or sabotage the work they are forced to do. In this case, the French soldiers wore prisoner uniforms and were clearly exploited by Germany; yet their own government discouraged them from attempting escape or sabotage. By negotiating with Germany from a position of weakness, the Vichy government, as Durand points out, "inevitably had to be drawn into concessions which at times left the POWs themselves in an ambiguous situation in which they no longer knew exactly where their duty lay."[11]

Although Vichy backed down over the use of prisoner labor in war industries, it intervened successfully in other cases. Scapini, to his credit, resisted German efforts to send Jewish prisoners of war to separate camps, insisting that as French soldiers they should receive the same treatment as the other prisoners.[12] Germany, although it did nothing to prevent a typhus epidemic among Russian prisoners of war, permitted France to send huge quantities of vaccines to its own prisoners. Further, the Vichy regime obtained the release of some 200,000 prisoners by 1944 (see table 3.1).

The Germans deliberately used the prisoners of war to encourage a pro-collaboration attitude in France. For example, in August of 1941 Rudolf Schlieir, from the German Embassy in Paris, claimed that Germany had already repatriated five hundred thousand French prisoners, a generosity he attributed to "the Führer's esteem for the French soldier." The prisoners of war, once informed of Hitler's esteem, should "turn France resolutely away from what has proven to be a very unfortunate line of conduct of hostility towards Germany. The liberated prisoners will thereby contribute to the reconstruction of a successful Europe."[13] A more gruesome example of Germany's use of the prisoners occurred after the assassination of German soldiers in Nantes and Bordeaux in October 1941. The commander-in-chief of the German occupation troops announced that he would consider liberating all prisoners whose families "cooperated with the ongoing investigation to find the assassins of Nantes and Bordeaux."[14]

That the Germans used the French prisoners to entice collaboration is hardly surprising. That the French government exploited its own captive soldiers, trying to win over the public, was a strange twist. A media blitz, which the government censors obligated newspapers to carry, accompanied every return of prisoners to France. Photographs showed the happy prisoners in trains covered with such slogans as "Vive Pétain" and "Vive

TABLE 3.1   *Liberations before 1945*

Obtained by Vichy	
Veterans of World War I	59,359
Fathers of four or more children	18,731
Career military	1,422
Specialists	14,490
Relève	90,747
Public administration	17,751
Widowers	123
Cultivators	18,127
Railway workers	1,710
Agricultural engineers	381
TOTAL	222,841

Released for Other Reasons	
Escapees	71,000
Medical services	32,740
Sick and wounded	183,381
Deceased	4,216
Rescuers	232
Services rendered	81
Prisoners from Alsace-Lorraine	7,681
Prisoners from Dieppe	1,580
Humanitarian Cases	273
Reward and Propaganda Mission	12
Undetermined reasons	81,076
TOTAL	382,272

Source: Yves Durand, *La Captivité*, 324.

Laval," along with the more obvious "Vive la France."[15] Speeches by General Huntziger (chief of the Armistice Army), Pétain, and Scapini described all liberations as proof of Vichy's efficacy. In fact, the first prisoners to return—those interned in Switzerland, the sick and wounded, and medical and sanitary personnel—were covered by the Geneva Convention. Vichy could legitimately claim responsibility for liberating veterans of World War I, members of certain services—railroad, post office, electric, and gas company employees—and fathers and eldest brothers of families with four or more children. About three hundred thousand others either escaped or were repatriated under provisions of the Geneva Convention. But the media blurred the distinction between those liberated under the Geneva Convention and those liberated because of Vichy's efforts (see table 3.1).

Vichy deliberately took credit for all POW liberations in order to inspire the "correct attitude" in France. As Scapini insisted after the return of prisoners held in Switzerland, "Never forget that the problem of the prisoners cannot be isolated from the whole of general policy." Havas, the official French press agency, described the return of another group of prisoners (veterans of World War I and sanitary personnel) as a "new and tangible result of the policy followed . . . by the Marshall."[16]

The press and the government also interpreted release of prisoners as a sign of Germany's goodwill toward France. If the Germans let French soldiers return home, perhaps they were not so bad after all. Hitler liberated veterans of World War I, *L'Illustration* explained, because "the Führer himself is a war veteran. . . . He more than anyone is open to pity for those—whatever uniform they wear—who will always be brothers in arms to him."[17] More relevant to Germany was the fact that, because these men were already fairly old, their value as laborers was not worth the manpower necessary to intern them. The same can be said of the sick and wounded. Employees of France's railroad company, post office, and public utilities could serve Germany just as usefully in France, where they maintained the infrastructure, thereby freeing German manpower. As for fathers and brothers of large families, they cannot have been a particularly large group, for fathers of four or more children were generally exempt from mobilization.[18]

Government collaboration, as Stanley Hoffmann points out, provided a springboard for the more rabid forms of collaborationism that developed in Paris.[19] In the same way, private collaborators imitated the government's use of the prisoners to garner public support. The Rassemblement national populaire (RNP), a collaborationist party founded by Marcel Déat in February 1941, shamelessly exploited prisoners' wives to fill out its membership. One prisoner's wife remembered hearing on the radio that a certain number of prisoner of war wives who signed a list at a certain place at a certain time would get their husbands back. "How many of us abandoned our meager lunch to rush over, with hope in our hearts." When she arrived a huge crowd had already formed. Nothing came of the episode, however, except that Déat obtained an artificially inflated RNP membership list.[20]

In October 1941, Eugène Deloncle broke off from the RNP and formed a splinter group, the Mouvement social révolutionnaire (MSR). Again, prisoners' families were tricked into joining his Amicale des familles de prisonniers de guerre with the false promise of liberation. The MSR asked prisoners' families to fill out a "Questionnaire for the eventual liberation of a Prisoner," which closed with the statement, "I declare that I belong to the Amicale des familles de prisonniers de guerre, MSR." One prisoner's wife sent a copy of the questionnaire to the government asking if she could hope for the liberation of her husband, a member of the group.[21]

La Relève

There is no way of knowing how many desperate families were taken in by such false promises. Unfortunately, playing on the desire for the return of a prisoner husband or son was not unique to rabid collaborationist groups. The French government itself drew on the same emotions, hoping to avoid the institution of compulsory labor (which was nonetheless imposed eight months later).

Through an agreement called the *Relève*, France and Germany together endeavored to make the French public aware of the connection between collaboration and repatriation. The Relève represented a return to Scapini's initial idea of demonstrating to Germany the mutual interests of the two countries. In 1940, Scapini had proposed that the Germans exchange three POWs for every worker who went to Germany. The Relève reversed the proportion: every three skilled workers who went to Germany voluntarily enabled one prisoner of war to return to France. Although the ratio was not made explicit to the French public until mid-August 1942, two months after the Relève had been inaugurated, Laval made the connection with collaboration explicit from the beginning.[22] When he announced the Relève in June 1942, Laval stated, "I hope for a German victory."[23] Otherwise, he continued, bolshevism would take over in Europe. Germany needed all its men in the struggle against bolshevism and therefore sought outside labor to run its factories. Every French worker who went to Germany contributed both to the defeat of bolshevism and to the return of the prisoners. The prisoners became a reward for collaboration.

The French press billed going to Germany as an act of solidarity with the prisoners, who had already worked in Germany for two years and deserved a rest. Vichy propaganda appealed directly to women to send their men on the Relève, thereby expressing their solidarity with prisoners' wives, mothers, and fiancées.

> You who have the great good fortune of keeping your sons, your husbands and your fiancés who work in factories near you.
> You more than anyone can understand the pressing need to counsel these same sons, these same husbands, these same fiancés, that the HOUR OF THE RELEVE HAS COME.
> That other mothers, other wives, other fiancées will be infinitely grateful to you for having given them back the absent loved ones they have been awaiting for two years.[24]

The government even called on prisoners' wives to work in Germany. "You can rejoin *him* in Germany," promised a publicity poster, by signing a "spouse" contract for one full year of work in Germany.[25]

The press created the impression that the prisoners themselves solidly supported Laval. On the front page on 29 June 1942, *Le Temps* published "the moving call of a prisoner for the Relève." That prisoner happened to be André Masson, a notorious collaborator. A "liberated prisoners' action committee in favor of the Relève" addressed Laval on behalf of those prisoners still in Germany. "In the camps and barracks the conversations are feverish and . . . every one of us feels a surge of joy in his heart. . . . You are responsible for much joy and renewed courage. We thank you on their behalf."[26] A prisoner from Stalag II C insisted that the prisoners in Germany reacted to the Relève "with a unanimous and profound feeling of joy and of earnest gratitude for the marshall and President Laval."[27]

In fact the Relève damaged morale, both in camps and at home. In the prison camps the Relève created bad feelings, jealousy, and suspicion among prisoners.[28] In the same way, although the Relève supposedly demonstrated French solidarity, evidence indicates its extreme divisiveness in France.

For most wives, the Relève brought misinformation, false hopes, bitterness, and jealousy. In July 1942, letters began pouring in to Pétain as a result of publicity about the Relève. Many families mistakenly believed that the Relève would liberate a prisoner whose family members volunteered to work in Germany. "I am writing to ask if you would be good enough to do something for my husband who is a prisoner of war in Germany, having read in the papers that if three members of a family were working in Germany, the prisoner could be liberated. That is my case."[29]

Pétain's office forwarded these letters to the Scapini mission, which responded bureaucratically, "The Relève is collective and not individual." Desperate families became easy prey for the false hopes raised by the Relève. "Since the Relève was announced we have been waiting in vain for him. Every time a train arrives we say, 'This is the one!' and he still has not returned."[30] Families wrote to Pétain pleading with him to send their men back on the Relève long after it ceased to operate.

The Relève created a sense of bitterness and jealousy toward those prisoners who did return. The whole thing seemed to be arbitrary and unfair. One prisoner's wife wrote, "At times we are very unhappy to see returning young men without family responsibilities while those who have children remain behind barbed wire." Another told Pétain, "Believe me, it is more than a little revolting to see young men returning around you who have no children and [are] unmarried."[31]

Prisoners' wives wrote to Pétain because he projected a warm, fatherly, omniscient image. They had faith that he could obtain their husbands' release. "You, you could give him back to us—I am sure of it. I have confidence in you. . . . Do not destroy that confidence, I beg of you." The letters were hardly impartial or disinterested since the wives were trying to get something out of Pétain. Nevertheless, that the women wrote to him personally and the terms they used (for example, their request for his "intercession" to get their husbands home) illustrate the continued current of reverence for Pétain.[32] One wife wrote, "I am revolted to see how the Relève is done with so much injustice. Certainly, *Monsieur le Maréchal,* you have not been informed of this. So here I am to tell you all about it."[33]

Germany's labor needs continued to grow and French workers did not volunteer for the Relève in large enough numbers to satisfy the Germans. By the fall of 1942, French factory workers were being designated for labor in Germany and escorted to the trains by the police.[34] Officially, however, Germany introduced forced labor only in February 1943.

Even after it became compulsory, the Germans continued to link the prisoners of war to French labor. Every compulsory laborer who went to Germany enabled one prisoner of war to be "transformed" into a so-called free worker in Germany. Free workers wore civilian dress, earned regular wages and a two-week vacation, and fell under civil, not military, authorities in Germany—not altogether an improvement, as this substituted the Gestapo for the military high command.

Once again, Vichy refused to learn from the failure of the Relève that collaboration benefited Germany more than France. The Germans gained the increased productivity of free labor. German soldiers, freed from guard duty, could be sent to the war fronts. A total of some 221,000 prisoners were transformed, freeing thirty thousand German soldiers.[35] Vichy promoted transformation because it brought prisoners home, if only temporarily, and seemed to be progress in the direction of cooperation on equal terms.

Given the decline of Germany's military position during the spring and summer of 1943 in North Africa, Italy, and the Soviet Union, the error of abandoning both a uniform that classed the prisoners among Germany's enemies and the protection of the Red Cross should have been clear to the prisoners. Yet not all of them were well informed about the military situation. Furthermore, the transformation contract promised them two-week vacations in France with their families (although after the first contingent was sent to France and very few transformed prisoners showed up for the return trip to Germany, the vacation policy was discontinued).[36] Higher wages may also have attracted many prisoners whose families needed the additional income. (Ironically, after 6 June 1944, D-Day, they were again cut off from their families and unable to send money.) In some cases, the prisoners had no choice: their labor detachment was transformed as a group.

Like the traumas of war and defeat, Franco-German relations shaped the lives of POW wives but were beyond their control. Although foreign policy had an impact on them, it was primarily concerned with the POWs and only secondarily with their families.

But Vichy did have a domestic agenda. Saving the French family was a central part of its plans to reshape France. Prisoners' families constituted special objects of concern in two of Vichy's dearest projects: protecting prisoners' interests in their absence and reinforcing the traditional, patriarchal family.

Vichy's National Revolution

The new state at Vichy represented the first "postwar" attempt to restore order and return to normalcy. It was not a puppet regime enacting policies imposed by Germany.[37] Neither was it a monolithic regime. On the contrary, the number of different groups and ideas competing for ascendancy throughout this period led one historian to suggest that Vichy should be presented in the plural, as "the governments of Vichy."[38] Furthermore, scholars continue to draw distinctions between state collaboration and collaborationism, between those who collaborated for personal gain and collaborationists motivated by ideology, between *attentiste* and activist interpretations of collaboration, between all forms of collaboration and the Vichy regime as a whole, and so on.[39] In spite of the variations, some basic generalizations about the Vichy regime, and therefore about state collaboration, can be usefully made.

Vichy has been aptly described as "the revenge of the minorities."[40] For the most part, those who came to power had been part of the prewar right wing, people alienated from and antagonized by the Third Republic, who shared such characteristics as anticommunism, antiliberalism, and an acceptance of the defeat. The various personalities can be grouped into three basic competing schools of thought: the traditional conservatives, the technocratic experts, and the radical right fascists.[41]

The traditionalists' spokesman, Pétain, maintained that France had been a great power under the Old Regime. Democracy had ruined France, as had the "false idea of the natural equality of man."[42] France needed a "national revolution" to return to its pre-1789 greatness. Traditionalists disliked the materialism, individualism, and égoism fostered by the republican system. The new French State was based on a paternal vision of power. The state revolved around, if not a king, at least a strong, regal, authoritarian father figure—Pétain. Rather than guaranteeing individual liberty, it demanded sacrifice from people to rebuild a strong and populous nation. To signify the new order, Vichy replaced the republican motto "Liberty, Equality, Fraternity" with a new one: "Work, Family, Fatherland."[43]

Traditionalists yearned for a return to a society based on small family farms and shops and led by a natural elite. Industry, big cities, and the modern mass culture they bred caused France's decadence and international decline. Vichy traditionalists wished to reverse the concentration and depersonalization of modern industry and agriculture. Vichy's "return to the soil" program attempted to halt the rural exodus and rebuild the family farm, "the principal economic and social base of France."[44]

Corporatism was the traditionalist principle of industrial reorganization. Ideally, employers, managers, and workers would organize into natural economic groupings by branch of industry. Each corporation would govern itself, attenuating the chaos of the free market system and, as all members shared an interest in the well-being of their corporation, eliminating class struggle. Just in case, Pétain outlawed strikes and dissolved all unions and syndicates.[45]

Pétain represented only the foremost of the many traditionalists who came to power at Vichy, including General Maxime Weygand, at the Defense Ministry; General Paul de la Porte du Theil, in charge of the Chantiers de la jeunesse; and Georges Lamirand at the Ministry of Education. Their opinions echoed those of such traditionalist writers as Charles Maurras, Gustave Thibon, and Jacques Thierry-Maulnier. Many army officers approved the military flavor of Vichy's leadership.[46]

Catholic church leaders appreciated the overall tone of moral regeneration as well as the attempt by the government to strengthen Catholicism and ease long-standing church-state tensions. As Pétain put it, "A good mass never did anyone any harm."[47] Church schools received state financial support. Further, Vichy expanded the public school curriculum to include religious and moral instruction. Public schoolteachers, long considered apostles of the Republic, were required to take an oath of loyalty to Pétain. Free Masonic and Jewish teachers were to be purged.[48]

Pétain and the traditionalists held the most prominent, publicly visible positions at Vichy. Behind the scenes, however, the technocrats gained key positions and increased their power as the war went on. After Laval was fired and Pierre-Etienne Flandin fell from power, Navy Admiral François-Xavier Darlan took over as virtual head of state in February 1941. He represented the technocratic orientation of many of France's highest ranking civil servants and big businessmen.[49]

Although right-wing, authoritarian, antiliberal, and anti-egalitarian like the traditionalists, the technocratic experts rejected the traditionalists' backward-looking orientation. Educated for the most part at the *grands écoles,* the technocrats worked to rationalize the economy and the state in the interest of efficiency. Men such as Pierre Pucheu and François Lehideux, successive ministers of industrial production, and Yves Bouthillier, minister of finance, were not filled with poetic longings for a return to the Old Regime. Rather, they pushed France away from small, inefficient production toward centralization and economic concentration. Many of them hoped to integrate France economically into the German-led New Europe.[50] Darlan brought most of them in, and their real influence increased throughout the war, owing to German requisitions and the resulting scarcities.

Overjoyed to be freed from the meddling of poorly educated elected officials, the technocrats welcomed Vichy as their opportunity to administer France as efficiently as possible.[51]

Opposing both the traditionalists and the technocrats but combining elements of both, another ideological group initially competed for power at Vichy: the fascists. With the traditional conservatives, the fascists shared antiliberalism, anti-egalitarianism, and authoritarianism. Yet fascism yearned for a system different from the traditionalists' pastoral vision, preferring, like the technocrats, a modern, efficient, and powerful state.[52] What set the fascist right apart from the other groups was its revolutionary nature, its populism, and its propensity for violence. In the summer of 1940, Marcel Déat, prewar right-wing leaguer and director of the newspaper *L'Oeuvre*, proposed that Vichy establish a single party. When Pétain rejected the proposal and repulsed the radical right, most fascist intellectuals and party leaders (Déat, Jacques Doriot, Eugène Deloncle, Pierre Drieu la Rochelle, and Robert Brasillach) left Vichy. They returned to Paris in disgust and became vociferous critics of the lack of activism at Vichy. Until the appointments of Darnand, Henriot, and Déat in the final months of the Occupation, the fascists had little real power or influence over the state.[53]

Pétain, a popular figure, symbolized Vichy to the majority of the French. His brand of regressive, Catholic traditionalism, although unable to triumph against the technocrats, continued throughout the war to be the face and the voice of Vichy.[54] But traditionalism could not hold out against the exigencies of the occupier, whose demands only increased over time and whose repressive and brutal presence grew more and more evident. Thus by 1944, traditionalists at Vichy, whose hold on reality had always been tenuous, had completely lost touch with it.

Vichy Family Policy

The family policy of the Vichy state illustrates perfectly what happened to most of the goals of the national revolution. Vichy had ambitious plans for restoring the traditional French family and reversing the population decline.[55] Pétain blamed the defeat of 1940 on "too few babies" as well as too few allies and too few weapons. "Family" was at the center of France's new motto and in theory was central to the national revolution. Pétain believed that "a people is a hierarchy of families." Rather than the individual, the family "is the essential cell: it is the very foundation of the social edifice; on this we must build. . . . In the new order we are instituting, the family will be honored, protected, aided."[56]

Although Vichy traditionalists blamed the Third Republic for destroying the French family, the Vichy government did not replace the 1939 Family Code with one of its own. Vichy had no argument with the assumptions and goals that informed the Family Code and adopted it in its entirety.

The activism of Vichy distinguished its family policy from that of the Third Republic. Vichy intended to conduct a national crusade against the vices that weakened the French family. Despite his brief tenure, Jacques Chevalier, family and health secretary from February 1941 until August 1941, proved to be a key actor in Vichy family policy. His appointees, Léon Husson, Paul Huary, and especially Philippe Renaudin, survived Chevalier's departure and shaped Vichy family policy until the Liberation.[57] Vichy family policymakers championed a Catholic, conservative, and patriarchal vision of the ideal family, from which French families had strayed with disastrous consequences. The policymakers placed much of the blame on women.

In particular, traditionalists at Vichy believed that there had been a social revolution in women's status between the wars—a situation they intended to remedy. By restoring the patriarchal family, Vichy hoped to reverse the perceived increase in female employment. Conservatives in and out of Vichy stressed the harm female employment had done to the French moral fiber by creating delinquent children, alcoholic husbands, and flirtatious women. Women's work had also weakened France by lowering the birthrate. In November 1941, to focus public attention on the problem, the family and health secretary sponsored a public competition that presented a list of factors responsible for the fall in birthrate and asked the public to number them according to importance. The top three causes, according to the respondents, were the absence of religion, the "difficulties of raising a family," and female employment.[58]

Vichy support of Catholicism in church-run and public schools worked to reverse the absence of religion, while family and single-salary allowances mitigated the financial difficulties of raising a family. Vichy traditionalists responded to female employment by proclaiming that they would "return women to the home" ("la femme au foyer"). Georgette Varenne, in *La Femme dans la France nouvelle,* agreed: "I am convinced, with Marshall

Pétain, that women, as wives, as mothers, in the family and in society, must return to the place that nature assigned to them." Varenne asserted, "Women must understand: the happiness of the world is in their hands."[59]

On 11 October 1940 Vichy passed "one of the most important laws developed by the Marshall's government," according to Darlan.[60] The law prohibited state administration and services from hiring or recruiting married women, except women whose husbands were unable to support the household. A quota limited the number of women each branch could employ. Bonuses were paid to women who quit when they married; married women already employed whose husbands were able to support them could be placed on leave without pay. Women over the age of fifty were to be automatically retired with a pension. Although only applicable to the public sector, the law promised similar dispositions for personnel in private enterprise.[61] A closer look at the policy reveals its inconsistency.

The preface to the law explained that it was passed primarily "with a view to fighting unemployment." The demobilization of the army combined with the massive movement of population from the industrialized north to the rural south of France left the south facing a serious unemployment problem. The October 1940 law was thus a somewhat feeble attempt to create jobs for unemployed men by sending married women with working husbands home.[62] Further, the law was ineffective and was inconsistently enforced. Vichy never provided specific instructions on how to apply the law or how to determine a husband's capacity to support his family; nor were the proposed measures for private industry ever passed. Many upper-level directors considered the law disruptive of their personnel. While it remained in effect, the law resulted primarily in uncertainty for employed women and financial claims on the state as women retired or quit and collected their bonuses. A law in September 1942 finally suspended the law of October 1940. The cry of "return women to the home" faded as unemployment disappeared. German labor demands forced Vichy to consider conscripting female labor.[63]

Another Vichy profamily initiative was the creation of the Commissariat général à la famille (CGF) in September 1941, led by Philippe Renaudin, to coordinate all aspects of public policy directed at families. As this move showed, in its early years Vichy was more vigorous than the Republic had been in promoting its family goals by means of propaganda and moral exhortation.[64] The CGF sponsored the production of brochures, posters, traveling expositions, cartoons, newspaper inserts, and radio programs such as *France-Famille*, which promoted large and traditional families.[65]

The Third Republic intended, but never managed, to include a new school curriculum on the family. Vichy mandated, along with other educational reforms, educational programs to teach children about the joys of a large family and the proper roles of mothers and fathers. Vichy also resuscitated another Third Republican creation: Mother's Day. A propaganda blitz in the schools, on the radio, and in the press accompanied its approach.[66]

Vichy not only promoted its family ideology more vigorously than the Republic had, it also intervened more actively in people's private lives. Although birth control and abortion were already illegal, Vichy prosecuted both offenses more rigorously and stiffened the penalties against abortion, making it a crime against the state.[67] Vichy also intervened to stop the increase in the divorce rate. A law of 2 April 1941 prohibited divorce within the first three years of marriage and tightened judicial leeway in determining sufficient grounds for divorce.

The magnitude of state resources devoted to satisfying German demands limited the ability of the Vichy regime to follow through on its ambitious programs for the family.[68] Much as Vichy leaders wanted to believe that the war was over for France, Germany was still fighting and intended to extract as much from France as possible to feed its own war machine. The war also intruded on Vichy family plans by keeping over one million POWs in Germany, as well as 730,000 forced laborers and 138,000 political and religious deportees.[69] Families were separated, not strengthened, and Vichy was forced to deal with hundreds of thousands of families that could not attain the family ideal. More than anything, families separated by the war demonstrated the failure of Vichy to live up to its ideological pronouncements.

Protection of Prisoners' Families

Under international law, POWs remain mobilized soldiers. The Third Republic, basing its policy on World War I precedents, acted immediately after the declaration of war in September 1939 to provide for families of mobilized troops. At first the Vichy regime merely expressly extended these measures to POWs. Career officers, noncommissioned officers, and other reserve officers with at least two years of active service were entitled to a monthly salary based on their rank, function, marital status, number of dependents, and years of service. Up to three-quarters of that monthly sum could be paid directly to their wives or parents. Regular soldiers whose families relied upon them for support could be eligible for military allowances, which included a daily sum of money for the wife or dependent parent and additional sums per child, varying with location. A commission established in each canton examined applications and decided which families needed allowances. In May 1941, POW families on allowances were given an additional two francs a day (approximately six dollars a month) to allow them to pay for goods sent in packages.[70]

Other measures taken before the armistice were also extended. Laws exonerated prisoners' wives with incomes below five thousand francs a year from all taxes except the land tax, reduced rents by three-quarters for prisoners' families that remained in their prewar homes, and suspended the collection of back rents. Farm leases had to be renewed on the same terms to prisoners' families, and actions for recovery of commercial debts were suspended. All these measures remained in effect for six months after demobilization. Prisoners were reassured that the families of those who died in captivity would receive the same benefits as the families of those who died in battle and that they themselves would be considered on an equal basis for military honors. The government guaranteed reimbursement of the special camp money (*Lagermarks*) paid them for work on German labor detachments and promised a "liberation bonus" to all POWs except officers and civil servants who received their monthly civilian salary in France during their captivity (schoolteachers and other civil servants continued to receive their salaries). The bonus, equal to one-half the average monthly salary in their department, was to allow repatriated POWs a two-week vacation before returning to work. Employers also had to permit prisoners' wives to take a two-week vacation at the time of their husbands' return.[71]

None of these policies represented any real innovation beyond those developed during World War I on behalf of soldiers, prisoners of war, and their families. As with so much of the activity concerning POWs, the general expectation in 1940 that they would return quickly meant that a full year passed before the state decided to supplement these minimal measures.

Prisoners' families made up a large enough constituency that Family and Health Secretary Jacques Chevalier eventually decided specific family policies were needed for them. In July 1941, Chevalier explained in a letter to

Darlan, then head of state, that POW families presented the government with a problem of such profound repercussions for French society that it engaged the entire family policy and even the general policy of the government. Chevalier felt that "the nation has a debt to prisoners' families and this debt has not been paid." Prisoners' families, for whom the collectivity had charge during the captivity of the heads of the family, were suffering.[72]

Initially, Vichy responded incrementally to the growing problem of prisoners' families. As prisoners' children were clearly dependent and unable to work, raising benefits for them proved to be fairly easy. Between June 1941 and March 1942, benefits for prisoners' children were raised three times.[73] Also in March 1942 a national solidarity fund was established to provide emergency funds for which prisoners' wives could apply to supplement their regular allowances. Prisoners' families with two dependents were given bonds entitling them to free bread within the ration allotments.[74] But those at Vichy concerned about the possible political and social ramifications of the difficulties faced by prisoners' families believed such limited measures were inadequate.

The policies that finally emerged were riddled with contradictions. State policy toward prisoners' wives involved two essential elements of the broader Vichy program: its family policy and its desire to protect the prisoners' interests while they were away. Vichy insisted in its pronouncements that it would look after prisoners' families, considered to be wards of the state in the absence of the heads of households. But the traditionalist rhetoric of a patriarchal state protecting the wives of its prisoners of war was belied by the unwillingness of the technocratic "experts" to pay for such protection.

The Battle to Raise Military Allowances

Chevalier's letter marked the beginning of a battle within the government to reform the existing system. Chevalier enunciated the idea that France had not fulfilled its obligation to prisoners' families. Military allowances were inadequate. He wrote, "A prisoner's family with children is condemned to the most severe deprivation, or to seeking unspeakable resources." Widespread deprivation resulted, according to him, in the "considerable development of prostitution of women and minors and the large number of actual or expected births . . . of children whose fathers are German."[75] Chevalier proposed giving prisoners' families the means to survive either by increasing monetary aid or providing aid in kind and jobs. Perhaps the government could temporarily replace female employees with POW wives and generalize part-time work. Although nonsalaried wives were not legally entitled to family allowances, many caisses d'allocations familiales had continued to pay them on the basis of their husbands' prewar salaries.[76] Chevalier encouraged all caisses d'allocations familiales to follow this initiative; he also hoped that the single-salary allowance could be paid to non–wage earning wives of formerly salaried POWs.

Chevalier's letter persuaded Darlan, who quickly sent copies to the entire cabinet with a note stating, "You will certainly agree with me that we must put an end to these situations immediately, no matter what the financial consequences of the necessary measures might be."[77] Darlan asked Chevalier to coordinate a meeting to discuss possible measures and draft proposals for the next cabinet meeting.

The meeting to discuss measures for POW families was held on July 30. Chevalier and Yves Bouthillier, the minister of finance, agreed on only one measure: increasing the sums paid per child for the first two children. Bouthillier vetoed Chevalier's idea of paying a single-salary allowance to POW wives. Against such a veto, nothing could be done. All the ministers and secretaries agreed to give hiring priority to POW wives and to increase part-time jobs for "auxiliary personnel," meaning cleaning women.[78]

Chevalier requested that René Belin, the minister of labor, rescind his prohibition of paying family allowances to those not legally eligible.[79] Chevalier also asked that social security reimburse medical costs for POW families, that the Ministry of Education provide free books, paper, and scholarships for children of prisoners, and that the Ministry of Provisioning allow POW families to buy goods wholesale. These requests and the higher allowances paid per child were all that came of Chevalier's effort.[80]

A second attempt to make changes took place six months later, this time led by Maurice Pinot, in charge of the newly created Commissariat général aux prisonniers de guerre rapatriés (CGPGR). Another meeting was held 16 December 1941 to discuss raising military allowances. Pinot insisted that the amount of the present allowances was "clearly insufficient. . . . One of the most disastrous consequences of this insufficiency is that, in big cities, many prisoners' wives have turned to prostitution." Furthermore, he asserted that in Paris, 75 percent of all prostitutes were POW wives.[81]

One month later, in early January 1942, the new family secretary, Dr. Serge Huard, sent Darlan a letter parroting Chevalier's letter of July 1941, starting with the painful and tragic situation of POW wives with children and the insufficiency of military allowances which condemned POW wives to severe deprivation or to seeking "unspeakable resources." Huard reminded Darlan that Chevalier had already raised the issue six months earlier, but he declared that the problem had since become agonizing. "A study of prostitution done early this month in Paris has shown that approximately 60 percent of prostitutes are prisoner of war wives, most of whom have fallen out of hunger and not vice." Six months later, in June 1942, the new family secretary, Raymond Grasset, claimed that "50 percent of those who turn up at police court examinations every morning are prisoner of war wives."[82]

The accuracy of these figures is impossible to determine: none of these so-called studies can be located in the National Archives, and the police court archives are closed for 1939 on. The only figures on the total number of prostitutes in Paris during this period appear in a book by A. Schieber published in 1946. Schieber took his figures from "the administration," explaining that the estimated number of "clandestine" prostitutes was based on the common knowledge of local prefects and police services. He points out that such estimates were probably low; the larger the city, the less accurate these guesses were likely to be.[83]

Schieber reports that in the department of the Seine in 1939 there were 6,881 prostitutes, 4,926 "card-carrying" and 1,955 "clandestine." In 1945, he reported a total of 11,073 prostitutes, 4,750 card-carrying, 6,323 clandestine.[84] In the winter of 1942, an estimated 30,000 POW families in Paris lived entirely on military allowances—less than 1,000 francs a month.[85] Assuming that these POW wives would have been the most likely to resort to clandestine prostitution and, estimating conservatively, that they constituted 50 percent of the 6,000 clandestine prostitutes, it is therefore possible that 3,000 POW wives out of 30,000, or 10 percent of those living entirely on allowances, turned to prostitution to survive.

The accuracy of these estimates is less significant than the fact that the issue of prostitution came up within government circles in one context only—that of raising military allowances—and was raised by those sympathetic to POW wives. Not only were all three estimates given by those who wanted to raise military allowances, but the issue of prostitution apparently never arose in the many discussions held within the government about preventing adultery of prisoners' wives.

The issue of prostitution and the frighteningly large figures given were thus a scare tactic used to gain Darlan's support and especially to force the hand of Bouthillier, who was fundamentally opposed to any increase in funds paid to POW families. It was one thing to try and gain sympathy within the government for the suffering and deprivation of the POW wife. It was another to contribute to the break-up of marriages and female vice. Ministers were asked to imagine the disgust POWs, and society as a whole, would feel toward a government that drove prisoners' wives to selling themselves just to have enough to eat.[86]

This tactic eventually succeeded, although Bouthillier put up a fight: "As to the misconduct of certain prisoners' wives, raising the allowance does not seem to him to be the complete solution." As usual, he preferred aid in kind, setting up extra stocks of nonrationed goods to be distributed to POW wives free of charge. Pinot pointed out that public opinion tolerated unequal rationing poorly. Although the representative from the interior doubted that "misbehavior" was due solely to economic causes, he recognized that economic causes were the only ones the government could remedy immediately, and he worried about what would happen if the POWs felt the Vichy government had, by neglecting their wives, left these women prey to poverty and temptation.[87]

Two days later the War Ministry again asked Darlan to raise allowances.[88] Negotiations over allowances continued. The finance minister suggested that if aid in kind were given to POW families, the value could be deducted from the additional sums paid per child. In January, however, the minister of finance informed the CGPGR that he had decided against accepting any change in military allowances. He did not want to "knock down the laboriously constructed edifice of the budget."[89]

Meanwhile, various solutions to the problem were proposed. The CGF had already, for other purposes, proposed that each prefect set an "essential minimum salary" for each region. Once this amount was determined, a commission could examine POW wives' financial situation to determine their total resources. If those resources fell below the essential minimum, the government would make up the difference with allowances for the wife and children. The CGF, officially in favor of returning married women to the home, also suggested that POW wives without children be given 10 to 20 percent below the minimum "to inspire the wife in question to find paid professional work."[90]

The Secours national's proposal was similar. The Famille du prisonnier (the branch of the Secours national that provided social services for prisoners' families) insisted that the families should not be obliged to receive charity when they had a right to adequate state support. The Secours national (SN) would solve the problem by having the state pay a salary to the person the prisoner of war normally supported. The situation of prisoners' families would thus return to what it would have been if the husbands were home, thereby keeping these families within the general framework of Vichy social policy. The wife would receive 40 percent of the "average departmental salary" set by her husband's corporation—50 percent if she had one child, 70 percent with two, and 90 percent with three or more. The state would also pay her social security taxes, so that the family would be covered, and she would also be eligible for family allowances. To prevent the salary becoming a "subsidy for laziness," prisoners' wives capable of working were to be offered jobs "in conformity with their aptitudes and their normal standard of living."[91]

Both proposals represented a radical departure from the system of military allowances, ensuring that all POW families received adequate support based on variable payments, either by setting a minimum level below which no family could fall or by paying amounts equivalent to what the POW would earn if he were there. In contrast, the CGPGR proposal stayed within the previous system. Instead of receiving military allowances, POWs would collect captivity pay, regardless of need. All prisoners who did not receive a monthly salary as officers or civil servants and who were married or had children had the right to captivity pay, which could be delegated fully to their wives or children. After declaring captivity pay a right, the CGPGR then proposed setting a ceiling of resources above which the salary would not be paid: for example, for one person, resources equivalent to one-and-a-half times the average departmental salary; for two, twice the salary; for three, two-and-a-half times; and so on.[92]

Drawing up proposals took time. Meanwhile, the Vichy government had undergone a major shift in personnel. In April 1942, Pierre Laval returned as head of state; he took a more active role in deliberations about military allowances than had his predecessors. The meeting on 8 June 1942 to discuss the three proposals took place in his office. Laval believed that the radical changes proposed by the CGF and the SN could take longer to implement—as much as six months or even a year—than it would for the POWs to return. He insisted that the reform would have to be implemented immediately "so that the government benefits from the psychological advantages created in the public opinion by improving the situation of pris-

TABLE 3.2   *Family Allotment in Francs per Day*

	Wife	1st child	2d	3d	4th and up
Paris and Seine	20	15	16	18	25
Seine-et-Oise, region within 25 km. of Seine	17	12	12.50	14	20
Seine-et-Oise, cities of 100,000 or more	14.50	12	12.50	14	20
Seine-et-Oise, cities of 5,000 or more	12	12	12.50	14	20
Cities of less than 5,000	10.50	7	7	11	13

Source: *Journal officiel,* 25 July 1942.

oner of war wives."[93] In this atmosphere, Pinot pushed his captivity pay idea, which was less radical than the other plans.

The new finance minister, Pierre Cathala, objected to making captivity pay a right, as in that case it could be given to unmarried POWs. All present agreed to add the word "family" to the new designation. All but the representatives from the CGPGR agreed to Cathala's condition that the actual number of beneficiaries of the new salary not increase over the number of families already receiving military allowances.[94]

Laval, a more effective head of state than Darlan, saw important political reasons to improve the situation of POW wives and so forced the minister of finance to back down. The law passed in July 1942 referred to the new payments as a "family allotment" (*délégation familiale*). The amount was finally increased in the Seine from sixteen to twenty francs a day for the wife, with similar 20 percent increases for the rest of France (see table 3.2). Because Laval considered it politically essential to act quickly, no reexamination of resource levels for prisoners' families, which the CGPGR pressed for, took place.

Although the new system that emerged on 20 July 1942 declared every

POW's right to the family allotment, it was essentially the same as the previous system of military allowances. It differed only in that resource level ceilings, rather than being set randomly by departmental commissions, were decreed for all of France, varying with region and population.[95]

The resemblance of the new system to the old did not escape public notice. One letter criticized the law for not changing the "spirit" of assistance, as it pretended. In response to these criticisms, the judicial service of the Maisons du prisonniers explained, "The principle is indeed one of a salary paid to men in their country's service. . . . Nevertheless, the present circumstances have led us to exclude from the benefit of these provisions those families who do not have a true need." Thus families were excluded because of governmental fiscal constraints and not as a matter of principle. Set ceilings made distribution equitable rather than dependent on local commissions.[96]

After one full year of fighting, the CGPGR had won a major victory: allowances were raised. Inflation quickly swallowed up the value of the increase, however, and within a year, prisoners' wives again began to ask Pétain for higher allowances. "So it is not with ten francs a day that I can provide for my needs and send packages to my husband," wrote one wife. If he could not raise allowances, then he should "get my husband back from Germany."[97]

Pétain could not satisfy either of her two requests. Allowances did not increase again until after the liberation. Family allotments changed only minimally after July 1942. Despite rampant inflation, the most the Finance Ministry conceded was reducing the resources that determined eligibility for allowances to three-quarters of the family's total resources and raising the resource ceilings so that more families became eligible. In May 1943, a Family Ministry circular set up differential payments to families in which the wife worked and received a family allowance lower than the payment she would have received per child had she been on military allowances. One year after the increase in allowances, the assistant secretary general of the CGPGR complained that for three months he had tried, if not to increase family allotments, at least to improve the "methods of application," but that once again the minister of finance had blocked all his initiatives. As of June 1943, families dislocated by the war could receive both the family allotment and the "refugee's allowance." In March 1944, the struggle continued, this time over lowering the family resources taken into account and allowing POW families on family allotments to receive the single-salary allowance as well. In the meantime, the official price index had risen 185 percent, and unofficial prices had increased as much as 600 percent.[98]

Compared to the imperative to return women to the home and to its self-proclaimed duty to protect the wives of its captives, Vichy policy was a failure. The battle over military allowances reveals the contrast between the traditional, Catholic exterior and the practical considerations that actually governed Vichy policy. Vichy promoted the return of married women to the home. Owing to lack of funds, however, it never paid prisoners' wives enough to allow them to stay there.

In fact, the combination of policies intended to bolster domesticity for women actually encouraged prisoners' wives to work for pay. A salary, which meant eligibility for family allowances, the single-salary allowance (ironically called the "mother in the home" allowance), and social security coverage, more than made up for the possibility of losing military allowances. Even those who believed firmly that a woman's place was in the home ignored the contradiction in their thinking when they considered POW wives, because the CGF and the SN proposals set up penalties for not working. The actual policy toward prisoner of war wives contradicted both the ideas behind Vichy family policy and the notion that the state had a duty to replace the POW heads of households as providers for their families.

Thus, for prisoner of war wives, the impact of Vichy efforts was minimal, if not the exact opposite of the traditionalists' intent. In effect, the Vichy government had two imperatives, which proved to be mutually exclusive: the national revolution, and occupation costs, which took up some 58 percent of government income.[99] The strain on the budget sabotaged social policy by limiting the money available to pursue social goals and by putting power in the hands of the technocrats of finance and industry, who cared little about grandiose plans for French society. Just as constant efforts in negotiations with Germany failed to obtain the release of the French prisoners of war, so Vichy failed to fulfill its theoretical obligations to the families of those prisoners.

Kedward has recently suggested that historians explore the actual effects, rather than the ambitions, of Pétain's national revolution in such areas as family life and women's employment.[100] Because the state failed to back its ideological pronouncements with real benefits, it left open the question of how prisoners' wives were to survive. In the next chapter I shall explore the ways they found to do so.

The Daily
Life of Prisoner
of War Wives

I'm alone tonight, with my
    dreams.
I'm alone tonight, without your
    love . . .
I will wait, day and night,
I will wait forever for your
    return . . .
Time runs on and on,
Beating sadly in my heavy heart,
And yet, I will wait for your
    return.
—Louis Poterat, "J'attendrai"
(I Will Wait)

The lyrics to this song, extremely popular during the war, express two of the fundamental qualities of the life of a prisoner's wife: loneliness and waiting. A prisoner's wife had to adjust both to the initial separation from her spouse and to his prolonged and indefinite absence. In this chapter I shall delve into the more personal aspects of what it meant to be the wife of a prisoner of war in Vichy France.

Surviving the separation demanded hard work, ingenuity, flexibility, and emotional resilience. Sandra Gilbert describes the impact of World War I on English women as liberating, "offering a revolution in economic expectations, a release of passionate energies, a (re)union of previously fragmented sisters, and a (re)vision of social and aesthetic dreams."[1] Prisoners' wives in France during World War II certainly learned new behaviors and skills, experienced unaccustomed independence, and united with fellow prisoners' wives. Yet the war years impressed most of them not as an era of liberation but as a time of overwhelming physical and emotional hardship whose passing they greeted with relief.

External Conditions

Being the wife of a prisoner of war was both an internal and an external reality: the internal emotional state reflected to a large extent the external conditions of war, the German occupation and their husbands' captivity—events that shaped the women's existence but that they could not control. The initial period of trauma began in 1939 with the general mobilization and continued through 1940 with the war, the collapse of France, and the capture of prisoners.

Once most prisoners' wives abandoned the expectation, fed by Vichy propaganda, of a quick return and accepted their situation as long-term, they gradually made the necessary adjustments. For the next few years, life settled down into a more stable pattern. The damage done by Vichy propaganda, however, emerges in letters written to Pétain by prisoner of war wives. First, many women clearly lacked an awareness of the global war. All of the wives wrote hoping to obtain the liberation of their husbands, yet none of the letters even mentioned the war in Europe. Without any other reasonable rationale for their husbands' continuing captivity, many wives apparently accepted, or at least echoed, Vichy's rhetoric of redemption through suffering as it applied to the prisoners of war. For those who interpreted the crushing defeat of 1940 as punishment for the sins of Republican France, the prisoners of war would be purified by their suffering in Germany, return to France, and lead the movement of national regeneration.

If the prisoners were in Germany to atone for France's sins, many wives wondered why they did not return once they had atoned sufficiently. "Many people have forgotten that for four years [the POWs] have been suffering and atoning. . . . Sometimes I am astonished that it has been so long and yet no agreement has been reached for their liberation."[2] Prisoners' wives played on Vichy's own propaganda. If, as Vichy claimed, the war had ended in June 1940, then why, prisoners' wives demanded insistently, did their husbands remain captive?

After the trauma of the Battle of France ended and wives reestablished contact with their husbands, life stabilized for most prisoners' wives, settling into a more manageable pattern. Laure's diary reflected the cycle of trauma, stability, and renewed trauma. While there were only three entries in the summer of 1940, Laure wrote more and more regularly throughout the fall of 1940, almost daily in December, January, and February. By the spring Laure only wrote weekly, twice in July 1941, then once a month, finally only once between February 1942 and February 1944. At that point she confessed: "Over a year since I last wrote in this notebook. I must confess that from disappointed hopes to deflowered illusions (*illusions dé-foutues*) I find nothing more to say."[3]

Life settled into a manageable, or at least a predictable, pattern, inter-rupted by occasional moments of intensified loneliness, and such events as the Relève. Also during the era of general stability from 1941 through early 1944, certain prisoners' wives experienced specific kinds of trauma. Jewish wives of prisoners, discriminated against from the passage in October 1940 of the Alibert laws, faced the prospect in 1942 of arrest and deportation. Other POW wives faced the same threat owing to their Resistance activities. Allied bombing raids uprooted some POW families as early as 1942.

The vast majority of POW wives experienced a period of relative stability until the summer of 1944, however, when the final year of trauma began. Rather than disruptive and life-threatening shocks, there was a steady in-tensification of the hardships to which they had grown accustomed by 1941.

Living from Day to Day

Daily life was trying for most people during the war, but being alone multiplied the difficulties for POW wives. Financial hardship was the rule, with few exceptions. Prisoners' wives relied either on military allowances, on a salary that was generally lower than their husbands' salary, or on a combination of the two.[4] In two districts in the Paris area in 1941, ap-proximately 75 percent of all prisoners' wives received military allowances.[5] Of the twenty-two cases presented in *Femmes d'absents . . . Témoignages,* seven of the women received military allowances alone and another eight received both military allowances and a salary for a total of 68 percent on allowances, which matches closely the government estimate. None of the wives I contacted reported living on military allowances alone, although six received military allowances and a salary. Of the twelve whose main income was a salary, some may also have received allowances. Five claimed to have received allowances for a time and then either found a job or became eligible for officer's pay after their husbands had been in active service for two years.

Over 50 percent of this group of women worked outside the home or took in such work as laundry and sewing. Including those wives who ran the family business or farm raises the number of employed women in my group to 80 percent. In comparison, only about 30 percent of the total female population worked for pay in France in the late 1930s, including women working on the family farm.[6] Such a large number of married women and women with children working outside the home would have been extraordinary before the war, but during a period of crisis, women's role as protector of the family included taking such extraordinary measures as working outside the home for the sake of the family.

Even in his absence, the husband's prewar situation determined the wife's wartime situation, most obviously for farmers' wives. When asked about their resources during the war, several farmers' wives echoed Agnès Minot: "Six cows, corn, beans, vines." Although most farm wives worked alongside their husbands before the war, in some cases they were forced to take over the farm without that experience. Fernande Damart, whose husband raised cattle, explained that before the war "it was his business" and that she did not even know "the extent of our land." The decisions I made were by intuition, by dint of having heard tell of various solutions."[7]

Women whose husbands owned small businesses before the war usually took over the shop. One woman who had legal training took over her husband's notary practice. Her main difficulty was her husband's partner, who believed that "the clients would not like having a woman know what was in their accounts." For that reason, "He arrogated excessive rights over the bookkeeping and I had a great deal of difficulty controlling the movement of assets."[8]

In some cases, wives took over their husband's position. Henri Peletier's employer asked Monique Peletier to learn to drive so she could replace her husband delivering goods at the market depot in Chatellerault, which she did for five years. Francine Louvet's husband was a judicial bailiff at the Bank of France. In his absence, the bank director asked her to collect bankers' drafts and bills of exchange, which she did by car and then, when the Germans requisitioned her car, by bicycle.[9]

In addition to his prewar position, the husband's military rank also determined the wife's financial situation. State policy exhibited class bias: officers' wives, regardless of their other resources, were eligible to receive one-half to three-quarters of their husbands' military pay. According to Estelle Sergent, wives of career military officers such as her husband were expressly prohibited from working outside the home.[10] Officer pay, although it varied with rank, number of dependents, and years of service, was higher than military allowances and generally provided enough to live on. Six of the prisoners' wives I interviewed lived entirely on their officer pay, though many non-career-officers' wives also worked outside the home (nine in my group). Some prisoners' wives received three monthly checks. For example, one prisoner's wife was a professor of physics, and her husband was a professor of history and an officer. Thus she received her own salary, part of her husband's officer pay, and his salary, because the state as a matter of policy continued to pay the salaries of civil servants during their captivity.[11]

Worst off were soldiers' wives without a family farm or a shop. Military allowances were not indexed to the rampant inflation. A POW wives' journal appealed visually for increased military allowances with a drawing of a tiny woman looking up imploringly at a man four times her size, who represented average salaries, and another man six times her size, who represented "normal" salaries.[12] Soldiers' wives who worked outside the home rarely had the advanced education or training that would have enabled them to make a decent salary.

A comparison of resources to costs highlights the difficulty most POW wives had in making ends meet. In Paris, for example, allowances were raised for the last time in July 1942 to 20 francs a day for a woman without children, or 140 francs a week. One week's worth of basic food at official—not black market—March 1944 prices totaled 93.90 francs, leaving only 46.10 francs for everything else.[13] My total does not include any fresh fruits or vegetables; nor does it take into consideration housing or heating costs. As for clothing, the Organization Committee for Textiles fixed the prices of basic articles. In August 1943, a woman's shirt cost 117.35 francs; a dress was 544.20 francs—practically the entire month's allowance. Prisoners' wives faced the additional strain of sending their husbands the monthly five-kilogram care packages to which they were entitled.[14] Vichy added two francs a day to POW wives' allowances for the express purpose of paying for packages for their husbands. Yet given the cost of food, it is unlikely that sixty francs a month ever sufficed. In fact, many wives listed the cost of each package at 250 francs and up.[15]

Prisoners' wives, like everyone in France, had to make do with severely restricted quantities of food, as almost everything was rationed, yet they received no additional rations to put aside for their husbands' packages. Whatever they sent they took from their own or their children's allotments.

Unless they had relatives in the country, many urban prisoner of war wives had no choice but to bring their package address labels to the local Red Cross and have them send a standard package. Many wives hesitated to go to the Red Cross because it further restricted communication with their husbands. Standard Red Cross fare replaced a personalized package with special objects, favorite foods, and photos.

The wife's financial situation depended not only on the husband's prewar career but also on geography. City wives of prisoners of war, although their budgets were probably tighter than other city dwellers due to their husbands' absence, faced the same major difficulty of *ravitaillement* (provisioning). The food situation, especially in big cities and in the Midi region of the south, was desperate. The Family and Health Ministry reported in January 1942 that "the French population has suffered in general from malnutrition." On the average, people lacked one-quarter to one-half the necessary daily calories. A report written after the war tallied French wartime rations and concluded that they provided no more than 1,200 calories a day; during the winter of 1942–43, they dropped to 1,100 and even 1,000 calories a day.[16]

The key to adequate food in the city was having family in the countryside, buying on the black market, or controlling goods that could be exchanged for food. The only other way to increase one's food supply was to produce it oneself. In cities, some women raised rabbits and chickens on balconies or maintained small gardens in back yards.

City dwellers in general also suffered from a lack of fuel. Most places were heated with coal or wood, which became nearly impossible to find in cities. Unless wood could be gathered somewhere, many people did without heat in the wintertime. Catherine Michel claims, "There was ice on our bathroom mirror." Jeanne Capel obtained wood scraps from a sawmill and had to carry them down into her cellar herself—harder labor than she had been accustomed to. "But the hardest thing was that I had to saw and split the wood to get it into my oven and believe me, it was no fun at all."[17]

Not only were clothes extremely expensive, they were also in very short supply. Eventually, clothes were rationed with a system of textile points. Each person had a total number of points that he or she could distribute among articles of clothing, each of which was assigned a point value. Buying a new pair of shoes required an application for permission. One woman wrote in 1943 that, like many others, "I am still wearing my old, shabby clothes from before the war." The war years inspired great creativity in procuring clothes. One prisoner's wife wrote, "I had to cut up a bed sheet to make blouses and dresses." Martine Lombardi unraveled sweaters to make clothes for her daughter. Women's magazines constantly suggested new ways of making do: turning an old tablecloth into a bathing suit, even saving poodle fur clippings to knit sweaters.[18]

Prisoners' wives, unlike their fellow citizens, had to obtain clothing not only for themselves and their children but also, on occasion, for their husbands as well. The Germans did not always provide prisoners of war with clothing, as required by Article 12 of the Geneva Convention. To make up for this, the French government and the Red Cross sent huge quantities of it to the camps. Still, a prisoner of war might request a sweater or long underwear—or worse yet, a pair of shoes. Prisoners' wives received no additional textile points for their husbands. This proved to be an especially sore point after the men returned and could not obtain civilian clothing. The textile-point issue even sparked a massive POW demonstration in Paris on 2 June 1945.

In a less serious way, the clothing shortage could be demoralizing for prisoner of war wives in such a fashion-conscious country as France, and especially in Paris. In 1940 a prisoner's wife wrote to a women's magazine that because she only had her military allowance to live on, she could no longer dress elegantly.[19] Germaine Doucet explained that then, more than now, "you had to follow [fashion]; otherwise people looked at you funny. So, intelligently, fashion dictated that in '39 jackets were very short, and in '41 they were very long." If it had been the reverse, she continues, they could easily have shortened their old jackets, but lengthening was impossible. "So we were twenty-five or twenty-six years old, we must have been crazy! But we felt like we were behind the times." In retrospect, "it has a somewhat ridiculous, petty side to it," but at the time it was hard on her morale.[20]

Unlike urban dwellers, prisoners' wives who lived on farms generally did not face the same shortages. With the exception of the viticultural region in the south, rural areas had adequate food supplies. Rural prisoners' wives faced their own hardships, however. Small family farms were the rule in France at that time. The Ministry of Agriculture estimated late in 1941 that 680,000 POWs were farmers. Hence many small farms lacked 50 percent of their labor force, which created "numerous material difficulties due to the fact that there was one less man to make the farm survive."[21]

Rural day labor, in short supply in France even before the war, became increasingly difficult to find. Prisoners' wives such as Hélène Noiret "could not always find workers to help." With the German imposition of forced labor in 1943, the situation worsened. Rural POW wives wrote dozens of letters to Pétain complaining that, in their husband's absence, they had hired a worker to help on the farm but now even he had been sent to Germany.[22]

Requisitioning created another major problem for rural prisoners' wives. Animals used to work the land—horses and oxen—were requisitioned, as were the trucks and cars needed to deliver goods. On top of that, Germany siphoned off huge amounts of France's agricultural production.[23] The French government, to ameliorate the severe food shortages in the cities, tried to improve the distribution of food by requisitioning farm produce as well. "We had to produce. Requisitions piled up: oats, straw, hay, milk, potatoes, cows, calves, pigs all had to be delivered to the occupier with no regard for our situation as prisoners' wives on the part of the town's residents who feared having to contribute our portion."[24]

In addition to requisitions and a labor shortage, rural prisoners' wives also faced shortages of agricultural tools, fertilizer, seed, and food for livestock. All of this added to the challenge of farming without their husbands. Small farms often rely on loans to carry them over slow times of the year or bad years. But until the law of 22 September 1942 appointed the wife the head of the family in the husband's absence, an agrarian wife could not take out loans without a written power of attorney from her husband.[25]

The difficulties faced by POW wives on the farm did not escape the attention of a government promoting a "return to the soil." Conservatives at Vichy hoped to reverse the prewar trend of urban migration within France, but the failure of POW farms could potentially aggravate the rural exodus.[26] The Ministry of Agriculture and the *Corporation Paysanne,* an agricultural producer's guild created by Vichy, both appointed experts to study the problems of POW farms and to make policy recommendations.

The first step in keeping prisoner of war farmers on the land was preventing urban migration of their wives during captivity. As usual, many studies were completed and suggestions made to the government on specific laws and projects, but very little was actually accomplished. Laws required the renewal of leases to POW farmers until their return and exempted them from the land tax.[27] The agrarian study groups suggested that the lack of farm labor would best be remedied by "peasant mutual aid adapted to local conditions," which was difficult to legislate.[28] Typically, Vichy sent large quantities of "return to the soil" propaganda to the POW camps in Germany.

The studies, of little practical use at the time, confirm the wives' complaints about shortages, lack of labor, and the heavy burden of requisitions. They also point out additional problems faced by rural prisoners' wives, "favored because they generally have enough to live on from the farm, disadvantaged because they are isolated and often succumb under the very hard labor." Being isolated meant little help on the farm and few opportunities to meet with and gain the support and friendship of fellow POW wives, as frequently happened in cities. Although they had easier access to food for their husbands' packages, mailing packages was more difficult because the post office was often far away.[29]

Given the long, hard days for rural wives and the lack of adequate food and heat for urban wives, it is not surprising that many women complained of being "run down," or *fatiguée*.[30] Few women experienced serious illness. In my group, only five prisoners' wives had serious health problems during the war, nine had minor health problems, and three said they were overtired and underfed. Thus, unlike being a prisoner of war, which studies have linked with a series of specific health problems, being the wife of a prisoner did not create serious or lasting health problems.[31]

Emotional Life

Life in occupied France was a constant struggle to survive for most people. In the end, the external conditions of life for prisoner of war wives paralleled those most people in France faced, with similar variations. Their husband's absence intensified the difficulties for prisoners' wives, generally reducing their income and halving the number of adult family members available to cope with difficult circumstances. But being a prisoner's wife was also an internal reality, and their emotional landscape distinguished these women from the rest of French society. Although each woman reacted differently to her situation, similar themes emerge from studying the sources.

Most prisoners' wives agreed that loneliness was "the hardest thing." Sixteen women in my group mentioned loneliness as their primary emotional difficulty. Even those who lived with their parents or had children felt lonely, because other family members could not replace the husband's companionship. The women felt they had no one to talk to or share their troubles with. Martine Lombardi, for example, lived surrounded by her family—mother, grandparents, and children—and worked full time in an office; yet she felt "alone to face all the difficulties, no one to give me moral support. On the contrary, I had to help my family to bear their sorrow and moreover I had to hide in my letters to my husband how badly I felt about his absence and my loneliness." Loneliness went beyond the lack of companionship. It was also "the unfortunate absence of someone I loved very deeply."[32]

Their husbands were not just absent, however, they were prisoners of war, and many wives lived in a state of constant anxiety about their husbands' welfare. Louise Cadieu "for six years experienced a great anxiety for my husband." Contact was limited to two letters and two postcards a month. That the letters took anywhere from two weeks to a month to arrive left Camille Cassan with an "immense concern about what had become of him." "Scarcely had we read and reread them," writes Josette Lorin of the letters, "than we asked ourselves, 'is he still alive?' " Some wives worried that perhaps their husbands did not tell them the whole truth. Nicolle Bouchard lived "in permanent anxiety about my husband's condition and health; he urgently asked for bread . . . and said he had lost 25 kgs [55 pounds] in a month."[33] Although some wives' worries centered on their husbands, others experienced a more general sense of anxiety that could result in insomnia. "The nights were the worst, because I could not sleep."[34]

Rather than experiencing tension and anxiety, some prisoners' wives responded with depression. One wife wrote during the war that she underwent several "nervous depressions." Though none of the women in my group experienced clinical depressions, many described the war years as a period of "great sorrow." In addition to generalized anxiety or depression, prisoners' wives worried also about themselves. Nicolle Bouchard felt "an insidious anxiety, would I hold up? If not, if the slightest thing should have happened to me, what would have become of my children, and my husband . . . ?"[35]

Many prisoners' wives felt overburdened by work and by their new responsibilities. Stéphanie Thibault lists as her emotional difficulty "keeping up with the work (land, animals, house and raising the children)." Agnès Minot wanted her husband to return "to help with raising our child and to bring in some money so we could make it."[36]

One emotional response to the separation from their husbands was mentioned by several women: a sense of envy or jealousy toward united couples and families. Two women from the 1943 study described feeling "almost envious of united homes." The women resented both the happiness of other people and the loss of their own youth. Sylvie Crouet described the war as "six of the best years of our lives when we saw around us happy couples, and when we found ourselves still alone." Marthe Jolliet felt that "all of our youth was wasted, our most beautiful years lost forever." Lucette Nauman and her husband felt that "the most beautiful years of our lives were the ones we 'gave to France!' We were very bitter about that!" They had an additional reason to feel a sense of loss: "We regretted never having had any children." During the war, women without children worried as the years went by that they would not be able to have any. One POW wife wrote to Pétain in 1943 that her husband had to come home because "soon we will be too old to have children, for we have not yet had that good fortune."[37]

Marguerite mentioned a problem one would expect to hear more often. "It was not easy to function sexually without tenderness or caresses or any of what is the high point of a couple's life." Only one other wife, Lisette, mentions this problem: "As for sexuality, I suffered, no more, no less." That so few women mentioned sex does not necessarily indicate that few perceived the lack of it as a problem. As Jacqueline Deroy has aptly pointed out, "Discretion about this theme is characteristic of that generation."[38]

Specific categories of prisoners' wives—Jewish wives, for example—suffered special dangers that created particular emotional problems. Sarah Lisik had to wear the yellow star and was considered "the Jew" of the town. In addition to being a prisoner's wife, she suffered from isolation and persecution. Although she had hoped for special consideration from the Vichy government as a prisoner of war wife, "I was sadly mistaken about that point, since I was arrested by French police accompanied by German soldiers." She and her son were deported to Bergen-Belsen. Another Jewish prisoner's wife who had immigrated to France with her husband from Poland in the 1930s concealed her Jewish identity, but she and her son felt like "hunted animals." Monique Becht, whose husband was Jewish, wrote, "Since I hid some Jewish people, I lived in fear for them. I myself was not Jewish but I felt fully with them in danger."[39]

Some prisoners' wives experienced the war more directly, because they lived in areas of Allied bombing or became involved in the Resistance. One of the wives I interviewed joined the Resistance "because I wanted to fight for my husband." Her husband returned ill in 1942. After an operation, he joined the Organization civile et militaire, a resistance group. In 1944 she saw her husband arrested by the Gestapo and deported to Neuengamme, never to return.[40] For other prisoners' wives, involvement with the Resistance derived less from ideology than from circumstance. After hiding an escaped prisoner of war, for example, a woman might intensify her involvement with the Resistance.[41] However it came about, working in the Resistance, like being Jewish, meant living in constant danger.

Loneliness, preoccupation with their husbands, depression, anxiety, fatigue, and a sense of deprivation were the main emotional responses to living as prisoners' wives. Only one wife wrote that she was so busy with her full-time job and taking care of her children, mother, mother-in-law, grandmother, sister, brother-in-law, and a live-in housekeeper that "there was little time left for me to think about my personal problems." Her emotional difficulty was "lack of news."[42]

Relationship between Husband and Wife

Aside from memories, thoughts, and photographs, letters and packages were the only link between husband and wife. Francis Ambrière, a French POW who worked in a postal sorting station during his captivity, wrote of his job sorting mail for some twenty thousand French POWs: "We put heart and soul into this job, because we knew from experience what a letter meant in the life of a prisoner."[43]

But letters were not especially satisfying. Correspondence was limited to two letters and two postcards a month, with twenty-seven lines per letter and seven lines per postcard. Most couples developed a particular kind of minimalism in their writing. As Raymond Doucet recalled, "One could not be very precise." German rules prohibited writing between the lines. Jean Doremus cheated occasionally. "What did we risk? Not much. Sometimes we wrote in between the lines." Furthermore, the German authorities censored every letter that passed into or out of POW camps, violating any privacy in communication between spouses. Certain things were difficult to express knowing a stranger would be reading them. Doubtless like many other wives, Florence Morin believes that her husband "certainly did not tell me everything."[44]

Information of a political nature or news about the war or German occupation was sure to be censored. Many couples therefore devised secret codes, which they used with more or less success. Raymonde Moulin, for example, worked before the war for a British firm. When she referred in her letters to her "former employer," her husband understood she was passing on information about the British. Another wife used a similar ruse: "news from David," one of her husband's prewar colleagues, meant British bombs. However, she admitted that the codes were not always easy to interpret. "Sometimes we were completely mistaken."[45]

One particularly resourceful POW wife worked for the civil status registrar. When she heard that an agreement had been reached with Germany to repatriate widowers with three or more children, she forged her own death certificate and three birth certificates for children they did not have. Once she began the procedure to get her husband repatriated, she wrote to him "as his sister and I gave him news about his three children." She had meanwhile hidden a letter in a package explaining what she had done, but it was so well hidden that he found it only three months later. "So he wondered when he got my letters if I had not lost my mind." Ultimately her ruse worked and her husband was repatriated.[46]

Although the Germans explicitly forbade letters in packages, many wives hid letters—for example, in hollowed-out cigarettes.[47] Jean Doremus had a friend who received notes in cans of preserves. Michelle Dupuy hid letters in balls of wool and wrote her husband on the official stationery, "I am sending the wool you requested for your socks." He understood the hint.[48] Roger Ariel, whose wife sent him secret notes in a cigarette, wrote after a German guard found one of her notes that she was never to put secret notes in cigarettes again. He went on to ask her to send some good homemade jam in her next package. Her next note was hidden in plastic on the bottom of the jelly jar. Gabrielle took her secret notes to the bakery and had them baked into a loaf of bread. When her husband wrote, "Thank you for the end, but not for the middle" of the bread, she understood that the notes were discovered in the middle of the loaf, as the Germans cut the bread in two before giving it to him. Roger Ariel, suspecting that his wife had baked a note into a cake, cut the cake into crumbs before he realized that there was no note—and no cake left, either.[49]

Some wives did not send secret notes because they worried that "it was too risky." Christiane Motte says of clandestine notes, "They were discovered immediately and we did not try again, knowing that it would cause trouble for our prisoner." On the other side, some prisoners' wives tried to encourage their husbands to escape, primarily by concealing items in care packages. Jacqueline Ariel once sent a detailed map with an escape route indicated. She concealed it, cleverly, behind a framed photograph of Pétain. Her husband puzzled over the gift but did not take the frame apart.[50]

Less direct ways of communicating existed for those afraid to hide notes in packages. Photographs could be included in a package, although no writing was allowed on the back. Children's drawings could be sent. Nicolle Bouchard learned with surprise that censors had not removed one of her son's drawings, as it clearly, if naïvely, indicated the presence of a German airfield near the small northern town where they lived. Christiane Motte sent parts of a diary she had kept in her youth. A prisoner of war wives' organization suggested sending books on topics of mutual interest, with particular passages underlined.[51]

As important as this communication was to both husband and wife, it was minimal, just barely enough to keep them familiar. Many wives found, as the years went by, that "we forgot their features, their expressions."[52] Patricia Longet during the war could only see her husband as a photograph.

The Prisoner's Perspective

Wives and families were a constant preoccupation of the prisoners. Initially, the men's reactions mirrored those of their wives: After their capture, they endured a traumatic period of months not knowing what had happened to their families. Finding out that their families were alive lifted a huge weight. For both husbands and wives, the initial relief faded into new concerns and anxieties. The wives wondered when their husbands would return and how they were being treated. Ambrière claims that the prisoners "were devoured by the need to know what they [their families] were thinking. We wondered how they were taking our absence, a crafty, acute torment which we were wary of talking about to others (scarcely did we dare admit it to ourselves) and which followed more than one of us through every day of those five deadly dull years."[53]

The prisoners worried about the health and security of their families, how they were surviving, whether the wives would wait for the prisoners to return. Yet more than one former prisoner claims that the men did not discuss family matters among themselves. "It's almost a sacrilege to talk about them here."[54] Raymond Doucet found it puzzling. "It's strange but there was great modesty about those matters. . . . We were shabby, rude, vulgar, as badly behaved as it's possible to be . . . but there was this other, modest side. . . . Never did I see anything at the time that could have made someone doubt the good behavior [of the wives]. *Never.*"[55]

Although many prisoners were reluctant to discuss family concerns, the hours they spent reading and rereading letters and composing responses testifies to the importance of their families. "What precautions, what mental erasures before inscribing on paper the summary reminder of an eternal entente! Six weeks to note a complete agreement. Two and a half months to correct a misunderstanding. Over three months to know that all of the clouds have cleared up. That's the drama of our situation."[56] Just as the wives reserved a special place for their husband's photograph, most prisoners tacked pictures of their wives and children up on the wall next to their bunks.

Prisoners' Wives and Others

The marital relationship, although central to the experience and even definition of being a prisoner of war wife, made up a minimal part of daily life. In contrast, relationships with other family members—parents, in-laws, and children—grew in importance. Relationships with women's parents often became more intense.

Many prisoner of war wives could not have survived financially without their parents' support. Elisabeth Doremus was refused military allowances because her father had a pension. She had nothing to live on but the money she and her husband had saved before the war for a car they never bought. She relied heavily on her parents' support. As a result, when her husband returned, "He had much, much more respect for my parents." Nelly farmed during the war. "If I had not had my parents, I don't know how we would have come through, my baby and I." Estelle Sergent said she had fewer problems than many POW wives in part because "my parents provided me with a great deal of support."[57]

But some women paid a price for that support. Madeleine Capot, like the other prisoners' wives helped by their families, appreciated their support, yet she alludes to the problem of her lost autonomy. "I lived with my mother because we got married on March 23, 1940 and were never able to settle down. I should explain that I come from a family very attached to traditions and to social conventions and that my mother would not have liked me to live alone. I was young and had to be protected to remain worthy and faithful."[58]

Some parents maintained control over their daughters during these five years. A number of POW wives resented the lack of autonomy, the inability to grow up and assert their independence. The situation was especially acute for fiancées such as Yvette Giraud, whose parents maintained total control over her social life until she turned twenty-seven.[59]

Tension with parents arose for various reasons. One wife, who had moved back in with her family when the war started, left "to avoid aggravating our little misunderstandings." Several prisoners' wives from the 1943 group complained of differences of opinion on child rearing. The most frequent problem was that the grandparents spoiled the grandchildren, paid too much attention to them, or undermined the mother's authority. "My child hardly fears me at all, his grandparents fawn all over him—a child who gets too much attention . . . becomes overbearing. His whole family gives in to him and anticipates his every whim, which is a disaster." In a similar vein, a prisoner's wife wrote that if she could live in her own home "it seems to me that my little girl would be less spoiled and have fewer airs. Her grandmother and her aunts put up with all her whims. And then I abhor their flattery when I have just scolded her, or else I catch it if they think I'm too strict." Forty years later, Marguerite believes that her oldest daughter, who lived with her in-laws during the war, "was over protected, raised like an only child. That left its mark on her."[60]

Only Fernande Damart mentioned the opposite problem, excessive strictness. Her parents, and especially her great-aunt, "from a generation even beyond that of my mother-in-law," were very strict with her two children, insisting on proper manners and behavior. "There was a certain constraint, perhaps a bit excessive."[61]

Trouble was most likely to arise, however, with the husband's parents. Patricia Longet explained that in the family hierarchy a woman was expected to defer to her husband's mother, which often created trouble between the generations. Problems arose over such things as letters from the prisoner. Because prisoners could send only a limited number of letters, some wrote jointly to their wives and their parents. One wife called this practice "a cause of disputes, for then there is no longer the same intimacy in the only bond that unites us." Prisoners' parents could resent a daughter-in-law's refusal to allow them to read the letters she received. An article addressed prisoners' mothers about the letter problem. "And if, sometimes, we hesitate to let you read all of a certain letter received from over there . . . Mother dearest, do not be among those who get annoyed." The author of the article also discourages, in the gentlest terms, another potential source of trouble. "Oh! Mothers, how grateful we are for your consideration in not opening our letters . . . before we get there."[62]

Simone felt that the hardest thing for her to cope with during the war was living with her in-laws because they "absolutely did not understand our difficulties." Several wives in the 1943 group also complained of a "lack of understanding" from their in-laws. Difficulties with in-laws occasionally went beyond disputes over letters or lack of understanding. Catherine Michel, for example, sent her oldest son to live with his paternal grandmother so he could attend high school. Michel's mother-in-law, "eager for profit," charged her grandson three hundred francs a month for room and board—half of the officer's pay Michel received every month. Gisèle Desbois's in-laws lived in a rural area but refused to send her food in Paris as a way of exerting pressure on her to move in with them. Odette Keller, from the 1943 group, also claimed "my in-laws are not very understanding, and even though they are farmers, they don't help me or my children much with food."[63] There are even cases of in-laws who misinformed their sons about their wives, unjustly accusing the wife of adultery in order to break up a marriage they disapproved of. But such extreme difficulties with in-laws were probably rare.

In addition to the importance of relationships with the adult members of their families, for POW wives with children (the majority), relationships with their children took on added importance and new levels of complexity. Most prisoners' wives, whatever the problems presented by the additional responsibilities of child rearing, found companionship and support in their children. Fernande's children "were a tremendous consolation to me, especially compared to people who were alone. Children provided us with company and helped our morale." Another prisoner's wife wrote, "My little girl is very affectionate to me. . . . If I let her see my grief, it affects her deeply. Her thoughts are a consolation and support to me." One wife summed up her testimony, "If children to raise alone are a great worry, a torment, what a consolation! I pity with all my heart the wives who don't have any." Nicolle Bouchard, with the perspective of time, feels that the experience brought her closer to her children. "Thus the two little ones and myself were united by a great tenderness, and even today there are privileged bonds of confidence and friendship between us, woven from memories of austerity and shared loneliness."[64]

Nineteen of the prisoners' wives in my group had no trouble raising their children alone. Sixteen, however, cited problems. Some children, for example, became anxious or fearful. Martine Lombardi's daughter became happier and more relaxed after her husband returned, but "she still has an anxious character." Dominique Filasto felt her husband's absence provoked "fear and insecurity" in her children. Some children felt acutely their mother's stress. Francine Louvet's children suffered because she was "rarely available and irritable due to the heavy responsibilities of the very difficult life I had to lead." Anne Devron believes her son felt the lack of a man in the house. "When my son became conscious of the world around him, it was only to be surrounded by two unhappy women." Despite such difficulties, only one wife reported a child that suffered severe psychological disturbances.[65]

The description of problems of child rearing varies with the timing of the testimony. A number of POW wives who wrote in 1943 were concerned with an issue rarely mentioned forty years later—discipline and authority. In *Femmes d'absents,* seven of the women with children stated, in one form or another, "I lack the desirable authority." One POW wife even wrote to Pétain that she needed her husband back for this reason. "My oldest son . . . is already a very headstrong child who needs all his father's authority."[66]

She was not the only prisoner's wife to miss the father's authority. The difference between mothers and fathers was noted by Jacqueline Guy: "At first I did not react. I was weak, and for the sake of peace, I gave in."[67] Perhaps more prisoners' wives mentioned the problem of authority in 1943 because the questionnaire to which these women responded raised the issue of children specifically in terms of authority, asking, for example, "Do you have the necessary authority over your children?" That discipline concerned such issues as bedtime, meals, homework, and so on, whose significance faded over time, also accounts for the difference in testimony from the 1980s.

One problem mentioned both during and after the war was that at times children became too attached to another relative, usually a grandparent. "My daughter without a doubt became too attached to her grandmother to the prejudice of her father." The Doremuses had a similar problem with their oldest daughter, and Estelle Sergent's daughter even called her grandfather "daddy." Such a situation could also undermine the mother's authority, making the child demanding and capricious. In the case of a Jewish family, Sarah Lisik's son was emotionally disturbed because he lived "in a family idle due to the proscriptions of Vichy's laws. . . . The child alone polarized the family's interest . . . he had no friends of his own age."[68]

Prisoners' wives were primarily responsible for maintaining the relationship between children and their absent fathers. They had to explain to their children why their fathers were gone and what it meant to be a prisoner of war. Young children with no prewar memories of their fathers often became confused on this point. Several wives reported that, because their husband's photograph showed him in military uniform, their children saw any man in uniform as a potential father. Anne Devron described a situation in which her son saw a German soldier on the street and asked her, "Mommy, is that man there Daddy?" The incident caused her great embarrassment at the time.[69]

Fathers occasionally wrote notes to older children on one of their cards, and the children could write back directly. Children could also help put together packages for their fathers. Marie Patin wrote that her two girls, eleven and twelve years old in 1943, "think about their father, they count the days until the next letter arrives, think of saving biscuits distributed at school to include in the packages, ask for a card from time to time to write to him themselves." For Fernande Damart's two children, "Everything was for Dad. Their chocolate was for Dad, their whatever was for Dad."[70]

Children could feel closer to their fathers by contributing to the packages themselves. Michelle Dupuy and Marie-Louise Mercier realized, however, that at times their children resented these sacrifices. Dupuy took all the chocolate they were allowed and melted it down into a tin for her husband's package. Her son finally asked her, "Why is it that we always send Dad all the chocolate and then I don't get anything at all, I'm only allowed to lick the pan?" Dupuy was taken aback but from then on saved him some chocolate.[71]

Children of POWs also wrote letters to Pétain. At certain key times of their lives they felt deprived of a normal childhood by their father's absence. "I am in great pain because my father is a prisoner and my mother has been sick for four months. Other years my mother was able to work and we had a nice Christmas, but this year misery has settled upon us and there's a lump in my throat because I have nothing." Two children wrote asking Pétain if he could arrange to have their fathers return home in time for their upcoming First Communions. One boy of twelve wrote in a more theoretical vein that he "would be happy to see [his father] again because for four years I have had maternal love but no paternal love."[72]

Whether children felt the lack of paternal love or not, it was difficult to create in their minds a real image of their fathers. Nicolle Bouchard's husband "had become to his sons a MYTHICAL person. Every day I talked to them about their father, I showed them pictures . . . but when he came back, the youngest did not recognize him." Gilberte Voisin, whose two children sometimes wrote directly to their father, "considered their distant father to be a hero they were proud of."[73]

Although family relationships came first for prisoners' wives, sources from both the war years and present day recollections indicate the significance to these women of their treatment by members of the society in which they lived, from close personal friends, neighbors, and co-workers to acquaintances and even strangers. One might expect that people outside of the family would be solicitous of these women and would help them overcome some of their hardships or at least be supportive in general. Certainly the press portrayed an image of the entire nation helping the POWs and their families.

Some people did help. Marie-Thérèse, who ran a small shop, writes, "One thing was satisfying: the other merchants organized to help me out." Several prisoners' wives describe the help they received in obtaining food or other goods for the packages they sent. Jeanne Capel wrote, "I will never forget the grocer I walked by every day telling me to come by in the evening when she had received some canned goods." Anne Devron and Patricia Longet both mentioned doctors who refused to charge them for medical care as a matter of principle. Raymonde Moulin returned home one day to find on her doormat a package put together by one of her husband's former colleagues. Though it was not very much, she "was very touched by it."[74]

Moulin stressed, however, that this colleague was Armenian and not French. "Otherwise, from the standpoint of solidarity, there wasn't any." Common among former prisoners' wives is a sense of bitterness about their treatment during the war. Usually, people exhibited a more or less passive attitude toward prisoners' wives. "The fact that I am a prisoner of war wife by no means inspires my colleagues, directors or bosses to be considerate of me or to help me."[75] The general explanation for the fact that "society as a whole has no interest at all in prisoners' wives" was that people had become "perverse and egotistical."[76] Raymonde Moulin felt that during the war "it was every man for himself." Such an attitude is understandable in hard times, when almost everyone has difficulty finding enough to eat. One of her father's colleagues told Anne Devron, "We are much better off if they stay put because if the prisoners return, we would have even less to eat."[77]

In some cases, the attitude toward POW wives went beyond selfish egoism and lack of concern to become actively negative. Prisoner of war wives resented and continued to resent that they were closely watched by their neighbors, their behavior subject to easy criticism. Dupuy stated emphatically, "They watched us like hawks, but no one helped us." Hélène Noiret asks, "What to say about the gossips who spied on you and slandered you if you had on a new dress or a hat or if you talked to a man? . . . Never any help, never any sound advice." Fernande Damart agreed, "We were watched and listened to more than most."[78]

Even some people the women had considered friends before the war shunned them during their husbands' captivity. Moulin explained this as egoism. Estelle Sergent, whose prewar friends of her age were "not *very* nice" to her during the war, offered another explanation. She was rarely invited into her friends' homes because they were uneasy in her presence. It was not that they felt guilty for not helping her, but, Sergent claims, "I had the impression that I was like an unwed mother. . . . I was not welcome when families entertained."[79]

Negative treatment created in prisoners' wives a heightened sense of affinity for each other. They were drawn together not only by their shared experiences but also by the lack of support and understanding of others. As Patricia Longet said of the Roanne Association of POW wives, "It was *entre nous,* because we were treated as outsiders."[80]

The final phase of the war in Europe ended the relative equilibrium for most POW wives. A new series of traumas began with the intensification of Allied bombing raids, the Allied landing in Normandy, and renewed fighting after June 1944. The symmetry of the war years for prisoners' wives—trauma, stability, and trauma—was expressed in an unusual way in the interview with Gisèle Desbois. She lived in Paris but left the city both in 1940 during the exodus and again in 1944. In telling about her two excursions, she jumped freely back and forth between the two periods, sometimes confusing them. At one point, after telling of hiding on a farm in 1944 while the Germans evacuated, she finished by stating, "and then I got the card saying my husband was a prisoner."[81]

Paris was liberated on 24 August 1944 and the rest of France by October 1944. While most of France rejoiced at the end of an ordeal, Germany had not yet been defeated and the prisoners of war remained captive. One article in a POW wives journal asked, "Our Liberation . . . and Theirs?"[82] Intensification of the war and the deterioration of conditions in Germany along with Allied bombing raids of factories, train depots, and other communications sites meant that many women found themselves once again cut off for months at a time from news of their husbands. With Allied war bulletins no longer censored, the women learned of bombing raids in areas where their husbands lived and worked. Just as the possibility of a return became real again, so did the possibility that their husbands might be killed.

As Allied armies advanced, many POWs in western parts of Germany were liberated and quickly repatriated. Other POWs had to wait for the total capitulation of Germany in May 1945. Those in eastern areas were repatriated slowly because the fighting had been so destructive and disruptive. Many prisoners were not repatriated until June, July, or even August 1945.

Even the long-awaited return of their husbands did not always mean the end of hardship for these women. Many POWs returned in poor health, having been undernourished and overworked for five years. Some were seriously ill. Four women in my group lost their husbands shortly after their return owing to such deadly diseases as cancer and black lung. Those women whose husbands were ill continued to face serious financial difficulties.

Shortages, rationing, and requisitions of farm produce continued in France long after the war ended, through 1949 or 1950. Having been away for five years, many prisoners of war returned to find themselves without a job. Almost all POWs suffered to some degree the psychological aftereffects of captivity. They returned bitter or else tyrannical and aggressive, prone to rages. In some cases they fell into a depression and seemed to lose all initiative and drive. Almost all the returned prisoners felt disoriented in a France so changed by the war years that it had no relation to the homeland they imagined while in Germany. Many felt bitter or at least disappointed by their reception in France.

Hence even after the return of the POWs, prisoners' wives had to care for their husbands, keep the family going, and in some cases bend to what they considered unreasonable demands from their husbands. The women not only smoothed things over at home, they acted as intermediaries between their husbands and the outside world, which had become unfamiliar and overwhelming to the prisoners. Eventually, however, life stabilized for most prisoners' wives. War and their husband's captivity were behind them.

Power, Class, and Gender: Public Agencies and Prisoners' Wives

To act as the interim head, or supporter of the family, such is the goal we have assigned ourselves.
—La Famille du prisonnier

We do not have the right to leave these mothers alone before the serious problems they have to face.
—CGPGR circular

Prisoners' wives did receive outside moral and financial support from two agencies created during the war: the Famille du prisonnier and the Commissariat général aux prisonniers de guerre rapatriés et aux familles de prisonniers de guerre. The sincerity of each agency's desire to help prisoners' families was matched by the determination of both organizations to extend their power, leading to constant friction. True philosophical differences also divided the two agencies. What these agencies fought about reveals the deep tensions in Vichy France. Ideological differences over paternalism and class relations became highly divisive. The story of these two agencies also belies the supposedly apolitical nature of the regime. Just as collaboration proved to be a dangerous game for the Vichy regime, so the attempt on the part of these agencies to work with the Vichy government on social policy but steer clear of politics also proved unwise.

But the groups shared without dispute the profound and unquestioned paternalism of French social attitudes toward women. That the politics of gender never became an issue of contention signifies how deeply beliefs about the nature of women were held in France. Both organizations believed that prisoners' wives needed not only financial help but someone to replace the absent head of the household.

77

The Famille du Prisonnier

The wife of the Armistice Army chief, Madame La Générale Huntziger, created the Famille du prisonnier in April 1941 as an autonomous, private agency. Huntziger led the national committee in Paris, which appointed one delegate in each department, usually a prominent citizen, who relied on teams of social workers to visit the homes of POW families.

To Huntziger's dismay, another agency swallowed the Famille du prisonnier in August 1942. The Secours national, a semipublic agency paralleling the Red Cross, had originally been created during World War I to coordinate relief efforts for civilian victims of the war. It was recreated by law in October 1939. The Secours national justified taking over the Famille du prisonnier because it already provided most of the funding. Furthermore, growing numbers of POWs were beginning to return and needed personal loans, credit to restart their businesses, and training for jobs. The SN explained that this was no longer a matter of "feminine problems, or of children's problems." Men's problems surpassed the "somewhat feminine framework of what is called the Famille du prisonnier de guerre."[1]

The Famille du prisonnier became the "Prisoner" delegation, a bureau within the Secours national. Henceforth, each department would have a "Prisoner" delegate who replaced the delegate of the Famille du prisonnier, although in many cases the same person stayed on in the job. The SN recommended that, whenever possible, the prisoner delegate should be a repatriated POW. The new system put the SN in control of budget, administration, personnel, and decision-making, while the former Famille du prisonnier executed decisions only. Each decision to help a particular family required approval from the top. Disgusted, Huntziger stepped down.

One year later, in November 1943, the new system was abandoned as too bureaucratic. The SN restored the Famille du prisonnier, which regained its former autonomy over decisions and distribution of aid, although the SN still hired and paid personnel. For the purposes of this chapter, I will refer to this agency throughout as the Famille du prisonnier.[2]

The Famille du prisonnier sent social workers to visit prisoners' families to determine if they were in distress and, if so, to distribute money or aid in kind. Directors insisted, however, that it was not a charity office. They would have "to account to the prisoners whose families are our responsibility. We are the guardians of these families and we must replace for them the absent head of the family."[3]

The Famille du prisonnier could not be accused of a lack of thoroughness in the duties it felt compelled to fulfill. The wives needed much more than money. Discouraged and overwhelmed, they needed "men who are strong to guide them, kind to love them, courageous to protect them and understanding of their weaknesses."[4] Famille du prisonnier delegates and social workers guided these women and helped them overcome their difficulties.

Although paternalism in modern industrial society usually refers to class relations, the Famille du prisonnier illustrated that this attitude also governed gender relations. The *International Encyclopedia of the Social Sciences* defines paternalism as "a type of behavior by a superior toward an inferior resembling that of a male parent to his child." The encyclopedia describes the motivation of paternalistic systems: "First, since a 'child' is defenseless and lacks property, he requires assistance and support. Second, since a 'child' is not fully aware of his role and therefore not fully responsible, he requires guidance."[5]

The Famille du prisonnier description of its role could have been modeled on the French Civil Code description of the duties of the head of the family, the very definition of paternalism. Famille du prisonnier social workers took over the role of husband and father, providing for the family, deciding how money should be spent, where the family should live, and whether the wife should work. They were to guide the wife who, in their view, was not fully responsible and needed leadership. They were to prevent infidelity, oversee the education and discipline of the children, and decide the children's future career and schooling needs. The Famille du prisonnier considered prisoners' wives incapable of fulfilling these duties alone.

Although initially created by a woman, the Famille du prisonnier was taken over by men. But male leadership alone does not explain the attitude toward women, because the social workers who executed the Famille du prisonnier policies were women. Paternalism toward working-class families motivated the very creation of the social-work profession in France. Most social workers were educated, single, bourgeois women who assisted working-class families. The profession, a secular equivalent to becoming a nun, provided an acceptable way of life for a bourgeois woman unlikely to marry. Many of the women carried two prejudices—one about women and one about the working class. As single, professionally trained women, social workers considered themselves capable of handling responsibilities, but in their view, housewives or mothers without professional training were not. As for working-class family life, it was in ruins, largely because working-class wives and mothers worked outside the home. Social workers could reverse the disintegration of working-class families by reawakening buried maternal instincts in working-class wives and mothers.

Hyacinthe Dubreuil's history of the development of social work as a profession, *A L'Image de la mère: Essai sur la mission de l'assistante sociale,* clearly elaborates these assumptions, prejudices, and goals. According to Dubreuil, the Industrial Revolution had destroyed the working-class family by separating home from workplace. Women who worked in factories lost their desire for motherhood and developed a taste for liberty. The social worker's function was to restore the family by substituting herself for the mother and reconstructing the family until such time as the real mother was ready to resume her responsibilities. Working-class families would be strengthened and would also benefit from contact with a cultivated person. Social work not only made up for the lack of an adequate mother in working-class families, it also provided an outlet for single women, allowing them to fulfill their natural calling as mothers even though they had no families of their own.[6]

In other words, social workers had always considered that their role went beyond material assistance, and Famille du prisonnier social workers were no exception. Over and over, Famille du prisonnier social workers were advised to take on intimate duties within these households. The Famille du prisonnier insisted, for example, that it was up to its social workers to keep the memory of the prisoner alive. While the prisoner was gone, the social worker, not the wife, was to ensure that the "house becomes more beautiful, but only better to receive him." In fact, the Famille du prisonnier should make sure that the prisoner's wife "remains attractive, but only because her loves her"—not, it is implied, to attract other men.[7]

In advising a prisoner's wife about an important decision, delegates and social workers were to ask themselves, "What would the prisoner do if he were here?" How were they to know what he would do? The Famille du prisonnier reassured its social workers that because they were educated and enlightened, they might often find a better solution than the POW himself would have.[8] Whenever possible, they were to press wives to consult with their husbands before making decisions. By doing so the Famille du prisonnier fulfilled its task of keeping husband and wife together and of preparing for the prisoner's return.

The Famille du prisonnier also assumed responsibility for preventing infidelity, and if that failed, for saving the marriage by reforming the wife.

"We must try to have the wife climb back up the slope, even if it seems that she is completely lost."[9] The Famille du prisonnier encouraged the prisoners in these situations to forgive their wives. The monthly bulletin frequently printed examples of desperate situations salvaged by the tact and diligence of a Famille du prisonnier worker.

> In Calvados, a prisoner's wife is expecting a baby. She bitterly regrets her mistake. Her husband, urged on by his family, filed for divorce, but he wrote to our village representative, telling her of his concern about his two children. Our representative wrote him that his wife regretted her behavior and still loved him. She closed by imploring him to be generous, to have pity on the innocent child about to be born.
>
> During this time, our representative supported the unhappy wife, encouraged her good resolution. Her efforts were finally rewarded in the form of a letter from the prisoner to his wife forgiving her and renouncing the divorce.[10]

Keeping husband and wife together only exceptionally involved preventing infidelity. The national leadership praised the initiative taken by a local Famille du prisonnier agent. Considering that the sole remaining tie between the POW and his wife was their correspondence, the social worker "is doing everything she possibly can to raise the level of the letters sent by the wives, helping them to include more interesting things in their letters than they normally do." The Famille du prisonnier felt that this effort "merits encouragement. Too many letters are totally insignificant, more out of ignorance than out of unwillingness."[11] The irony that suggesting phrases and things to write about might actually strengthen the bond between the POW and the social worker rather than between him and his wife went unnoticed.

The Famille du prisonnier focused special attention on prisoners' wives with children. Huntziger stated that the Famille du prisonnier "is watching particularly over prisoners' children. The Famille considers them to be its own children, and will not allow the father's absence to be a cause of inferiority for them."[12] Mothers certainly had a role to play in child rearing, yet one Famille du prisonnier leader, Lalande, insisted, "It is up to us, maybe even more than it is to the wives and mothers, to try and replace the absent father."[13] The Famille du prisonnier helped young boys choose their careers and provided occupational therapy and scholarships. Girls, not to be neglected, were offered home economics. "Never lose sight of the fact that these are future mothers that *we* must train."[14] The Famille du prisonnier also tried to protect the health of children and mothers by sending children to stay with rural families and mothers to special rest homes.

The Famille du prisonnier, as the "interim head of the family," had to guide wives, keep the memory of the husband alive, prevent divorce, and make sure wives consulted husbands and wrote interesting letters. At times prisoners' wives resented this intrusiveness. "Mothers can be so jealous of their prerogatives that our attempt at Montlhéry to educate the children and through them the mother caused nothing but trouble."[15]

The Famille du prisonnier not only treated women as incapable minors, but its paternalism also ran along class lines: the social milieu of the family determined how the agency responded to each set of circumstances. The Famille du prisonnier frequently stated that one of its goals was to "maintain the level" of each family, neither raising nor lowering the status of the families. It justified class distinction in its policies by pointing out that working-class families finding themselves better off with Famille du prisonnier aid than they had been on the husband's salary could end up resenting the POW's return. Class distinction went beyond the question of how much money should be given to a particular family: it colored many attitudes within the Famille du prisonnier.

The agency did not restrict its charitable efforts to working-class prisoners' families. Though bourgeois prisoners' families often received officer's pay, the Famille du prisonnier believed it would be a mistake to assume that bourgeois families did not face hardship. Decline in status, not lack of money for food, was the difficulty for these families. The Famille du prisonnier worried about wives who lived honorably before the war on their husband's income. With their husbands gone, such women had the same expenses but only half or three-quarters of their husbands' officer's pay for income. The Famille du prisonnier knew of "tragic cases; wives of intellectuals, artisans, engineers, even industrialists who found themselves obliged to change their lives totally." Working outside the home represented a definite decline in status for a bourgeois wife.[16] The Famille feared that even accepting help represented a decline to these families, who, it was assumed, would go to great lengths to hide their misery. Hence the agency needed to exercise tact and diplomacy to persuade bourgeois families to accept help. "One such woman, for example, would refuse money, but will accept having us pay her child's educational expenses."[17]

In the case of working-class families accepting help, the Famille du prisonnier expressed a different concern. "The distribution of assistance was causing the development among the families of a hand-out mentality which we must prevent." Thus the Famille du prisonnier ran *ouvroirs* (charity workshops), where working-class POW wives could earn money and, in some cases, gain skills. One workshop in Paris taught prisoners' wives marquetry, an artisanal trade they could, after a three-month apprenticeship, practice at home. By 1941, the Famille had opened over two hundred workshops which employed some fourteen thousand POW wives, most often in repairing used shoes and clothing. The Famille du prisonnier preferred sending working-class wives to the workshops to earn money rather than simply giving them money on a regular basis. Unfortunately, the Famille reported of POW wives that "most of them are getting used to doing nothing, to receiving cash as the reward for their idleness, and they no longer want to work."[18]

The Famille du prisonnier insisted that providing part-time work in a place with a good atmosphere and a day-care center would allow these women to help themselves without having to neglect their children or their homes. Furthermore, the workshops gave the Famille du prisonnier another opportunity to exercise moral guidance over working-class prisoners' wives. The agency organized many activities in the workshops, "such as household management sessions (child rearing, hygiene, cooking, family morality)." Unfortunately, at the congress, Lalande reported ruefully that the attempt to train wives in household management was not a resounding success; "Only the very young women proved to be at all receptive."[19]

Still, the Famille could not abandon household instruction, as it had reconciled blatant class prejudice with another, contradictory tenet. The Famille du prisonnier asserted that female employment in the twentieth century had precipitated the decline of the French family by destroying women's taste for housework. "In recent years women too often have renounced the tasks for which they were born." To harmonize its denunciation of the decline of love of home and family among working women with the contradictory expectation that working-class POW wives should work, the Famille included education about the home in its program of part-time work.[20]

To its credit, the Famille du prisonnier distributed large sums of money—168 million francs as of November 1943 (approximately 16 million 1978 dollars). In addition to distributing direct financial aid, the Famille ran a variety of programs. One, for example, sent prisoners' sickly children to recover in country homes. The luxurious Hotel la Savoie became a rest home for prisoners' wives in need of convalescence. The Famille provided scholarships to prisoners' children for higher education or apprenticeships and reimbursed POW families for medical expenses not covered by social security. It acted as advocates for prisoners' wives on an individual basis, lobbying the provisioning office to obtain adequate raw materials for a wife running her family shop, intervening at city hall on behalf of wives who were not receiving allowances, and so on. It also held meetings for POW wives, with talks on such relevant topics as making the most of available food. Prisoners' wives, facing the immense difficulties of life in occupied France alone, appreciated the help. A Parisian prisoner's wife wrote the Famille du prisonnier to thank the agency for its help in sending her convalescent daughter to the countryside. According to her, until the Famille came along, she received "not one human, helping or charitable gesture from anyone in the world. At times I found it hard never to find a helping hand. . . . Your gesture did my heart and soul good."[21]

The Famille du prisonnier's class prejudice offended the repatriated POWs at the CGPGR, its main rival. The CGPGR did not, however, object to the Famille's attitudes toward women. Rather, the two groups feuded over which agency should exercise patriarchal authority over prisoners' wives in their husbands' absence.

The CGPGR

Some months before the Famille du prisonnier was created in April 1941, lawyers and other professionals in the POW camps began to consider what would happen to the POWs when they returned to France. Study groups in several camps explored the issues of concern. In November 1940, the government received a proposal, "Preparing for the Return of the Prisoners," which warned that without careful advance planning, the liberation of 1.5 million POWs could create a "new cataclysm" in France. To prevent social upheaval, the government needed information on each POW's occupational, medical, and family history. No government agency existed to coordinate measures for repatriated POWs who, after demobilization, would no longer be under the aegis of the Ministry of War. The proposal suggested appointing a General Secretary for Prisoners.[22]

Eventually, the Vichy government obtained the release of several of these administrators and jurists, including Maurice Pinot and Pierre Join-

Lambert. Together with repatriated prisoners from a variety of backgrounds, they created the Commissariat général au reclassement des prisonniers de guerre in September 1941. Pinot became commissioner, Join-Lambert was general secretary, Bernard Ariès director in charge of family matters, and Henri Guérin director and Georges Baud assistant director for the occupied zone.[23]

The commissioner initially hoped to protect prisoners' jobs while they were away. Most employers would have hired replacements in the absence of the prisoners. The commissariat's first law, which appeared in February 1942, guaranteed that "every prisoner, when he returns, will automatically be rehired by the business that employed him before the war." The law guaranteed the job for six months. POWs whose enterprises had closed during their absence were guaranteed placement or retraining by the state.[24]

The commissariat's attention then turned to the situation of self-employed POWs, artisans, shopkeepers, and farmers. They would need loans to restock or to repair damage done by neglect or by the war. While they were gone, the commissariat wanted to prevent new shops from taking business away from the prisoners' shops. A law required potential shopkeepers to apply to the government before opening a new business that might compete with a prisoner's business.[25]

Examining the problems confronted by the self-employed revealed the importance of the prisoner's family. If the prisoner was married, his wife usually took over the shop or the farm in his absence. Originally, the law creating the commissariat limited its function to reemployment and retraining of prisoners themselves. But protecting the prisoners' interests often required acting in favor of their wives; thus Pinot increasingly felt the need to "take charge" of prisoners' families. The Commissariat général au reclassement, to indicate its broader interests, became in July 1942 the Commissariat général aux prisonniers de guerre rapatriés et aux familles de prisonniers de guerre.[26]

Pinot also hoped to reduce the confusion bred of the multiplication of agencies concerned with POWs and their families. Along with the Famille du prisonnier and the CGPGR, the Red Cross, the Comité central d'assistance (CCA, the equivalent to the Red Cross in the northern zone), the War Ministry's Direction des services de prisonniers de guerre, and the Scapini mission (Services diplomatiques de prisonniers de guerre) all dealt with matters pertaining to POWs or their families. A prisoner's family with a problem could spend days running from office to office, never sure which was the appropriate agency. Pinot wanted a central location, a Maison du prisonnier, in every major city to house all POW-related bureaus and agencies. Prisoners' families and repatriated POWs could then go to one place and be directed to the appropriate service.

In November 1941 Pinot asked the Secours national to establish a Maison du prisonnier in every departmental capital. Every service concerned with POWs or their families would be invited to set up an office in each Maison, and a repatriated prisoner would be named director of each Maison by the Secours national in agreement with the CGPGR. The director was to coordinate the various services located in the Maison. The first Maison opened in Paris at the Place Clichy early in 1942. By April 1942, there were forty Maisons, and by 1944, there were 151.[27]

The ambiguity of having each Maison paid for by the Secours national and directed by one man responsible to both the SN and the CGPGR proved unmanageable. The CGPGR decided, rather than relinquishing control to the SN, to transform the Maisons into public nonprofit organizations, thereby entitling them to public funds. As of 1 January 1943, the Maisons were run entirely by the CGPGR, although the local SN representative automatically sat on the administrative council of each Maison.

Finally, Pinot created a prisoners' mutual aid network, the Centres d'entr'aide (CEAS). Repatriated prisoners of war often experienced a sense of guilt. Fortunate to be going home, they felt an obligation to their friends remaining in Germany. Many repatriated POWs believed they had a mission to keep the issue of the prisoners of war alive in France and especially to help their friends' families. As more and more POWs returned in 1941, informal groups developed. According to Pinot, in the northern zone the German occupying authorities forbade meetings of any groups other than those of collaboration parties. In the southern zone the Légion française des combattants, which by law had the exclusive right to "bring together veterans and manage their interests," opposed any POW group separate from the Légion.[28] CEAS kept POW groups independent of politicized groups, gave them a cover, and still allowed "repatriated prisoners to fulfill the promises they made to their friends when they left camp."[29]

The CEAS, established officially in May 1942 and open to all repatriated POWs, helped recently repatriated POWs and the families of those still in Germany. Headquartered in the local Maison du prisonnier, CEAS collected goods to send to POW camps, met with recently repatriated POWs, sponsored exhibitions about life in the prison camps, and visited POW families.

Dueling Agencies: Paternalism, Power, and Politics

By the summer of 1942, two national agencies assisted prisoner of war families while their husbands and fathers were captive. To the outside world, articles and brochures painted a picture of solidarity, the two organizations working hand in hand, united behind their leader, Pétain, to promote the welfare of POWs and their families.[30] But as the CGPGR expanded, added families to its title and domain, and even sent repatriated prisoners to visit POW families, tension mounted between it and the Famille du prisonnier. Behind the scenes a picture emerges of constant squabbling and rivalry between and even within organizations, of frequent petty disputes over matters of seemingly little import. In the spring of 1943, for example, a bitter fight broke out between the CGPGR and the Famille du prisonnier over mail. The issue was whether mail sent to any of the agencies located in a particular Maison could be opened first by the director of the Maison.

In April 1943 the CGPGR received complaints about Maison du prisonnier directors opening the mail addressed to departmental representatives of other agencies. The general director of the Maisons sent a circular to Maison directors to clear up the conflict. A director could only open mail sent to an agency in a Maison "when the wording of the envelope is impersonal in nature," meaning addressed to La Famille du prisonnier and not to Mr. X.[31] Having established that directors could not open mail addressed personally to a representative of another agency, the CGPGR complained about letters addressed personally to representatives of other agencies, because they bypassed the Maison director's control.[32] In November 1943 the issue continued to rage. Léger stated categorically at the Famille du prisonnier congress, "I do not want Maison du prisonnier directors opening the mail addressed to our delegates."[33]

What was the fighting really about? Bureaucrats can get carried away by such questions of protocol as the mail issue. But underneath this and several similarly picayune disputes ran deeper conflicts. According to Jean Vedrine, original director of the Centre d'entr'aide, repatriated POWs primarily disliked the Famille du prisonnier's "certain paternalism." Indeed, in 1942, one director of the CGPGR complained, "It is the badge of paternalism which we ask the Famille du prisonnier to remove as soon as possible."[34]

The paternalism of the Famille du prisonnier as well as its aura of charity offended the sensibilities of repatriated prisoners who insisted that France had an obligation to these families while the prisoners, captured in the line of duty, remained in Germany. The repatriated prisoners objected to a charitable institution of bourgeois notables helping needy families when, they insisted, the prisoners and their families had a right to public assistance. "The services we render to the absent men and their families we owe them by rights, proportional to their needs."[35] Repatriated prisoners also objected to the bourgeois "charitable ladies" of the Famille du prisonnier who visited and meddled with working-class prisoners' families under the guise of helping them. For this reason, the CEA demanded that its members, repatriated POWs, be sent to visit fellow POWs' families.

Although the dispute erupted over paternalism of a class nature, everyone assumed that, as women, prisoners' wives needed outside direction. The Famille and the CGPGR fought over which agency should act as the head of the household in the prisoners' absence. No one suggested that the wives might be capable of doing so themselves.

The Famille du prisonnier, rather than refuting the charge of paternalism, justified its position by defending the principle behind paternalism. The Famille declared that it knew what was best for prisoners' families. First of all, its social workers were trained professionals who knew their jobs. Second, it objected to having repatriated prisoners visit prisoners' wives because it perceived men visiting women alone to be a situation fraught with danger.[36] It eventually did agree to allow CEA members to visit families. But it retained the right to appoint the CEA members allowed to conduct visits and required them to undergo a "minimum of social training," provided by SN social workers. Finally, the Famille du prisonnier did not deny that notables ran its departmental offices; rather, it asserted the superiority of such a system. Léger insisted, "The 'Prisoner' delegates are always prominent citizens in their Department who absolutely refuse, with good reason, to be superseded by people generally less qualified than themselves."[37]

Much of the friction between these two agencies arose over matters of control. Although such agencies exist to serve certain clients, charity is never neutral; an agenda lurks behind the façade of unselfish help to those who need it. To begin with, the giver, whether a private organization or a state bureaucracy, gains power over the recipients. Second, the way in which benefits are distributed—who receives them, what proof is required, how much is received, and how often—all give the agency power to try to shape the recipients and control their lives. In this case, the size of the constituency, nearly eight hundred thousand prisoners' wives, also conferred national power on the agency that controlled policy toward them.[38]

The Famille du prisonnier keenly resented the intrusion of the CGPGR and its various branches into what the Famille defined as its sphere. Several of the disputes—the mail dispute among them—can be interpreted as an attempt by the Famille du prisonnier to maintain control over what it had carved out as its domain and to prevent the CGPGR from intruding. Hence, the Famille du prisonnier defended its position not only on the grounds of professionalism but also on the grounds of precedence. It had been there first, and CEA members annoyed Famille delegates by acting as if "nothing had been done before their existence."[39]

All social welfare costs money, and that is the issue over which the most serious power struggle developed. Leaders of the two agencies fought bitterly over which of the two groups should be allowed to raise money and which of them controlled the distribution of funds. Not only were the sums involved enormous—millions of francs annually—but the agency with the purse strings controlled its rival. The Vichy government, short on funds for social programs, granted certain organizations a monopoly over public fund-raising campaigns rather than directly supporting semipublic agencies.

Each organization argued that the law gave it exclusive rights to raise money. Although the Secours national received grants from the government, it relied primarily on private donations, on money raised by the national lottery (which it sponsored), and on one national publicity campaign held in November and December. The law creating the Secours national conferred on it a legal monopoly over publicity campaigns to raise money for civilian war victims, among whom it counted POW families. The CGPGR, however, felt that the POWs' military status extended to prisoners' families, who thereby fell under its jurisdiction by the decree of 2 September 1941.[40]

To clear up the confusion and end the feuding, Laval empowered the prefects in October 1942 to oversee and authorize all publicity campaigns raising money for POWs or their families. Each department was to establish a commission of public events for the prisoners with representatives from the War Ministry, the CGPGR, the Famille du prisonnier, the Red Cross, the CEAs, the CCA in the northern zone, and the Légion française des combattants in the southern zone. The commission would advise the prefect on each fund-raising event, but the prefect alone had the final say. Any event that raised over twenty thousand francs had to turn 20 percent of the money over to a departmental fund for the prisoners of war and their families. The remainder of the money was left to the organizers of the benefit if the prefect approved of their proposed use of the money.[41]

Unfortunately, although the circular allowed prefects to resolve local disagreements over fund raising, it did not end the disputes on the national level. The CGPGR objected, for example, to the use by the Secours national of the POWs as a theme in their campaigns unless the money went exclusively to the Famille du prisonnier or toward sending packages to POW camps rather than into the general budget of the agency.[42]

In turn, the Famille du prisonnier objected to the CEAs controlling any money at all. The Famille du prisonnier originally set up a system of visits to prisoners' families by social workers who conducted investigations to determine need. When the CEAs insisted on sending their repatriated POWs to visit families, the Famille du prisonnier eventually relented; but it intended to keep a close watch over the CEAs. It insisted that the CEAs fell under its control insofar as visits to prisoners' families were concerned. The Famille du prisonnier decided which repatriated prisoners could visit families, then trained them, sent them to specific neighborhoods, and laid down a plan of action. The Famille also specified that it alone distributed any and all financial aid to POW families. The CEA visitor could only propose cases. The Famille du prisonnier would consult its card index, conduct its own investigation, decide whether or not the family needed help, and then notify the CEA of its decision.[43]

Because all CEA members were volunteers, they could distribute any money they raised directly to prisoners' families, bypassing the Famille du prisonnier. To prevent CEAs from escaping its control, the Famille du prisonnier needed to prevent the CEAs from raising money on their own. Hence the SN sent another circular in February 1943 instructing its delegates that CEA activity "must not consist of raising funds and distributing them to our friends' needy families." The CEAs could only help other agencies raise money. Although they could set rules for the use of the funds they raised, the CEAs were not to receive any part of the money raised.[44]

The SN sent the exact same circular around again in July 1943. When the director of one CEA saw it, he complained to the general secretary of the CGPGR about "the Secours National's state of mind and the fact that it assumes it has the right to give orders to people outside its own services." The Secours national, however, had the next victory. Laval sent another circular to all prefects, reminding them that the Secours national, by the law of 4 October 1940, had the exclusive right to appeal to the public for money. No appeal to public generosity by any other group, including the CEAS, could be made without the prefect's authorization in consultation with the SN delegate.[45]

Not content to let things stand, the CGPGR struck back two days later, insisting that the SN only had a monopoly on raising funds for civilian war victims. POWs were military personnel, not civilian war victims. Furthermore, the law of 2 September 1941 mandated that the CGPGR was to coordinate the activities of other agencies dealing with POWs. In light of this mandate, the assistant general secretary of the CGPGR reported to the minister of the interior that rather than slowing down during the SN Winter Campaign of 1943, he had asked "all 'Prisoner' organizations to intensify their mutual aid efforts."[46]

The direct challenge by the CGPGR hardly escaped the notice of the SN. Lunven, the Secours national director of collections, reported at the Famille du prisonnier congress in November 1943 that the SN had specifically requested during its winter campaign that "competing groups, if I may put it that way," reduce their own activities "to leave the coast clear for us." Instead, "Opposite instructions were issued . . . to intensify activity precisely during the period when we asked them to slow down." Lunven warned that, although the SN preferred to work amicably with other groups, the Council of State would suspend delinquent groups.[47]

The very creation of the CGPGR entailed such disputes over jurisdiction. Once the Maisons du prisonnier were established and all groups had to work in the same building, the disputes trickled down to the local level. Did the director of a Maison du prisonnier "coordinate" all the services located in the Maison? Or did each agency's representatives answer to their own central authority? Were prisoners' families civilian or military victims of the war? The Famille du prisonnier and the CGPGR needed clear and precise definitions of their functions and hierarchies, but the laws were contradictory. Each organization could legitimately claim direction of efforts for prisoner of war families. Each also resisted efforts to be coordinated by the other.[48]

The Famille du prisonnier insisted that it was an autonomous agency in no way subordinate to the CGPGR. Whereas the Famille du prisonnier was a private relief agency with a social mission, the CGPGR was a government bureaucracy whose activity was, or should be, primarily administrative.[49] Moving into a Maison du prisonnier as a service to repatriated POWs and

POW families did not diminish the Famille's autonomy. Any other solution meant that the Famille delegates worked under the orders of one of the CGPGR bureaucrats, and "such dependence of our charity on subordinate officials cannot be allowed." The CGPGR disagreed. As the general director of Maisons du prisonnier explained, "The Famille's delegates are forgetting that our mission is to animate, control, and coordinate the activities of services in the Maison du prisonnier, including those of the SN." Directors of the Maisons du prisonnier were "the masters in their houses."[50]

On a national level, negotiations between the two agencies began soon after the commissariat was created. Jean Vedrine claims that despite initial clashes, their differences were settled in July 1942, after which everyone worked together happily. The evidence indicates, however, that the squabbling intensified in 1943–44, at which point Pinot, Vedrine, and their friends were officially out of the picture. Laval appointed a new commissioner in January 1943, and whatever modus vivendi may have been reached with the Famille du prisonnier fell apart completely. A new source of tension complicated the already sensitive issues of paternalism and power: politics.

Both the Famille du prisonnier and the CGPGR claimed to be completely apolitical. Pinot stated that the leaders of the CEAs should be motivated by a social spirit "outside of all political considerations." The Famille du prisonnier congress opened with the assertion that its delegates would "pursue, within the SN, their own eminently and uniquely social activities."[51] The fate of the CGPGR in particular illustrated the naïveté of such a belief. Any official organization concerned with POWs had to work with the Vichy regime. Given Vichy politicization of the prisoners of war to promote public support of its policies, it would have been extremely difficult if not impossible to stay clear of politics entirely. In spite of Pinot's efforts, a collaborationist eventually took over the CGPGR, using his position to encourage collaborationism among repatriated POWs.

Even before that happened, the leaders of both organizations defined apolitical within the context of the Vichy regime. Loyalty to Pétain, for example, was assumed. The Famille du prisonnier was founded by the wife of Charles Huntziger, the chief of the Armistice Army. Pinot, Join-Lambert, and the other original leaders of the CGPGR were also, during their period of official activity, openly Pétainist. Speaking at an exhibition of POW artworks from the camps, Pinot told the audience, "To think about the [prisoners of war], finally, means to form a strong and disciplined unity behind the Marshall in whom they and we place all our hope."[52] Until he was fired, Pinot, although never a collaborationist who hoped for an ultimate German victory, believed that France had to follow Pétain, pay for its sins, and rebuild a society resting on traditional Catholic values. The SN and the Famille du prisonnier held similar positions. Neither organization considered vague support of Pétain and his program to be political positions. But collaborationists found the CGPGR, and especially the CEAS, too tempting to leave alone. A group that attracted so many repatriated prisoners seemed the perfect vehicle to mobilize support for collaboration.

They had their chance after April 1942, when Laval replaced Darlan, who had been the head of state when the CGPGR was created. A repatriated POW named François Hulot, publisher of *Toute la France,* an openly collaborationist and pro-German journal addressed to POWs, convinced Laval's son-in-law, René de Chambrun, that Pinot was too reserved toward the Vichy government. Chambrun then lobbied Laval to appoint a strongly pro-Vichy leader at the CGPGR to win more repatriated POWs over to active support of the Vichy state and its policies.[53]

Laval officially asked Pinot to step down in January 1943 under the pretext that he had been back from camp for over a year and was no longer in touch with the prison-camp mentality. Pinot refused to comply, forcing Laval to fire him. The general public heard only the official version, and on 15 January the press announced that Pinot would be replaced by André Masson, just forty-two days after his liberation from Stalag V C. Prisoners already knew Masson as the author of numerous articles in the German-sponsored collaborationist camp newspaper *Le Trait-d'Union.* He had also published books and articles in France openly advocating collaboration with Germany to build a new Europe.[54]

Many POWs were probably initially Pétainist; they tacked up photos of Pétain in their bunks as an expression of French patriotism. The POW camps were isolated and officially received only the collaborationist press. With few exceptions, however, POWs separated Vichy from collaboration. To the prisoners, collaborators were discredited as being in the service of Germany. The prisoners' reactions in Germany to the news of Masson's appointment demonstrated both their disappointment and their confusion. From Stalag I A, "The news of Mr. Pinot's departure and his replacement by André Masson produced a disagreeable surprise among the POWs who wonder if those responsible for this nomination really are aware of the unfortunate articles that have appeared in the *Trait d'Union* under Masson's signature." The letter expressed a definite dislike of collaborationism combined with a certain naïveté about the Vichy regime and Pétain. Another prisoner wrote, "The POWs are disgusted to see that Masson, considered to be a 'collabo,' should at his liberation be put at the head of the General Commission." One group of POWs protested to the Scapini mission in January 1943, "We refuse to have the so-called politics of 'collaboration' extolled in our name.—We protest the nomination of a contributor to the *Trait d'Union* to the position of General Commissioner for Prisoners of War, and we protest the speeches in which he has already claimed to express our point of view."[55]

Meanwhile, back in France, at Pinot's departure the entire directing group of the CGPGR, the Maisons du prisonnier, and the CEAs resigned en masse. Pinot asked them to inform as many local CEA and Maison leaders as possible why he had been fired. At this point, he and many other founding members of the CGPGR tried to join the Resistance. Initially, the Gaullist POW resistance movement reacted with suspicion. In the first place, the former leaders of the CGPGR had made statements in favor of Pétain and had worked within the Vichy government. Furthermore, their first priority was to undermine André Masson rather than to encourage POWs in Germany to escape. The Gaullists denied the importance of the Masson issue, interpreting it as a personality conflict.[56]

Immediately after Masson's appointment, the former CGPGR group began to work against him. They set up a shadow CGPGR administration, the Committee of Five: Maurice Pinot, François Mitterrand, Jacques Benet, Jean Munier, and Marcel Barrois. They also created the Autonomous Federation of CEAs (Fédération autonome des CEA, or FACEA) to prevent Masson from using existing CEA groups. Mitterrand tried to discredit Masson publicly by calling out during Masson's speech to a house full of repatriated POWs in Paris that Masson had no right to speak in the name of the prisoners. What became known as the Pinot-Mitterrand (or Pin-Mitt) group eventually joined with the Gaullist and the Communist POW resistance groups to form the Movement national des prisonniers de guerre et déportés (MNPGD).[57]

Meanwhile, the new official commissioner hoped to use the CGPGR to promote active support of Pétain, the national revolution, and collaboration among repatriated prisoners. Masson immediately founded a new movement, the Mouvement "Prisonniers," for repatriated POWs "animated by the desire to serve with absolute discipline the Marshall and his government." The Mouvement "Prisonniers" included two teams: a social team which Masson designed to swallow the CEA and take over the task of mutual aid for POWs and their families, and a civic team to participate in "the work necessary for national renewal." Civic action included taking a "vigorous position against communism in terms of doctrine and combat," striking out against smugglers and black-marketeers, and spreading "information." In an internal note to directors of the Maisons du prisonnier and the CEA, Masson explained that a repatriated POW's duty was to denounce all aspects of communism, Gaullism, and attentism, "acting in a militant fashion."[58]

In April 1943, Masson decided to expand his horizons: "Within the Mouvement 'Prisonniers' wives, mothers and sisters will join into Unions of Prisoners' Wives" (Unions des femmes de prisonniers).[59] Each Maison director was to propose a POW wife who could become a departmental union leader. Her first responsibility would be to recruit members. Once a union formed, instructions would come from Paris about the work it was to undertake.

Article 2 of the union statutes defines the membership of this women's group: only mothers, wives, fiancées, sisters, and godmothers of "prisoners belonging to the Movement." As repatriated POWs entered France, they filled out sign-up sheets for the Mouvement "Prisonniers" along with myriad other forms. The results of the massive enrollment, however, were disappointing. The POWs did not show up for meetings. Masson's hope that wives would exert additional pressure on repatriated prisoners to join the Mouvement "Prisonniers" explains the emphasis the union put on recruitment and the occasionally unscrupulous methods the union used to gain members. In one town, for example, the union reportedly offered free potatoes to any POW wife who signed up.[60]

In addition to creating new groups, Masson tried to use existing structures to win active support of the Vichy government and its policies. A "Masson Letter" was sent to every repatriated POW. François Hulot, who became Laval's general secretary, instructed Maison du prisonnier directors to post Laval's speech about the Mouvement "Prisonniers" and reminded them that every Maison was to hang a portrait of Laval in the entrance. Directors were also to consider setting up a Mouvement "Prisonniers" as one of their "essential tasks."[61]

Masson's many attempts to form and use POW organizations for collaboration encountered stiff resistance from the beginning. Hulot complained in February 1943 that in spite of his own efforts, subscriptions to *Toute la France* were "just about negligible." Leaders of the CGPGR met in October 1943 to discuss why repatriated POWs refused to join the Mouvement "Prisonniers" and how to reverse that trend. Someone suggested tricking the prisoners into joining by not "shocking them with the term Mouvement 'Prisonniers.'" Once the POWs had begun to work with the movement—helping POW families with house repairs, gardening, and so on—then they could be told that they had actually been working "in the spirit of the Mouvement 'Prisonniers.'" The directors puzzled over the repatriated prisoners' "instinctive suspicion" of anything official.[62]

Many of the repatriated prisoners already active in local CGPGR organizations under Pinot reacted strongly to Masson. In the Gers Departmental Maison, all eleven directors of the Auch CEA resigned in June 1943, "considering that it was impossible for them to collaborate with the Maison du prisonnier whose directives seem to them to go against the goal of social solidarity." One week later, the CGPGR inspector called a public meeting to straighten out the mess; only fifteen people showed up. The prefect summed up the situation as a "serious crisis."[63]

The CEA director in Beziers described the "year long struggle of the CEA to maintain its opposition to all political initiatives and to retain a uniquely social role, despite the official pressure of the commissariat." A meeting in Lyons to promote the Mouvement "Prisonniers" was used by repatriated prisoners to denounce the movement and Masson.[64]

Despite Masson's lack of success within the CGPGR, his appointment added a new dimension to the Famille du prisonnier's mistrust and dislike of the commissariat and its affiliated groups. The Famille du prisonnier was highly suspicious of Masson and strongly opposed his attempt to politicize the prisoners in France. In fact, it was during Masson's reign that the mail quarrel and the dispute over the raising and distribution of money came to a head. By the November 1943 congress of the Famille du prisonnier, tensions had reached a climax, both within the CGPGR and between it and the Famille du prisonnier.

The issue was not clear cut. Masson's tenure was a miserable failure, beginning with the resignation of the entire directing committee of the CGPGR and extending to his inability to win repatriated prisoners over to active collaborationism. Mitterrand reported to resistance leaders in London that only thirty-five repatriated POWs had joined the Mouvement "Prisonniers." Masson proved so ineffective and counterproductive that within a year he was forced to step down. Thus, by the time of the Famille congress, Masson was on the way out and a new commissioner was about to be appointed. Jean-Pierre Maxence, representative of the CGPGR, spoke to the Famille du prisonnier congress. His statement—"It is inadmissible, and I insist on underlining this as a representative of the Commissariat Général, it is inadmissible that a social service should be used for any kind of political propaganda"—received "lively applause."[65]

In February 1944, a little over one year after Pinot's dismissal, Robert Moreau, a nondescript bureaucrat, replaced Masson. Moreau worked primarily to end the controversy, dissolve the groups created by Masson, and generally straighten out the chaos Masson had left. At the liberation, the CGPGR was disbanded in favor of a Ministry of Prisoners, Deportees, and Refugees, led by Henri Frenay, who retained some of the CGPGR institutions, notably the Maisons du prisonnier.

Furthermore, it would be incorrect to paint a picture of a politically pure Secours national-Famille du prisonnier opposing a tainted and collaborationist CGPGR. Neither group remained entirely free of political sin. The Famille insisted on a "perfect loyalty vis à vis the Marshall and the men he honors with his confidence."[66] But politics at the Secours national went beyond Pétainism. The Famille du prisonnier, for example, decried the fact that the prisoners were "returning most of the time . . . to contaminated households"—contaminated presumably by the Resistance. The Famille suggested distributing a brochure from the marshall to each prisoner "the minute he crosses his threshold" to neutralize the contamination.[67] In another instance, the administrative council of the SN met with Laval "on the subject of a liaison between the SN and the Milice Française" and decided to use the men and materials of the Milice. At another meeting, the SN discussed setting up a children's home in "Jewish property" that had been "requisitioned."[68]

Thus political distinctions between the two groups blur under scrutiny, illustrating the ambiguities of the occupation. Both groups accepted Vichy as an apolitical regime. Nonetheless, it proved impossible, no matter how strong the desire to steer clear of politics, actually to do so in the climate of Vichy France.

Both the Famille du prisonnier and the CGPGR served useful purposes, especially given the meager resources the state provided for the families of prisoners. These agencies distributed large sums of money and aid in kind, handed out scholarships, provided vacations, established rest homes for prisoners' wives and children, placed families from high-risk areas in country homes, passed laws to protect the rights of the POWs, and lobbied ministers on behalf of POWs and their families. The constant squabbling did not destroy the ability of either organization to act; however, neither group escaped untainted by the Vichy regime.

In the end, the political battles as well as the disputes over money were largely manifestations of the deeper conflict over control. Differences in philosophy, organization, and personnel only fueled mistrust and a desire by each agency to rule the other. Yet through all the battles and disputes, neither agency ever questioned the need for an outside organization to take over prisoners' families as the head of household. Although the CGPGR condemned the paternalism of the Famille du prisonnier, its leaders also spoke frequently of "taking charge of" prisoners' families.

Most prisoners' wives managed to survive the war and exodus without their husbands, and most of them made it through the lean years of the occupation as well. In spite of this overwhelming evidence of their abilities, paternalistic presumptions about women endured. Prisoners' wives demonstrated enormous resilience not only in merely surviving the war years but also in creating and sustaining an impressive self-help organization of their own, to which I now turn.

Prisoners' Wives United: Sisterhood and Solidarity

The Associations of Prisoners' Wives form amongst themselves a federation . . . , which shall be called the FEDERATION OF ASSOCIATIONS OF PRISONERS' WIVES. . . . This federation will be of limited duration. Its activity will cease . . . when all the prisoners have returned.
—Fédération des associations de femmes de prisonniers, 1942

Across France, prisoners' wives joined together and created support groups to deal with their many problems. A sense of female solidarity and shared identity developed; they defined themselves as *femmes de prisonniers,* women whose experiences set them apart from the rest of society. The groups demonstrate that prisoners' wives defended their own interests, belying many widespread assumptions about them. Prisoners' wives refused to remain passive clients of the state and public agencies or victims of the hardships of daily life. Instead, they overcame their isolation and eased their burdens through solidarity. They gained not only mutual support and friendship but also years of experience in organization, leadership, lobbying, publishing, and so on.

These activities, by mobilizing prisoners' wives, could have raised their consciousness, made them aware both of their own abilities and of the injustice of previous obstacles faced by women. Yet after the war the solidarity and activism ceased. Not only did the POW wives' groups disappear, but none of the many histories of Vichy France or of French captivity mentions them.

The disappearance signifies one of the limits of the groups of prisoner of war wives. Although the groups signified both the female solidarity and the activism of prisoners' wives, the women united on the basis of their husbands' status and justified their goals and tactics with reference to their husbands. When the prisoners returned, the women's common identity vanished, and most of them dropped out of the public arena to return to domesticity. During the difficult years of separation, however, solidarity rewarded prisoners' wives with friendship, understanding, and a public voice.

Prisoners' wives began to unite only in the spring of 1941, almost a full year after their husbands' capture. From the fall of France in June 1940 through October or November 1940, most wives awaited news of their husbands' fate. When they received word that their husbands were prisoners of war, most of the women believed, along with the rest of France, that because the war was over the French soldiers would return shortly.

After a year passed, most prisoners' wives realized that their situation would not soon change, and some of them decided to organize. Even then, many prisoners' wives intended their organizations to last "a few months."[1] The variety of groups reflected not only the territorial divisions of France in this period but also class and political divisions. In the occupied zone, three main organizations developed. Communist women in the Resistance created a special prisoner of war wives' section. In Paris, officers' wives created a group that eventually took the name *Femmes d'absents*. Because French army officers belonged more or less exclusively to a certain social milieu, their wives were *bourgeoises,* as one former member described herself. Led by Mrs. De Clinchamps, the women met in groups based on their husbands' *Oflag* (officer camp), and the director sent out a short newsletter signed "Quelques-unes parmi nous [some among us]."

For Christian working-class women in the occupied zone, the Service des femmes de prisonniers developed within the Mouvement populaire des familles (MPF), a Jeunesse ouvrière chrétienne (JOC) spin-off for married couples. While leader of the CGPGR, Masson tried with limited success to create a POW wives' auxiliary group, the Union des femmes de prisonniers, to support his Mouvement "Prisonniers." After Masson left the CGPGR, the Union des femmes de prisonniers renamed itself the Centre d'entr'aide féminin and joined the Centres d'entr'aide. In the unoccupied zone a Catholic movement created a service for rural POW wives that published a paper called *Avec lui, entre nous.*

The Fédération des associations
de femmes de prisonniers

The Lyons area of the southern zone gave birth to what became the largest and most inclusive group of POW wives, the Fédération des associations de femmes de prisonniers (FAFP). Starting in 1941 with several hundred members in Lyons, Roanne, and St. Etienne, the federation claimed by March 1942 to have 12,000 members—40,000 members by May 1943. After the liberation of France and before the liberation of the POW camps, the federation merged with the Service des femmes de prisonniers in the northern zone and the rural group Avec lui, entre nous, for a total membership of 150,000.[2]

The federation expressed POW wives' sense of shared identity. Even the way in which the federation started signaled the bonds they felt. The original leaders, most of them experienced organizers, marveled at the ease of launching groups of prisoners' wives. Andrée Aulas, eventual president of the federation, and two of her co-workers in Roanne decided in February 1941 to organize their fellow POW wives. They rented a room and hung signs in the local bakeries calling a meeting of all POW wives. To their complete surprise, some six or seven hundred women appeared for the meeting.[3] "We were astounded to see all these women arriving." The room filled to overflowing, with women standing in the aisles and out in the hall. Aulas and her friends quickly realized that they were on to something. "We were completely shaken up [*boulversées*] by these women who were like us, who were seeking, who were ill at ease, and who asked themselves, 'How will all this end?'"[4]

At about the same time in Grenoble, Suzanne LaPierre also began to organize POW wives. In Lyons, Agnès Griot organized a group of prisoners' wives before hearing about the groups in Grenoble and Roanne. "We were spurred on by the wives; there were too many women looking for something like support, action. . . . We easily had over a thousand prisoners' wives in Lyons. We did not have to go looking for them; all we had to do was put up a pretty poster."[5]

The sense of common identity shared by prisoner of war wives drew on both positive and negative emotions. Prisoners' wives felt alienated from the rest of society. Many of them experienced a "lack of understanding from [their] circle of friends." The POW wife "feels *alone,* in the margins of society. In the presence of single people, she is too rich in her love. . . . In the presence of united households, she is the poor relative."[6]

Prisoner of war wives, alone yet married, did not fit into any acceptable social category. Their husbands were away for an indefinite period of time, leaving the women's marital status unclear. Prisoners' wives in France felt that the entire community, even their own families, offered not support but "harsh judgment" on everything from leisure and clothing to "the way we live, . . . the way we raise our children."[7]

Even people not suspicious or hostile toward prisoners' wives were not particularly solicitous, because everyone faced difficulties during the occupation. Unlike most people, however, prisoners' wives were missing their usual companions. "Used to living with someone, they abruptly found themselves alone. The loneliness of nights with a sick child . . . loneliness of returning home in the evening, of the empty room, the bed too big." Loneliness, hardship and criticism opened the door "to all weaknesses."[8] Associations offered prisoners' wives the friendship lacking in the community and mutual support to help them overcome their loneliness and hold up under pressure.

Prisoners' wives also joined together out of a positive sense of community. As one brochure explained, "No one better understands a prisoner's wife than another prisoner's wife. Together, joining arms, we will be less cold and have less fear. We will struggle against misery and temptation, against loneliness and the blues."[9] As its motto, the federation chose, "Among ourselves, by ourselves, for ourselves."[10]

The three local associations from Lyons, Roanne, and St. Etienne formed a federation in August 1941, establishing headquarters in Lyons. In October 1941, the federation declared itself a public nonprofit organization under the law of 1901. By then over thirty local associations had joined.[11] After the total occupation of France in November 1942, the federation, hoping to create a national organization, contacted Jeanne Bajeux, director of the Service des femmes de prisonniers in the northern zone. The two groups worked together on publications until the liberation of France, when the two fused completely under one directing committee.

The independence of the federation from any other, male-run organization was exceptional. The committee of directors, local presidents, and all the leaders were women who not only ran an ever-growing organization but also dealt locally and nationally with public authorities and became increasingly adamant about certain demands. The public reacted to these groups with surprise. "Haven't you ever heard: that little woman from nowhere, who would have said, who would have believed it? Certainly it is wonderful to see them throw themselves like that into such an adventure . . . and succeed."[12]

The female solidarity and activism of the federation could have been feminist, except that the federation was not feminist in its rationale or self-conception. The federation based every demand on the women's identity as wives of prisoners and justified every action with reference to their husbands. The ultimate goal of the women in the federation was to preserve their marriages and families and ease the return to prewar family roles. The federation insisted that, rather than threatening the family, association activity represented "the 'family' note" in the husband's absence.[13] *Femmes de prisonniers,* the federation's monthly, constantly reassured members that their husbands would not be angry with them for joining such a group but would approve of their doing so. In an early bulletin, a POW from Stalag II D asserted, "In their spouses' absence, prisoners' wives should gather together and their voice should be heard." Another POW wrote, "The other night at dinner I explained to my buddies all the things you were doing together. They said to me, 'Those women are amazing!' "[14]

The federation considered the men's approval essential. When the three local associations united in 1941 and asked Aulas to be the president, she wrote to her husband for his permission to accept. But two months would have elapsed before her husband could have responded. Taking her mother-in-law's word that he would certainly approve, Aulas accepted the position before she received his reply. Even though she knew he would approve, it was important to her to ask his permission—more important than receiving it.

The federation leaders conceived of their role within the traditional bounds of femininity. For example, the local president should not just run the association, she should be its "mother." Under the president were the team leaders, the *responsables*. "What does it mean to be a 'responsable?' A 'responsable' is someone who responds to something, who carries the weight of something. Let's take an example: the mother of a family is responsible for the upkeep of her house."[15]

Of the Wives, By the Wives, For the Wives

That the federation was neither feminist nor an instrument of consciousness-raising does not diminish its significance. All the groups of prisoner of war wives demonstrated both the strong sense of female solidarity and the women's positive role in shaping their own destinies. The federation was especially significant because of its size and because, from start to finish, it was run entirely by women, who resisted at least one attempt by a male organization, the Légion française de combattants, to take it over.

Rigid social barriers, deep political and religious divisions, and a tendency toward excessive centralization characterized French society in the 1940s.[16] The federation tried to overcome those characteristics of French society, to build on an existing sense of solidarity; to cross the barriers of class, religion, and politics; and to remain responsive locally while working effectively on the national level.

The federation, which began as a grass-roots movement, successfully resisted the centralizing trend in France. Unlike the local-to-departmental-to-national hierarchy of most French organizations, each local association reported directly to the federation. Its leaders hoped thereby to maintain close contacts with the local associations, to share in their experiences while providing advice and support.[17] Aulas traveled constantly, visiting associations in cities and towns across France and even in Algeria, meeting with leaders, and keeping in touch with members.

The federation, run by a committee of directors, helped existing local associations when problems arose with other groups or agencies and promoted the creation of new associations across southern France and eventually throughout the country. The more associations the federation represented, the better it could speak in the name of all prisoners' wives.[18] The committee maintained contact with the Red Cross, the Direction des services de prisonniers de guerre of the Ministry of War, the Secours national, and the CGPGR. After the liberation, the federation held a seat on the Minister of Prisoners, Deportees and Refugees' advisory committee as he prepared for the imminent return of French nationals from Germany.

Locally, however, each association remained "of the people." The majority of activity took place at the level closest to each individual member's life. As prisoners' wives started new associations, the federation stressed that although a big public meeting was a good way to get started, small meetings by neighborhood or even weekly block meetings of five or six wives were preferable.[19] Aulas explained, "We have verified everywhere the value of these neighborhood contacts which are more real, where the women feel like a family, amongst themselves, where they get to know and appreciate each other."[20] Neighborhood meetings also brought together POW wives who lived near each other and who could, once they became friends, help each other on a daily basis, looking after each other's children, running errands, and so on.

Even the local associations avoided centralization. Each one was led by a president assisted by a group of team leaders called *responsables*. Each team leader chose a task and gathered a team of wives to take care of the organizational work. For example, one team was responsible for finding a meeting place, the next for planning the program. Spreading the responsibilities as widely as possible encouraged a deeper sense of involvement and commitment among the members. "Each women contributes the help she can and her personality to the others. Each one gives, each one receives." The personal enrichment gained from active involvement in a group allowed each woman to develop her abilities and personality, opened her to the problems of others, and taught her to give of herself.[21] The federation also believed that action prevented women from succumbing to temptation. As in Alcoholics Anonymous or Weight Watchers, prisoners' wives in the associations could call on each other in times of distress. They could count on their friends.

Because involvement with an association could even help women who had not resisted temptation, the associations remained open to women who had not remained faithful to their husbands. "We want all of them . . . the stylish, the less stylish, those who have done stupid things, who have compromised themselves, who have abandoned their little ones. . . . The envious, the bitter, the selfish, those who have lost all semblance of taste, the most miserable, the immoral, the neglected."[22]

Sharing responsibility with all members signaled trust. Having faith in wives who had "fallen" could be "the first step toward recovery." One prisoner's wife was about to abandon her home when the local association leaders "expressed their confidence in her by asking her to publicize our journal in her workshop. . . . She was touched by this confidence," began attending meetings, and soon "resumed a decent life."[23]

The federation sponsored a wide variety of activities. Of primary importance, it published newsletters, bulletins, and papers. Several issues of a three- to four-page newsletter entitled *Lettre aux femmes et mamans de prisonniers* appeared in 1941. By the spring of 1942 the federation had initiated two other papers, which appeared monthly. *Pages des responsables,* a bulletin for responsables, contained practical suggestions, reports from the associations, advice and instruction from the federation, as well as an in-depth analysis of one aspect of the POW wife's experience. The federation distributed the other journal, *Femmes de prisonniers,* to the associations to sell to members and other POW wives. They kept the price low: 1.50 francs in 1942, as compared to 3 francs for the woman's magazine *Pour elle* and 7 francs for *L'Illustration.*

Each issue of *Pages des responsables* and *Femmes de prisonniers* centered on a theme chosen by the federation's committee of directors. Articles were solicited from among the committee members, local leaders, and all members.[24] POW wives, not professional journalists, wrote the articles, although occasionally prisoners of war submitted essays or stories. Some of the themes recurred. "Fidelity" and "Hope" appeared twice; other themes included "Preparing for the Return," "Friendship," "Leisure Activities," and "Raising Children."

Both papers provided POW wives with a forum for expressing their opinions and suggesting ways of coping with matters of mutual concern. The papers contained practical legal information, recipes to prepare food for shipping, clothing patterns to extend the life of a dress, and so on. The papers publicized the federation, letting other prisoners' wives know of its existence and encouraging the formation of local associations.[25]

The federation also inspired the creation of central meeting places for prisoners' wives. Each local association set up an office to which any prisoner's wife could come for advice and support. If a Maison du prisonnier existed in a town, the association usually opened its office there.

Locally, the associations provided alternatives to family celebrations of traditional holidays, times when prisoners' wives most strongly felt their husbands' absence. Many wives experienced a seasonal cycle of ups and downs. Spring brought hope and renewal; summer meant a chance to relax and maybe take a vacation. But as autumn approached, the hope that the prisoner of war would be home for Christmas waned and depression set in. The newsletter of September 1941 already bemoaned the fact that "Christmas, the sweet celebration of intimacy, will not yet reunite the whole family." Almost every association held Christmas parties to permit "the isolated and all those interested to spend this holiday without sadness, in understanding and friendship."[26]

Associations also celebrated Easter as a group. The Easter program suggested by the federation enhanced the women's sense of identity with each other, with their children, and with their absent husbands.

1. Children's choir: "My little daddy" (by prisoners' children)

2. Word of Welcome—by a prisoner of war wife

3. Clown act for children (warning: ask for all the details of the act to avoid obscenities)

4. Folklore

5. Speech by the association president on education, preparation for the return, association services, etc.

6. Prisoners' Choir, "In Spite of Everything," by local troupe, traveling clan, group of prisoners, etc.

7. Snack for the children

According to the federation, this program incorporated the appropriate simplicity and "prisoner" spirit.[27]

In addition to hosting special holiday parties, local associations organized regular activities. One association reported that during the summer the women went on a "family walk" with their children every other week. The federation encouraged local associations to establish a "Leisure Team" to plan trips to the theater and outings to the countryside, or to stage theatrical shows and musical concerts using POW wives.[28]

Several issues of *Femmes de prisonniers* stressed the importance of leisure activities. The public expected prisoner of war wives to be in a state of mourning and disapproved if the women did not behave with the proper decorum. One *Pages de responsables* claimed that some people had "reproached prisoners' wives for getting together to sing." The wives themselves often felt guilty if they enjoyed themselves while their husbands suffered in prison camps. Joseph Folliet, a repatriated POW, wrote an article from the perspective of a POW wife who felt that whenever she allowed herself a simple pleasure, "I enjoy a momentary feeling of relief, but then I pay for it with remorse. . . . At the same time, I fear having scandalized my circle of relatives, neighbors, my acquaintances and colleagues. People are already so hard on prisoners' wives. . . . What will they think of me if they see me dressed attractively, a smile on my lips and a sparkle of happiness in my eyes?"[29]

The federation underlined the importance for POW wives of relaxation without guilt. The federation urged local leaders to discuss the issue and gave them questions they might use to start off the discussion. "To relax, does that mean to forget one's husband, forget that he suffers over there . . . or on the contrary, does it mean to love him by not neglecting anything that will allow him to return to a wife who has remained young and strong?"[30] A prisoner of war, having spent years in camp dreaming of the young, attractive woman he married, would not want to return to an embittered, prematurely aged wife. Therefore wives had to keep up their appearance, vitality, and strength. Relaxation and time off kept a woman attractive and healthy for the husband's sake.

The federation clearly justified its position with reference to the husbands. Not having fun was equivalent to neglect. Folliet wondered, "What would the absent one gain? Will he be happier knowing that you are sad?" Moreover, Folliet pointed out, although a prisoner's condition was sad, "He himself has distractions—fortunately, otherwise he would long ago have gone mad." The federation reminded its members that the POWs organized jazz groups and theatrical troupes in their camps.[31] Prisoners' wives should relax and enjoy themselves, as long as their distractions were "wholesome, honest, when they have nothing to do with dissipation."[32] Among the healthy ways to have fun, the federation listed walks in the country, reading, picnics, "feminine" sports, and, if one woman previewed the film for acceptability, going to a movie together.

In case some readers remained unconvinced of their husbands' approval, *Femmes de prisonniers* published favorable responses from the prisoners. "Of course it's a good idea to organize this little festivity. . . . But no, my dear, I don't mind if you act in the play. On the contrary, it makes me very happy." One husband from Stalag IV G even sent a poem, "Return," for his wife to recite. "You could learn it by heart, my dearest, if it would not be too much work, recite it with the proper tone of voice."[33]

The federation focused primarily on moral support through meetings, discussions, celebrations, and outings. Yet prisoners' wives faced serious economic and financial difficulties that the federation could not overlook. Rather than distributing money, the federation promoted mutual aid; locally the wives helped each other with available resources. Associations referred serious cases to the Famille du prisonnier, but every prisoner's wife, whatever her finances, could donate time and goodwill to help fellow wives. The federation especially emphasized visiting sick POW wives in hospitals and clinics. Healthy wives could bring their less fortunate sisters flowers or candy, send their husbands a package, forward mail to the hospital, and demonstrate in other small ways the "understanding friendship" and support of fellow POW wives.[34] The visitors also gained a new appreciation of their own fortune in being healthy.

The years of suffering experienced by POW wives entitled them to call themselves "elder sisters in suffering." But many people in France suffered during the war, and the federation wanted its members to be aware of and help all who suffered, not just each other. LaPierre explained at the March 1942 meeting that a preoccupation with one's own problems to the exclusion of outsiders ruined the best of groups.[35] At least, the women often reminded themselves, they were not widows: they still had hope. Becoming sensitive to the misery of others lightened the burden of one's own unhappiness. The elder sisters in suffering should support their younger siblings. "Be generous older sisters! Our suffering is great. Mixed in with the others, it is only one among the others."[36] By 1943–44, as Allied bombing of France intensified, a new form of mutual aid developed within the federation. Associations from untouched cities and towns collected money, clothing, and food to send to associations in towns hit by bombs. Rural POW wives housed city wives evacuated from war zones.

A less dramatic but constant preoccupation for prisoners' wives, the packages sent by families to the prison camps, were a natural focus of federation activity. The Roanne association organized an Easter package for the POWs as its first project. The association placed baskets in all the local shops where the citizens of Roanne could donate nonperishable food, cigarettes, and so on, to make up an Easter package for each POW from Roanne. One thousand packages were sent.[37] Despite the success of the Easter packages and similar appeals, the federation considered husbands' packages too essential to rely solely on public generosity.

In fact, the issue of packages for POWs had already sparked a public debate. The French government sent large quantities of food and clothing to the POW camps, as well as occasional individual packages at Christmas or Easter. The French Red Cross and its counterpart for the occupied zone, the Comité central d'assistance, coordinated regular mass shipments. But families of prisoners insisted on sending their own packages to their own prisoners. As goods became increasingly restricted in France, putting together a five-kilogram package every month meant additional trouble and expense; many wives and families gave up part of their own meager rations to fill the package.

Women's magazines such as *Marie-Claire* romanticized depriving oneself to send a package to a loved one, but in reality many prisoners' wives faced desperate situations. One woman asked the government for a supplementary food card for her husband's packages because she could no longer work without eating. "I do not doubt that you will honor my request, and that soon there will be a result. Thank you, otherwise the only way for me to escape my hunger will be to commit suicide." The government responded drily, "This issue has already been raised many times, but up to the present, we have not been able to comply."[38]

Many people had written the government requesting additional rations for prisoners' packages, but several key government officials opposed in principle special ration cards to help families send individual packages to POWS. They believed the POWS received their fair share of France's food from the Red Cross and the CCA. Collective shipments were more efficient, economical, and easier to transport. One bureaucrat even pointed out that collective shipments facilitated "the task of the various concerned German authorities." Still, some people in the government understood the emotional aspect of the package issue. "A prisoner who receives a package from his family or his town experiences a certain feeling of comfort from it. Besides, the families themselves must not be left out of the picture: it means a lot to them personally to give their prisoners a direct token of their regard and to lavish every possible attention upon them." The government resolved the issue to its own satisfaction in May 1941 by adding two francs a day to military allowances paid to POW wives. The solution ignored the problem of restricted goods, however, and the debate over a special ration card continued within the government, to no avail.[39]

Meanwhile, the Roanne association of POW wives, which believed wholeheartedly in family packages, devised another solution. It set up a special Package Center (Centre de confection de colis). Aulas negotiated with the Red Cross, which finally agreed to give the association enough goods to provide one package for each POW whose family belonged to the association. Members went to the Package Center on certain days and assembled their own packages. Although the basic items were the same, the wives preferred their own packages to the standard Red Cross packages, because they could add extra food, their husband's favorite candy, photographs of themselves or their children, articles of clothing, books, or whatever they wished within the regulations. The Package Center also provided an opportunity for POW wives to meet, talk, swap recipes for food that would not spoil, and otherwise encourage each other. Finally, the package was addressed in the wife's handwriting—something the prisoners considered important. "As for packages," wrote one prisoner of war, "we prefer those made up by our families, the beloved handwriting, the breath and the kiss of our wives or mothers, the touch of knowing hands and the look of the eyes we love are there. . . . Our gratitude goes beyond our bellies."[40]

As president of the federation, Aulas met with General Verdier, president of the French Red Cross, and extended the arrangement between local associations and the Red Cross to other cities. Verdier worried not just about the inefficiency of individual mailings but also about the possibility that wives would take the food home rather than sending it to their husbands. Aulas pointed out that Red Cross workers were susceptible to the same temptation, but she felt it was worth the risk of occasional stealing. Although Verdier agreed in principle to the arrangement, not every local wives' association set up a package center because some local Red Cross groups resisted.[41]

The package question illustrates how the federation represented, on both national and local levels, POW wives' interests to the rest of the world. Locally, as soon as an association had been declared, its president met with the prefect, the mayor, and all official agencies that had anything to do with the prisoners of war, "such that nothing is done locally without consulting the association."[42] Nationally, Aulas met with Pétain, negotiated with the Red Cross, and maintained contact with the DSPG, the CGPGR, and the Famille du prisonnier.

On behalf of prisoners' wives across France, the federation waged a continuous struggle to increase military allowances. "Families of prisoners must be able to live with dignity," Aulas declared. POW wives could not make ends meet on military allowances, and Aulas warned of disastrous consequences. One mother of two "deprived herself all winter long of her meat tickets and a portion of her bread tickets to send food to her husband. She went into a sanatorium and just died." Misery also led to temptation. "Who would dare cast the first stone at a woman who, one day when she was completely down and out emotionally and financially, no longer had the courage to refuse the offer that would momentarily end her painful nightmare?"[43]

The federation disapproved of work outside the home for prisoners' wives with inadequate resources if they had children. It also felt that government policy should avoid pulling the family apart more than it already was with the husband away. In France many working women sent children to a wet nurse (*nourrice*), separating wives not only from their husbands but also from their children. The federation stressed the potentially harmful effects of employment on prisoners' wives and families.

During its campaign for increased military allowances, the federation presented sample budgets to the CGPGR and the Ministry of Finance demonstrating the inadequacy of military allowances. The July 1942 increase, though appreciated, was too small to satisfy the federation.[44] Nevertheless, France did not raise military allowances again until 1945, after the liberation. Meanwhile, inflation quickly negated the benefits of the July 1942 raise. In 1944, the federation again collected sample budgets and put together a report demanding an increase of at least 50 percent in allowances.

As part of its effort, the federation dedicated the entire March 1944 issue of *Femmes de prisonniers*, "For Our Dignity, We Demand," to the allowance issue. Over and over the articles stressed both the poverty in which POW wives lived and its dangers: misery could lead to deprivation and illness; or to work outside the home, which was damaging to children; or perhaps even to infidelity. Although outside help was available to POW wives in financial difficulty, constantly having to ask for money humiliated and offended their dignity. It especially galled them that they had to beg for money when their husbands were gone precisely because they had served France in 1940. The federation thus called on the government to "remember the promises France made to her captive sons."[45]

The federation also played on Vichy's desire to win over the POWs. Sylvain Roche, a repatriated POW, journalist and brother of a federation director, warned the state that the POWs would be angry when they discovered what their wives were going through. He considered it an injustice suffered by the prisoner through the persons of his wife and children. "Indeed the prisoner will accept a great deal of suffering . . . but he will never tolerate the suffering, rancor and humiliation of his loved ones." Roche blushed to imagine the prisoners' reaction to the current situation. Likewise, the wives justified their claim to better treatment on the basis of their husbands' rights. "All the French are suffering. But are not prisoners' wives seniors in suffering? And this title, together with THEIR RIGHTS, permits us perhaps to claim what we judge indispensable to our dignity and to THEIR DIGNITY, to our life and to THEIR LIFE."[46]

Religion, Class, Politics

In the occupied zone, the Service des femmes de prisonniers closely resembled the federation in goals and outlook but chose to remain affiliated with the Mouvement populaire des familles (MPF) for political reasons.

According to Jeanne Bajeux, German presence in the occupied zone left little room for organizing and publishing free of censorship or interference. The MPF was a Catholic organization, and the Church was allowed to publish internal bulletins for its own congregation without German censorship. For this reason, the women active in the Service des femmes de prisonniers felt the MPF shielded them from the occupying authorities.[47]

The MPF grew out of the Jeunesse ouvrière chrétienne, a Catholic working-class youth movement established in 1927 by the priest Georges Guérin. The JOC worked to re-Christianize working-class youth and provide an alternative to such secular unions as the Confédération général du travail. Priests ran JOC meetings, which were organized along parish lines. A separate women's group, the Jeunesse ouvrière chrétienne féminine (JOCF), was created in 1928. The Ligue ouvrière chrétienne (LOC), similar in ideology, outlook, and organization, was formed in 1935, to keep members of either group who married from leaving the fold. But the LOC uniforms, medals, and other league trappings alienated many of its potential members. Hence in 1940, the leadership of the LOC renamed the organization the Mouvement populaire des familles, removing both league and the reference to Christianity from the title. The change created controversy, and in the northern zone it took another year before the LOC adopted its new title.[48]

During the German occupation, the MPF leadership split over defining its proper function. Some members felt that resistance to the Nazis should be its primary activity. The ruling majority, however, felt that the MPF had to help working-class families survive the hardships of the period. The increasing wage-price gap and the dissolution of the unions intensified economic difficulties for the working class. In the end, the MPF decided to focus on mutual aid, although many individual members joined the Resistance.[49]

The sensitivity of the MPF to working-class hardships led naturally to concern about the severe difficulties prisoner of war wives confronted. The Service des femmes de prisonniers, created in 1941, led originally by Anne-Marie Richard, claimed to have ten thousand members by 1942.[50] When Richard's husband returned in 1943, Bajeux took over.

The federation and the Service merged easily in 1944 because the two groups shared many features. The similarity was hardly coincidental, as the leadership of the federation came from the same milieu as that of the Service. Aulas joined the JOCF in her youth and, after her marriage, she and her husband joined the LOC. Griot, director of federation publications, joined the Jeunesse etudiante chrétienne, a sister organization for students, while she studied mathematics and science at the Ecole normale des jeunes filles at Sèvres. She also joined the LOC after her marriage, although because she married during her fiancé's last leave, he was not active with her in this movement. In Lyons, Griot's ties with the JOCF-MPF helped her set up the POW wives group. "It was easy to find leaders, women who had already taken on responsibilities."[51]

The federation leadership's prewar experience specifically in these Catholic social and family movements predisposed them to act. The LOC-MPF, for example, differed from most prewar family movements, which were open only to men and sometimes widows. Women not only joined the LOC, they were encouraged to take on responsibilities and leadership within the movement. The LOC-MPF divided itself into a masculine and a feminine branch to encourage women's activism; women, overwhelmed by men in mixed settings, were more likely to speak out, make their own decisions, and take on responsibilities among themselves. Women in the LOC-MPF, for the first time in any Catholic movement, held positions of leadership throughout the organizational hierarchy. Thus the LOC experience prompted many women to participate, to speak in public, write reports, and direct activities locally and nationally.[52]

Furthermore, the MPF believed that women's primary role as wives and mothers should not limit their horizons to the home and family. Rather, women should learn about and do what they could to improve the wider world in which they lived. Aulas, for one, claimed that her years in the JOCF and the MPF instilled in her the "habits of a militant activist, which means informing oneself, trying to understand and see what can be done."[53]

The JOC-LOC-MPF background also provided the women with practical ideas and experience in organizing. The JOC organized by neighborhood groups led by teams of responsables. The federation used the same terminology. The associations also adopted, informally, the JOC use of study circles to examine and report on matters of concern.[54]

In addition to experience and organizational structure, the federation rhetoric clearly derived from the prewar Catholic social movements. The centrality of the theme of salvation, albeit of marriages rather than souls, illustrates how deeply the federation rhetoric was colored by the experience of the leadership with Christian movements. The federation saved prisoners' families by keeping husband and wife together and by preventing unscrupulous men from taking advantage of the circumstances. Salvation resulted from involving as many members as possible in association activities, as action helped overcome difficulties. The idea that giving a member responsibility was a "wonderful way, the only way to safeguard, to elevate," derived clearly from a JOC tenet. A JOC training brochure stated, "The formative action of militancy rests on the collaboration required by entrusting responsibilities. . . . [This is an] excellent method even with regard to the most distant, for, sometimes the only way to save a soul in danger is to make it a saver."[55]

Federation papers referred to the benefits of its activities in such terms as ascension and exaltation, and many of its activities centered around Christian holidays.[56] However, although the wives' groups resembled the JOC-LOC-MPF in ideology, rhetoric, and organizational style, they differed in significant ways. While their Catholic movement experience motivated them to organize, prisoners' wives had another model of solidarity, the POW camp, which deviated from the Catholic movements.

To begin with, the federation was nonconfessional. Because prisoners' wives shared an identity based on their husbands' status, the prison-camp model mitigated the class and religious orientation of the federation leadership. Just as prisoners of war from all backgrounds shared a sense of identity by virtue of their experience, so prisoners' wives of all classes, religions, and political orientations shared certain preoccupations and understood each other solely by virtue of being a POW wife—according to federation leaders. Suffering "carves all prisoners' wives with the same blow of the chisel, rendering them all alike, all the same size. . . . Their hands thus brought together, reach out and clasp."[57] While some POW wives faced financial difficulties and others did not, the federation stressed that all their problems would have been easier to bear with their husbands' support.

Thus the federation hoped to attract all prisoners' wives, and not just active Catholic women. But because most members of the committee of directors and many local association leaders had been active in prewar Catholic movements, the issue of religion arose at the first major meeting of the federation in March 1942. Although their faith gave them strength, Suzanne LaPierre recommended not imposing Christian beliefs on the women who joined the associations, "for words have never convinced anyone, and at best we risk shocking them and scaring them off." LaPierre advocated demonstrating the love and charity of their faith through deeds instead. The federation agreed: "Rather than talking too much about [Christianity], we will live it."[58]

The associations were fairly successful in attracting nonreligious prisoners' wives. Bajeux, president of the Service des femmes de prisonniers of the MPF, which was explicitly Catholic, stated that joining with the federation in 1944 widened their horizons and opened up their groups. Join-Lambert, secretary of the CGPGR under Pinot and familiar with the Paris associations, claimed that "the vast majority of the membership is not Christian" and that priests "do not have open access to meetings."[59]

In the end, religion proved to be a less difficult issue than class. The model organizations—the JOC, the LOC, and the MPF—were openly working-class groups. What set the federation apart from other groups of POW wives, according to Join-Lambert, was its "popular stamp. These are wives of the common folk who want to remain amongst themselves." The class issue presented a dilemma both practical and intellectual. The federation hoped to reach as many POW wives as possible, but "they do not want charitable ladies."[60] The federation renounced the idea of charity, of having middle-class prisoners' wives helping the poor. The federation also feared associations led by bourgeois women; "Without even realizing it themselves they automatically overshadow women from the popular milieu who withdraw and do not take on responsibilities."[61] Opening the associations to bourgeois prisoners' wives could negate essential aspects of the associations, including spreading responsibilities widely, giving every member something to do, and making the aid given by the association mutual and not paternal.

But excluding bourgeois women denied the community of suffering that united prisoners' wives. So in theory the associations were not limited to women from the "popular milieu" and all POW wives were welcome to join. To sidestep the possibility that bourgeois wives might dominate an association, the federation recommended that the first and founding members of an association be of modest background and that responsibilities be given initially to nonbourgeois women. Bourgeois wives would understand and accept secondary positions, LaPierre informed the federation at its March 1942 meeting. "Moreover, many wives of superior officers have understood this psychological phenomenon and refused on their own to take leadership positions in our association's committees, all the while contributing valuable help to the associations."[62]

The federation eventually found another solution that allowed bourgeois wives to assume responsibilities without overwhelming the working-class members. A special group of officers' wives could be created within each association. Simone Demargne, leader of one such group, reassured the federation that the aim was not to pit soldiers' wives against officers' wives. "There are only prisoners' wives . . . all of them united by the bond of their common ordeal." Yet the associations existed not only to provide services and maintain morale but also "to elevate us in the true sense of the word: to make us go up."[63] All POW wives should learn from the experience of captivity and suffering, and the problems officers' wives faced differed from those faced by soldiers' wives, partly because of the difference in social background. Less likely to have financial difficulties, officers' wives, who usually did not work outside the home, were more likely to be isolated.

The different experience of captivity in officers' camps created another distinction important to officers' wives. Enforced idleness rather than hard labor characterized the officers' experience of captivity, because officers, unlike most regular troops, did not work for Germany.[64] Officers' wives had to prepare to face men returning with a different set of problems and needed to share ideas among themselves about how they would cope. Demargne believed that once bourgeois wives joined a local association, they would become interested in their fellow prisoners' wives. The association would promote solidarity and diminish prejudice between bourgeois and working-class women.[65]

To illustrate how the association helped both working-class wives and their wealthier sisters overcome prewar class prejudice, Marie-Louise Sévénier, an officer's wife, published a short story entitled "The Association is Friendship!" Two POW wives meet in line at a shop. Aline, a member of the association, takes an interest in Elisabeth, who looks discouraged, and invites her to come to the local association and put together a package for her husband. Several days later, Aline arrives to pick up Elisabeth for the association and finds, to her surprise, that Elisabeth lives in an elegant house. "She must not really need my help to put together her packages since she lives in a house like this." Finally Aline decides that Elisabeth had seemed awfully unhappy. Yet when she rings the bell, she worries, "What if this woman tells me at the door that I should stay out of her affairs!" But her fears are unfounded; Elisabeth is overjoyed to see her. Aline even teaches Elisabeth something new: how to knit her husband a pair of slippers. They become best friends and see each other daily. Elisabeth looks after Aline's son Jacques while Aline is at work; Aline manages to get eggs from a country cousin for Elisabeth. Most important, however, is the "solace they felt with each other, sharing their suffering, feeling understood."[66]

The federation in the south probably crossed class boundaries more successfully than the Service des femmes de prisonniers in the northern zone. The Service had been expressly working-class; there were enough officers' wives in Paris to sustain a separate organization, *Femmes d'absents,* led by De Clinchamps. No city in the southern zone contained a high-enough concentration of officers' wives, however, so those officers' wives who wanted to join a group went to the federation. In the northern zone, in contrast, even after the federation joined with the Service, *Femmes d'absents* remained separate.[67]

In addition to religion and class, politics presented another potential source of trouble. On this subject, what was clear in theory became ambiguous in practice. The federation statutes insisted that associations should "carefully avoid all deviation onto a political or partisan terrain." Demargne repeated the federation position at the May 1943 meeting: "We must remain strictly within the two following domains: moral and social; and we must systematically avoid anything that in any way concerns politics." The federation had many reasons for asking its members to avoid politics, but Demargne stated the one she considered most compelling: "Our husbands in their camps certainly prefer to see us stay away from these questions." Prisoners' wives should take advantage of the fact that because they were women "no one can ask us anything along those lines."[68] Members could hold personal political opinions, but they were never to engage the associations or the federation in any political camp. The federation also preferred that wives who intended to start up an association be "disengaged from all political influences."[69]

But wives defined by their husbands' military status could hardly avoid dealing with the state, especially as it acted as the protecting power for its own POWs. Aulas made a special trip to Vichy to meet with Pétain on 5 March 1942. Like the majority of French people, she believed that the war had ended in June 1940 and accepted the French State at Vichy as the legitimate government. Furthermore, the traditional Catholic rhetoric of Vichy undoubtedly appealed to one who had been active in Catholic movements.[70]

In retrospect, Aulas claimed she met with Pétain because "it could have been useful." At the time, she wrote about the meeting and the various practical issues they discussed: the difficulty of finding goods for packages, the inadequacy of military allowances. Pétain told Aulas "that he himself sends a great many packages, then he asked me for an address label so he could send a nice package to my husband." He also donated ten thousand francs to the federation and assured Aulas of his efforts to obtain the liberation of "those he calls his best children."[71]

Forty-three years later, Aulas admitted that, after the liberation, "I was not exactly proud of having seen the marshal" but pointed out that when they met "he had fired Laval," and she believed in him. (Laval returned to power one month later.) Aulas told her close friends that "he was really an old man; he may not have been bad in his own time, but . . . he was no longer himself."[72] To the public, she worded her impressions more tactfully. "I do not at all have the impression that I have just been received by a great Head of State. . . . Our Marshall is first, I believe, a true 'grandfather' who, while holding firm the reigns of the country, brings to his personal contacts a kindness so comprehensive that we can go to him and simply tell him of our distress."[73]

Aside from Aulas's article describing her visit to Pétain, the federation papers rarely refer to the Vichy government. As time went on, the federation became increasingly wary of Vichy. Local associations were warned to "avoid being taken over by a group or a charity which looks after prisoners' families in your city." During a meeting in 1943, Demargne alerted the federation that "we could be more or less led into the forbidden territory by one or another of the organizations with which we collaborate to help prisoners' wives. Be prudent and learn how to discern the tenuous line that separates the social from the political."[74]

Aulas stated without hesitation that the warnings referred to the Légion française des combattants, created by the Vichy government to unite veterans of both wars. Because the prisoners of war were soldiers, the legion insisted that it should be "the protectors of prisoners' families; it should sponsor, morally adopt prisoners' families, facilitate the creation of regional groups of prisoners' families."[75]

Aulas and the federation grew increasingly wary of the legion, which had become a politicized, openly collaborationist group. Both politics and gender were at issue. The legion clearly felt threatened by the independence of this all-female group, over whom it declared its paternal rights. Aulas admitted that, politics aside, "what was truly painful was that they wanted prisoners' wives to be part of their group." Aulas refused to have the federation join the legion, because then "it would have been their thing." The federation and the legion engaged in a series of scuffles before eventually reaching a cease-fire. The federation agreed to *"Intelligent and circumspect collaboration* with that which exists" but retained complete organizational independence.[76] Aulas was pleased to report that not one association ever joined the legion.

The war, another important political issue to POW wives, was mentioned only in passing and only when it had a direct impact on prisoners' wives or the federation. Federation publications referred to the Allied invasion of North Africa and the subsequent German occupation of southern France as the "events of November 1942." Because of these events, the federation lost contact with its North African branch but strengthened its ties with the Service des femmes de prisonniers in northern France. Most French newspapers described Allied bombing raids in 1943 and 1944 as the evil deeds of the Anglo-Americans. *Femmes de prisonniers* coverage of Allied bombing consisted entirely of appeals to help wives who had lost their homes.

Some prisoners' wives realized from the start that their husband's fate was tied to the course of the war and joined the Resistance. Four women active in the original Roanne association of POW wives became deeply involved in the Resistance, but they stressed that they joined as individuals and not as representatives of the association.[77] Aulas met both Pinot and Mitterrand in Paris when they were members of the CGPGR. She apparently stayed in contact with them after they went underground. Aulas also knew about resistance activities taking place at the MPF headquarters in Lyons, which were adjacent to her office. Members of the MPF used its placement service to save Jewish children, distributed the resistance paper *Cahiers de Témoignage Chrétien,* and so on.[78] The MPF resistance group decided not to involve the federation in its activities, however, because prisoners' wives had enough problems of their own.

Andrée Aulas encouraged certain forms of disobedience. In a large public meeting, Aulas told an audience of prisoners' wives to communicate openly with their spouses by hiding secret letters in packages. When one of her hidden letters was discovered by a German guard in a hollowed out cigarette, her husband wrote as instructed by his German guards that she was never to hide letters in cigarettes again. Aulas passed this information on to federation members in the newsletter.[79]

The federation of POW wives defies the historian's inclination to divide

France into collaborators and resisters. It maintained a certain ambiguity about politics for the same reason it was ambiguous about religion and class: it wanted to attract as many POW wives as possible. Just as the reality of POW camp fraternity was probably less idyllic than it has often been portrayed,[80] the federation probably did not attain completely classless, ecumenical, apolitical solidarity. Still, its huge membership confirms its success at overcoming the divisions that atomized French society. The very attempt to create such a group was noteworthy for a country as divided as France. Equally extraordinary, the federation, run entirely by women, remained independent and unattached to any male group.

After the liberation of France, the federation continued its activity, although with slightly altered rhetoric. In keeping with the politics of post-liberation France, the federation toned down its Christian rhetoric, praised the Resistance, and took a strong stand in favor of female suffrage. Its support of female suffrage did not, however, indicate radical new ideas about the role of women in society. Prisoners' wives were urged to vote because they were nurturing, because they were concerned about family issues, and, in this situation, because they were delegates of the husband in his absence.

The sense of sisterhood always rested on the women's identity as wives of absent men. No matter how active the leaders became, the federation always justified its existence by the absence of the prisoners of war. In the most fundamental indication of its limits, its statutes specified that it would dissolve itself once the POWs had returned. After May 1945 the federation simply disappeared. Their status as wives of POWs brought these women together; their husbands' presence pulled them apart.

The MPF launched a new group, Foyers de rapatriés (Repatriated Households), after the war. Foyers de rapatriés tried to build on the activity of the federation wives joined by their recently repatriated husbands; it dealt with the problems of readjusting to civilian and married life and pressured the government to meet repatriated POW demands. But this group fell into the Christian working-class category of the MPF, and those active in it eventually saw no reason not to work with the MPF, especially once they stopped defining themselves as "repatriated" households. By the end of 1946, the group fizzled.

An intriguing source indicates that the Fédération national des combattants prisonniers de guerre (FNCPG) considered asking the federation of POW wives to join, although neither Aulas nor Jean Védrine, who proposed it in 1944, recall anything about this.[81] The FNCPG until recently remained exclusively for former prisoners of war. (Widows can now join as full members.)

Not only did the federation of POW wives disappear as an organization, but it, along with prisoners' wives, disappeared from the past, escaping the notice of historians, even those writing about the impact of captivity on French society.[82] Yet, although it was not a feminist group, the federation provided thousands of POW wives with a way to act rather than being acted upon by various agencies. Denying that public agencies knew what was best for POW wives, that anyone other than a prisoner's wife knew what these women needed, the federation gave them a voice in the public arena; it expressed their solidarity and shared identity. The federation helped them overcome their alienation from society in a positive way. Rediscovering the federation corrects the prevalent picture of prisoners' wives as objects of policy and as individuals struggling in isolation against a cruel world.

Pour Elle

PRIX : 3 FR.
N° 69 - 3 DÉC. 1941

L'ABSENT

Prisoner of War Wife. Cover Illustration from *Pour Elle*, 3 December 1942. The entire issue of this popular women's magazine, dedicated to the absent prisoners, was filled with advice, recipes, sewing and knitting patterns, and so on. The prisoner's wife on the cover is holding a letter from her husband on the special POW stationery (see photo). The prominence of the letter and her wedding ring, the picture in the cameo at her neck all signal her devotion to her absent husband.

Ce que représente la D.F. : à peine le quart du salaire moyen, environ le sixième du salaire normal.

"What the Family Allotment Represents." Drawing from *Femmes de Prisonniers*. The FAFP presented graphically the deficiency of the family allotment (délégation familiale) for prisoners' wives. The amount represented one fourth of the average salary and one sixth of normal salaries.

Le Chic DANS LA SIMPLICITÉ

3. — ATTENDS-MOI, MON AMOUR.
Ce manteau vague, peut accompagner la robe précédente. Une guimpe à petit col en complète l'encolure. Manches raglan avec épaules arrondies. Fronces retenues par un petit poignet. (3 m. 35 en 1 m. 40.)

1. — POUR FÊTER TON RETOUR.
Quoi de plus simple et de plus élégant que ce costume coupé dans un tissu marine à pois blancs ? Tenue de ville idéale pour la belle saison. Blouse ou guimpe blanche.(4 mètres en 1 mètre.)

2. — TU RESTES DANS MON RÊVE.
Et voici, pour l'après-midi, une robe ou un deux-pièces en imprimé. Un plastron bas en forme de bavette souligne le décolleté en pointe et retient les fronces du corsage, ceinture nouée. Petites poches. Manches bouffantes. (4 mètres en 1 mètre.)

"The Chic in Simplicity." Illustration from *Dimanches de la Femme*, 15 May 1943, p. 8. Despite the hardships many prisoners' wives faced, this woman's magazine advised them to remain tastefully fashionable. "Letting yourself go would be as reprehensible as an uncalled-for extravagance." The first outfit was "To Celebrate your Return," the second dress indicated "You Remain in my Dreams," and the third ensemble promised the husband his wife would "Wait for Me, My Love."

Prisoner of War Wife Reading a Letter from Her Husband. Illustration from *Femmes d'absents*, "Fêtes et saisons" series. Compared to the cover of *Pour Elle*, this photograph provides a more intimate, private image. The prisoner's wife reads her husband's letter while she knits (something for him?) by the soft light of a lamp. (Courtesy Les Editions du cerf, 1943)

Sa place est gardée à la table et dans nos cœurs.

CLICHÉ FÊTES ET SAISONS

« Des colis, oui, nous en attendons. Vos chères
lettres, oui, nous les attendons. Mais nous attendons
autre chose encore : faîtes que nous ne devenions
pas chez nous étrangers, à force d'absence... »

"We Keep His Place at the Table and in Our Hearts." Illustration from *Femmes d'absents*, "Fêtes et saisons" series,
pp. 16–17. A prisoner's family at the table with the empty chair of the absent POW casting a shadow. Opposite, in his
barracks, the prisoner thinks to himself, "Do not let us become strangers in our own homes, by dint of our absence."
Prisoners' wives tried to maintain a presence for their absent husbands. (Courtesy Les Editions du cerf, 1943)

Associations de Femmes de Prisonniers
44, Rue Salomon-Reinach, LYON
2 fr.

sans doute début 1944

Femmes de prisonniers

Pour notre dignité NOUS REVENDIQUONS

DEPUIS trois ans qu'elles existent, les ASSOCIATIONS DE FEMMES DE PRISONNIERS ne se sont jamais écartées du but qu'elles s'étaient fixé à leur création : aider leurs membres à attendre et préparer « le retour » dans la fidélité et la dignité. Le premier adversaire de cette dignité, avaient-elles constaté alors, est la misère sous toutes ses formes, et elles avaient promis de lutter de toutes leurs forces contre la misère des Femmes de Prisonniers. Ce qu'elles ont fait sans relâche, sans découragement, sans tapage.

Depuis trois ans, peu de jours se sont écoulés sans que nos Responsables n'aient eu à résoudre des cas de difficultés matérielles pénibles. La misère est habituellement affaire de cas particuliers. Cela se résolvait la plupart du temps à l'aide des instruments fournis par la Loi, avec l'appui des organismes officiels de secours.

Or, aujourd'hui, la Fédération des Associations juge de son devoir de rendre publique la situation précaire à laquelle sont réduites les Femmes de Prisonniers.

On lira dans ce numéro les conclusions de l'enquête que nous venons de mener auprès de nos 50.000 adhérentes. On y verra la gêne des Femmes de Prisonniers ; les terribles difficultés auxquelles elles sont aux prises pour triompher de cette atroce lutte pour la vie où les pousse l'absence de l'époux ; l'héroïsme quotidien que doivent déployer les mères des familles de prisonniers pour assurer la subsistance et l'entretien des enfants. On y verra outre l'insuffisance des ressources normales constituées par la délégation familiale et même les délégations de solde, le grave danger moral que fait courir à leur dignité l'habitude, où elles s'enferront de demander, on serait tenté d'écrire : de mendier.

Nous avons cru bon de compléter ces revendications VITALES — à peine formulées, car les faits parlent d'eux-mêmes — par deux revendications que nous jugeons très opportunes, quoique peut-être de moindre conséquence ; l'une concerne les charges des Femmes de Prisonniers pour fournir leur absent en chaussures et en vêtement, l'autre, la prime de démobilisation.

Notre espoir est que ces appels tombent sous les yeux des Pouvoirs publics. Nous souhaitons qu'ils se laissent toucher par leur pathétique et qu'ils y fassent une place dans leurs préoccupations, dont nous imaginons sans peine le poids déjà écrasant. Mais nous les conjurons de se souvenir des promesses faites par la France à ses fils captifs, de se rendre compte de la responsabilité encourue à l'égard de ces innombrables jeunes foyers qui, demain, feront le pays, et de conclure que là gît, malgré les apparences peut-être, l'un des plus urgents problèmes à résoudre.

Tous les Français souffrent. Mais les Femmes de Prisonniers ne sont-elles pas des aînées dans la souffrance ? Et ce titre, joint à LEURS DROITS à eux, nous permet peut-être de revendiquer ce que nous jugeons indispensable à notre dignité et à LEUR DIGNITE, à notre vie et à LEUR VIE.

LA FEDERATION
DES ASSOCIATIONS DE FEMMES
DE PRISONNIERS.

"For Our Dignity, We Demand." Cover of *Femmes de prisonniers*, Fédération des associations de femmes de prisonniers (March 1944). This issue of *Femmes de prisonniers* argued that prisoner of war wives deserved better support from the state and society as a whole. (Gift to the author from Agnès Griot)

Andrée Aulas, President of the Fédération des associations de femmes de prisonniers. As president of the FAFP, Andrée Aulas traveled constantly to keep in touch with local associations. Her trip to Algiers was reported in the Lyons daily, *Le Progrès,* 14 March 1942. (Courtesy *Le Progrès de Lyon*)

The Return Half of a Prisoner of War Mailgram. Prisoners and their families could exchange two of these letters and two postcards a month. A wife could not write to her husband unless he sent her a mailgram first. All letters entering or leaving the prison camps were scrutinized by camp censors. (Gift to the author from Marcel Simonneau of the Union nationale des amicales des camps)

Repatriated French Prisoner Greeting His Family. This prisoner, repatriated in August 1942, was probably seeing his daughter for the first time. She does not look particularly happy about the meeting, a common reaction from prisoners' children. (Photograph: Roger-Viollet)

C'est le 114ᵉ qui me dit que j'ai « bonne mine » !..

"That's the 114th Person to Tell Me That I Look 'Fit'!" Cartoon from *Nos prisonniers*, Fêtes et saisons series. Many repatriated prisoners resented the attitude of much of French society that their captivity had not been particularly difficult. (Courtesy Les Editions du cerf)

Waiting Wives:
Representations
of Women Alone

Being prisoner of war wives placed a large group of women into a social category loaded with significance. Intangibles such as popular attitudes and social definitions, though difficult to resurrect, can be discerned in popular cultural representations of prisoners' wives such as books, movies, women's magazines, and pamphlets. The images evoked by the term *femme de prisonnier* provide valuable clues as to its social meaning. But popular culture in wartime France presented contradictory ideas about prisoners' wives, summarized in the following portraits of three very different kinds of women.

Three Visions: Arlette, Yvette, and Madeleine

A short story about a prisoner's wife named Arlette summarizes one image of the POW wife. "Après trois ans d'absence" appeared in a women's magazine, *Dimanches de la femme*. Married several years before the war, Arlette and her husband Yves had two sons when he was captured in 1940. Before the war Arlette had been a fun-loving woman, if a bit lazy about her housework, while Yves worked hard in his leather goods shop. But when Yves went to war, Arlette buckled down and did what had to be

123

done. Settled in a country home outside Paris, she continued to live there for the benefit of her two sons. When her elderly aunt could no longer support her, she reopened the leather shop, commuting to Paris daily, dropping her sons off at school on the way. With leather impossible to procure, Arlette, using her talent and imagination, concocted purses and bags out of old draperies, tablecloths, and bedspreads. She supported their sons, preserved Yves's shop, and waited faithfully with courage, dedication, and energy for Yves to return.[1]

Contrast Arlette with Yvette, heroine (if she can be called one) of *Le Chemin des écoliers,* by Marcel Aymé. "She was a pretty creature, with a delicately modelled face. . . . She had an air of languid grace, and there was something lingering in all her looks and gestures."[2] Yvette, whose husband was a POW, took up with a minor, Antoine Michaud, a seventeen-year-old high school boy. Because Yvette distracted Antoine from his studies, his academic standing declined, he began to lie to his parents, and he became deeply involved with the black market. Yvette encouraged him to earn huge sums of money on illegal deals because her cut enabled her to satisfy her extravagant, if somewhat tacky, taste for luxury and ease. Too lazy even to write to her husband, Yvette copied a letter Antoine had composed for her. When, toward the end of the story, Antoine's father discovered and put an end to his son's black marketeering, Yvette quickly dropped Antoine and picked up with a German soldier.

At first glance Madeleine, heroine of *La Guerre des captives,* by repatriated POW Sylvain Roche, resembles Yvette more than Arlette. In the first half of the book she committed adultery twice, living with two different men, one also a black marketeer, for extended periods. But Yvette calculated her affairs to preserve her life of ease and luxury, whereas Madeleine "fell" only when she was clearly at the end of her rope.

The book opened with Madeleine's attempted suicide in the Seine. Her rescuer discovered that both her parents had been killed in the bombing of Boulogne and that she was a prisoner of war wife, out of work, out of money, and all alone in the world. He took her in. After several months she broke off with him, moved out, found another job, and tried to live a decent life. But she lost the job by refusing her boss's sexual advances and once again found herself on the streets. Again she was taken in by a man she thought she loved but who in fact reminded her of her POW husband. Finally, the unconditional friendship and support of a fellow POW wife, Jeannine, whose husband was in the same camp as Madeleine's husband, saved her. Even though Jeannine discovered Madeleine living in another man's apartment, she extended a helping hand. Eventually, Madeleine left her lover, moved in with Jeannine, and helped with Jeannine's two children. She also joined a POW wives' association, in turn helping less fortunate prisoners' wives. By the end of the story, through the strength and support of sisterhood Madeleine had come to resemble Arlette. When Jeannine and her husband coincidentally died at the same time, Madeleine and her husband, Jacques, adopted Jeannine's two children.[3]

Each of these three heroines personified one element of thinking about women in general and women alone in particular. Although the three images seem contradictory, they can be viewed as three sides of a triangle. Each opens a window onto French society, revealing attitudes toward women, marriage, family life, and male-female relationships. In this chapter I shall explore the triangle of ideas about prisoner of war wives in Vichy France, an intangible yet critical aspect of life for POW wives. Understanding popular attitudes requires an analysis of the underlying social values that inspire them.

Traditional social norms and cultural assumptions about women and men and their respective natures and roles made up one side of the triangle. Although these social norms predated the war, Vichy propaganda and the official press promoted and reinforced them throughout the period. Social norms also survived intact the upheavals of war, occupation, and liberation in France. The second side of the triangle, popular opinion, in some ways reflected and in others seemed to contradict those norms. Prisoners' wives themselves made up the third side, reacting to both the norms and the popular attitudes and forging their own image of who they were and what it meant to be a prisoner's wife. Arlette corresponds to the normative view, Yvette to the popular view, and Madeleine to the self-perception of the prisoners' wives.

Idealization: The Cult of Domesticity

Prisoner of war wives fit into the social categories of women, wives, and often mothers. Thus social norms and expectations about gender roles and family life framed the idealized picture of these women. Ideas about what constituted a family, which children learned implicitly by the structure of their families and explicitly in school, at church, and through the media, received a tremendous amount of attention during the war years from traditionalists at Vichy. Concerned by both the threatened depopulation of France and by the seeming destruction of the social fabric and breakdown of the family, Vichy sponsored huge quantities of its own profamily propaganda, instructed schools to teach traditional values to children, and encouraged other traditionalist, profamily groups in their private propaganda and educational efforts.

In this view, society consisted of a hierarchy of families, its essential building block. Society and the family, both organic entities, perpetuated themselves through children. Within the family and in society husbands and wives filled different roles; they moved in separate spheres. Men entered the public sphere to earn a living, provide for their families, and direct public life. Within the family, the husband, the head of the family, had to "defend the family's interests, regulate its budget, . . . plan, insure and prepare the children's future."[4]

Women remained within the domestic sphere of the family, marriage, and children. If the husband was the head, the wife and mother was the heart of the family. To her belonged the following tasks: "control of the home, housekeeping, organization of daily life, education of the children and little ones, especially in its detail, accomplishing and directing all those activities which make a home intimate, warm, attractive, loved, clean, modestly comfortable, peacefully and gently ordered and disciplined." The wife filled the role of the "guardian of the family."[5]

Destiny ordained domesticity for women, the only way in which women could be happy and lead useful lives. Experts asserted that women needed marriage for their physical, economic, moral, and intellectual well-being. *Marie-Claire* answered a young girl who asked why she could not have a full life as an independent working woman, "A woman without a home or children has never completely fulfilled her mission."[6]

How did traditional norms apply to prisoner of war families? Vichy's preoccupation with the prisoners elevated both them and their families to a special public status. Pétain insisted that the prisoners were not to blame for their capture. "It was by clinging to the soil of France that they fell into the hands of the enemy." In fact, aside from those killed, the prisoners of war suffered the most from the defeat of France. Through their suffering, painful as it was, the prisoners would become "the purity of France."[7] Redemption through suffering, a favorite theme of Vichy, made sense of the defeat and humiliation of 1940. The prisoners, "defeat's ransom," embodied the process of purification through suffering. In their camps, the prisoners contemplated on and renounced the sins of prewar France, redeeming both themselves and their country. "You have reflected in a manly way, loyally meditated on the causes of our misfortune. You have felt the primordial need for those essential values which are: Family, Work, Fatherland, Religion."[8]

Thus, Vichy viewed the French prisoners of war as honorable captives serving a national function. What of their wives? Vichy propaganda, the Catholic press, and women's magazines addressed prisoners' wives directly and frequently. Arlette was the model *femme d'absent* whose "heavy task is to watch over the household so that when the absent one returns, he finds himself at home."[9] Ideas about the role of prisoners' wives without their husbands focused on the wife's role as guardian of the family.

The verb *garder* in French means not only to keep watch over but to preserve, to protect, to defend. Being the guardian of the home had practical implications; prisoners' wives had to keep the home going in the absence of the primary breadwinner. Here again, one French verb used to describe the duty of a prisoner's wife contains many implications: *se débrouiller,* to manage, to get by, to get out of difficulty.[10] "Celles qui se débrouillent," an article in *Dimanches de la femme,* described a prisoner's wife who opened a day-care center for the children in her apartment building, allowing her both to stay at home with her own child and to bring in extra money.[11] Similarly, Lucy Léger, a famous actress before the war, refused to act (*jouer* in French also means "to play") while her husband was captive. Instead, she took a lowly secretarial job until his return. "Eight hours a day, she who had already known success, typed and carried out her job with a determination bordering on despair." Another feature about a small rural village awaiting its prisoners of war described a woman who ran the family farm in her husband's absence. "Early to rise, late to bed, active and gay, she takes on the heavy burden of running the farm all by herself."[12] The phrase "active and gay" jumps out in contrast to the heavy tone of the rest of the sentence, emphasizing the enormous reserves of wifely devotion.

Being guardians of the home also meant keeping themselves attractive while their husbands were away. The husband's absence did not excuse sloppiness. "Yes, you are alone . . . but your duty is to remain worthy of the one whose thoughts always follow you. . . . Whatever the momentary difficulties, you must do everything you can to remain elegant and chic." To prevent husbands from being disappointed when they returned, wives should "attend to their features as well as to their hearts."[13]

Prisoners' wives fulfilled the traditional female roles of nurturing and self-sacrifice by sending their husbands care packages of food and clothing. Such packages represented more than just food for the body. With every package, a woman also sent "a piece of her heart." Women's magazines emphasized the theme of packages as loving self-sacrifice, frequently running features with suggested recipes or woolens wives could knit for their loved ones.[14] "Sometimes it is very difficult to make them as beautiful as one would like, but the heart's ingenuity has no limits, and depriving oneself for the person one loves is sweet deprivation." Packages were "a poem of tenderness," especially as the food was procured "by sacrificing your own bread ration tickets."[15]

Guardianship went beyond the practical matters of bringing in enough money, hanging on to the husband's business or farm, and remaining stylish and attractive. It was a moral task as well, which centered on the idea of waiting. Two women's magazines ran editorials entitled "Attendre," (To Wait). Marie Savinien explained in *Pour elle* that waiting meant more than existing, enduring each day, closing off emotions. Rather, waiting implied an active state of preparation for the future, a state of constant readiness for the return of the husband.[16]

Faithfulness, the cornerstone of waiting, went beyond not committing adultery. "Being faithful means: to keep the faith." Wives had to keep hoping their husbands would return and keep actively wanting them back. Ignoring the larger forces holding the POWs in captivity, many articles implied that wanting their husbands back badly enough might just bring them back. In a short story, the internal dialogue of a woman waiting for the return of the man she loves ended with the refrain, *"Feats of courage will bring him back, feats of courage."* Much popular advice encouraged such false hopes. Paulette Yves, advice columnist for *Notre Coeur,* answered a prisoner's wife who had lost hope, "We must, with all our force, think and hope that this year will be *for those we love, for those our thoughts never leave, the year of the return."* The daughter of a prisoner of war wrote to *Pour elle* worried about her mother's depression. She was advised, "Tell your mother that daddy will soon come home, you are sure of it, and, by dint of saying it to her and thinking every day, both of you, of the marvelous return, it will come to pass, perhaps sooner than you think."[17]

Fiancées, future guardians of the home, were also expected to wait, hope, sacrifice, and be faithful. Catholicism defined engagement for marriage as a sacred promise not to be broken. A Catholic fiancée's spiritual virtues of patience and suffering strengthened and purified her soul. The secular press, too, advised women engaged to POWs, even those who no longer loved or wanted to marry the prisoner, to wait. "You must, as a woman and a French citizen, practice the greatest of charity," wrote *Marie-Claire* to a woman whose pre-captivity letter breaking off her engagement never reached her fiancé. Her patriotic duty included supporting the courage of one of France's suffering soldiers. Besides, "Does not the sweetness of knowing you are the hope and reason for living of a man you admire suffice to fill your life?"[18] Women's magazines insisted that caring for a man, even an absent man, filled a woman's life and gave her the strength to face all hardships. The traditional, normative view expected great things of prisoners' wives without offering much real guidance.

Mistrust: The Double Standard

The normative, moralizing Arlette image of the prisoner of war wife dominated Vichy propaganda and the popular media during the war years. Arlette conformed perfectly to the profamily orientation of Vichy, which stressed traditional Christian values and forms of social organization. Vichy portrayed France as a nation of hard-working, self-sacrificing people. This vision of French society should not, however, be taken at face value. Undercurrents of a different popular attitude indicate that as the war and occupation dragged on, an ever-widening gap developed between the moralizing ideology of Vichy and real attitudes. Cynicism about Vichy, self-serving hypocrisy, and a lack of solidarity become apparent from a close examination of articles, popular humor, youth culture, styles of the period, and popular literature.[19] Yvette, of Aymé's book, more closely matched the image most people in France conjured up when the topic of prisoners' wives arose than the hard-working, long-suffering Arlette.

In fact, however, the negative image of the prisoner of war wife derived as much from general social norms about the nature of women as the positive image. The central assumption of essential gender differences between men and women that justified the notion of separate spheres also implied two human natures, one masculine and one feminine. Male human nature contained good, spiritual, moral qualities as well as evil, bodily appetites, including a strong sex drive. To be good, a man struggled constantly with the lower part of his nature. Struggle did not always end in victory, but an occasional lapse could be excused. "The man who yields to the weakness of the flesh is not the plaything of a caprice," explained Michel Audiard, "but the victim of a curse."[20]

Women, in the standard normative view, rather than having both good and evil within their nature, represented either one or the other. A woman could either be entirely good, pure, chaste—a saint—or entirely evil, vicious, unchaste—a whore. She could be only "housewife or harlot."[21] Chaste daughters, faithful wives, and mothers were saints. One false move, one lapse and a woman inevitably became a whore, with no possibility of returning to respectability. Women were protected from temptation by a weaker sex drive that derived primarily from the desire to please their husbands and to bear children. A wife's infidelity constituted a "deliberate transgression devoid of extenuating circumstances" and was therefore a much more serious offense than that of a husband.[22]

Given the assumptions of female innocence and lack of sexuality, why did some women "fall"? The explanation again rested on woman's special nature. Women, inherently weaker, more childlike, and softer than men, needed paternal control to keep them in line. Thus women alone—even prisoners' wives—became suspect. Without a husband's guidance and leadership, a wife was considered prone to infidelity.

These contrasting theories of male and female nature justified the double standard, which posited that "infidelity of a woman is an abominable thing, whereas that of a man is only a bagatelle."[23] Monique Beaulieu, advice columnist for *Notre Coeur*, explained that for "a wife worthy of that title, the very idea of passing the afternoon in arms other than the ones in which she will curl up at night has something incredible, intolerable, dirty about it. For a man . . . it has no more importance than the act of drinking a glass of water. . . . It's an occasional appeasement, a passing refreshment that he no longer thinks about an hour later."[24]

In France the Civil Code, which legally endorsed the double standard in the different treatment of adultery of husbands and wives, reflected widely held convictions. A survey of women conducted in 1959 by the French Institute of Public Opinion revealed that popular attitudes still manifested the double standard. One-third of the women polled considered adultery more serious when committed by a wife, and 40 percent judged a wife's submission to a passing weakness for another man "not excusable under any circumstances." On the other hand, half of the women polled deemed a married man's short, casual affair excusable; one-quarter claimed they would ignore such an affair; 17 percent would forgive the affair; and only 5 percent claimed they would leave.[25]

During the war, plentiful evidence of the double standard appeared in the advice columns of women's magazines, a prevalent form of didactic literature that both reflected and reinforced social norms and expectations. Women who wrote of their husbands' infidelity were urged to be tolerant. Advice columnists frequently explained to their readers the reasons for and appropriate response to a husband's infidelity. In fact, in response to a reader's complaint that she encouraged male infidelity, Beaulieu protested, "Do not make me say that I encourage male infidelity—it's just that I think confessors absolve it more easily because it is more in the nature of things and less serious in its consequences." She told "Georgette from Rouen," who discovered her husband's infidelity, "But Madam, you do not break up a marriage just like that, with one blow, for an infidelity. You forgive! . . . Between you and me, the physical infidelity of a man is much less serious than a woman's infidelity of the heart."[26]

Not only forgivable, a husband's infidelity could be the fault of the wife herself. "Look into yourself. In cases of marital conflict, a wife should try not only to reform her husband, but she should also look at her own mannerisms to find what might have driven her husband away." Aggressive, unfeminine wives, or wives who stifled their husbands out of excessive concern with neatness, drove husbands to seek comfort elsewhere. Once a wife corrected her faults and home became an "ideal haven," her husband would never again be tempted to stray. Even for wives not to blame for their husband's misconduct, "During the painful period we have just lived through, men have had plenty of excuses for their weaknesses."[27]

Women had no excuses. Contrast the very different treatment these seemingly indulgent advisors reserved for wives, and most especially prisoner of war wives, who confessed their own infidelity. "Heart in distress" wrote that her prisoner of war husband was a good man who loved her, but she loved another man, a good-for-nothing who would certainly make her unhappy. The response was blunt: "You do not deserve your happiness. It is women like you who deserve to marry the evil man who would make them suffer. . . . Be careful, if you betray your husband's confidence, if you take advantage of his distance to get close to the other man, you will be committing such a vile act that you will surely be severely punished for it one day." Another wife in a similar situation was told, "You do not seem to understand that you have committed a veritable abuse of confidence. If you want fate to be merciful, stay with your family, do not abandon your husband or your child. That is your duty as a wife, a mother and a French woman."[28] Women's magazines advised wives who admitted infidelity to drop the other man, not to leave their husbands, and if possible not to trouble their husbands by confessing their indiscretion. The tone of condemnation, absent in discussions of male infidelity, is quite clear.

Advice columnists also treated harshly fiancées who did not remain faithful to their prisoners of war. Sarcasm permeated the response to "Mado the undecided," a prisoner's fiancée who dated another man. "Does something trouble you? Does your nightly examination of your conscience worry and vex you? No? Are you happy with yourself? So? So, a prisoner has a little more or a little less pain, what does it matter?" "Loulou, heart in distress" had dropped her POW fiancé for another man, who then dropped her. Beaulieu responded, "You have used one of those infrequent letters where space is so limited to tell your prisoner it's over; the boy for whom you committed this atrocity 'dropped' you in turn. And you find him 'mean and vile.' Do you not have a mirror, young lady? What I think is that justice has been done. I have no other consolation to offer you."[29]

Women's magazines were unambiguously didactic. However, many sources confirm the widespread acceptance of the double standard with its corollary that women alone could not behave. Germaine, a former POW wife, claimed that when prisoners' wives dressed nicely or wore makeup, people said, " 'My goodness, they've found another man.' . . . All the men said, 'Prisoners' wives are easier than loose women.' " Several neighbors informed Patricia Longet that the prisoners whose wives worked at the local factory "are all cuckolds." While working on the survey of prisoner of war wives, Albert Robic reported being asked several times, "Is it true that prisoners' wives are not serious, that profligacy is the rule . . . ?" Even the Resistance press related shocking rumors about prisoners' wives. *Le Coq enchaîné* denounced Vichy with this story. "On June 1, 1942, there were 602 pregnant women in the maternity wards in Vichy, of those 435 were prisoners' wives. . . . Never has such debauchery ransacked the antechambers of a so-called government."[30]

Although the number of prisoners' wives who actually committed adultery can never be known, available evidence suggests that this phenomenon was not in fact widespread. Rather, the general mistrust and suspicion of these women, together with the propensity to jump to conclusions and to generalize, greatly exaggerated the public sense of the frequency of adultery among POW wives. Pierre Join-Lambert, for instance, estimated in 1945 that as many as 60 percent of the returning prisoners would ask for divorces upon returning and discovering their wives' misbehavior.[31]

Existing information discredits such estimates. The Paris courts received two thousand requests by mobilized soldiers or POWs to start divorce proceedings between 1939 and 1945, according to André Rouast.[32] Because two of the three grounds for divorce under French law were inadmissible under the circumstances, all two thousand requests could only have followed an "adultery complaint" against the wife. Two thousand may sound like a lot, but there were at least 140,000 POWs from the Paris area.[33] Based on Rouast's figure, only 1.4 percent of the POWs from the Paris area began divorce proceedings during the war. Admittedly, the accuracy of this figure cannot be confirmed, and wives had every reason to conceal their infidelity from their husbands. Still, 1.4 percent is well over a full order of magnitude from 60 percent.

Another clue to the frequency of adultery among prisoners' wives also pertains to the Paris area. After the war ended, a special committee conducted medical and social examinations of all repatriated POWs, forced laborers, and deportees in the Paris region. Summons were sent to 205,905 repatriated prisoners, deportees, and forced laborers; 115,475 eventually responded. The committee reported that there were 3,600 "abandoned homes" and 4,000 households experiencing "family difficulties" among the 115,475 repatriated households. Although three-quarters of those examined were POWs, it is not clear exactly how many of the 3,600 abandoned homes (3.12 percent of the total) or 4,000 homes experiencing family difficulties (3.47 percent of the total) were POW homes. But again, the total falls well below 10 percent.[34]

During the occupation, the Red Cross established homes that took in "adulterous children born in prisoner of war or deportee homes in the absence of the head of the family." When the husbands returned home, they could either accept the child into the family or have the Red Cross find adoptive parents. The Red Cross took in a total of 907 children across France, 254 of them from the Paris region.[35]

These figures hardly provide an accurate gauge of the number of wives who committed adultery while their husbands were captive. Because prisoners' wives had every reason to cover it up, not all husbands learned of their wives' infidelity. Moreover, many prisoners of war forgave it rather than demanding a divorce. Still, the order of magnitude suggested by the available data is considerably lower than the widespread rumors and the bad press about prisoners' wives would lead one to expect. All three figures for Paris fall well below ten thousand, and some come below one thousand.

The Adultery Law

French law defined a wife's marital infidelity as a crime. Again, the double standard led to harsher treatment of a wife's adultery than a husband's. Still, some leaders at Vichy asserted that the existing provisions of the Code did not do enough to prevent adultery among prisoner of war wives. In 1941 the Service diplomatique des prisonniers de guerre began fighting for a stringent law punishing adultery of prisoners' wives. Three fundamental assumptions motivated discussion of this law. First, owing to the feminine nature, wives living alone were at risk of committing adultery. Second, adultery of a prisoner of war wife constituted, not a private act, but a serious crime that compounded the pain of France's suffering sons. Third, documents reveal the prevalent assumption that the state had not only the right but the duty to take over the absent husbands' role of maintaining their wives' fidelity.

The notion of the state's responsibility in preventing infidelity of prisoner of war wives appeared originally in letters from the prison camps. Between July and November 1941, sixty prisoners of war in Stalag VIII C requested forms to start divorce proceedings, based on letters informing them of their wives' misconduct. Given the potentially "disastrous moral effect" of this "manifestation of immorality" on the men involved and their friends, the legal adviser to this Stalag recommended emergency measures. Courts in France should rigorously prosecute the guilty spouses and their accomplices. The "symbolic 16 francs" or fifteen days' suspended sentence equaled, under the circumstances, a joke, if not a form of complicity with adultery. Moreover, the legal adviser insisted on the need for new, tougher laws punishing adultery and abandonment of family.[36]

The prisoners' representative sent the report to the Berlin office of the Scapini mission, adding a key idea.[37] The prisoners, "unable to defend themselves here," were "counting on the state to take their place, punish the guilty ones and their accomplices and look after the children." Although most prisoners' wives deserved praise, the state needed to "inspire by fear the fidelity of some of the wives."[38] The Paris office of the SDPG led the battle for special legislation punishing adulterous prisoners' wives and their accomplices.[39]

The SDPG, the CGPGR, the Ministries of War, Justice, and Family, and head of state Darlan exchanged a series of letters in response to the camp reports. The SDPG stressed that the damage to POW morale resulted not only from the fear of losing their wives but especially from the men's inability to prevent their wives' infidelity, a duty essential to their role as head of the family. To remedy the sense of powerlessness created by their absence, the prisoners' representative from Stalag VIII C articulated the view that the state had a duty to act as the prisoners' proxy and punish adulterous POW wives.

Once the issue had been raised within the government, the ministers, secretaries, and commissioners concerned with prisoners or their families agreed to do something; but they disagreed over the appropriate solution to the problem. In the first place, they held conflicting assumptions about the nature of women, the reason women committed adultery, and which of the two parties to adultery held the greatest responsibility—the wife or the other man. The SDPG, deeming both parties to adultery equally responsible, proposed rigorous prosecution of both prisoners' wives and accomplices: deter adultery by striking the appropriate fear into the wives as well as by punishing unscrupulous men willing to take advantage of the husbands' absence. General Georges Revers from the Ministry of War, writing on behalf of Darlan, agreed that punishment should be severe and applied with rigor not just to the wife but also to the accomplice. On the whole, however, Revers placed more blame on the man, because he was the one "scandalously abusing the prisoners' situation." The wife, "poorly 'armed' for life, could have given in to a passing temptation for material (lack of resources) or psychological reasons."[40]

Disagreements also arose over how to handle judicial proceedings. Revers suggested empowering the prisoners' parents to press charges. The SDPG proposed that each town create a council, including the mayor and a group of repatriated POWs, to supervise prisoners' wives and, if necessary, bring charges against the guilty parties in the husbands' absence. The Commissariat général à la famille rejected the idea of anyone other than the prisoner taking the initiative in prosecution. "In the delicate area of marital fidelity, it is proper to leave to the injured husband an equal possibility of revenge or forgiveness."[41]

The fourth agency concerned with the prisoners of war, the CGPGR, disagreed with the SDPG, the War Ministry, and the CGF, placing full responsibility for adultery on male accomplices who took advantage of the prisoner's absence. The CGPGR, run by repatriated prisoners, feared that in trying to remedy the prisoners' loss of control over their wives, the state itself could infringe on the men's prerogative. The husband and only the husband should have the right to prosecute his wife. The CGPGR could accept a special law to facilitate prosecution of accomplices but did not want the prisoners of war losing control over matters pertaining to their own wives and families.[42]

In spite of the hostility of the minister of justice, Joseph Barthélémy, who asserted that women in general were "worthless" and required rigorous punishment, the CGPGR's emphasis on punishing the accomplice prevailed.[43] The law of 23 December 1942 stated that whosoever lived in "notorious concubinage" with the spouse of a person "absent from his country because of circumstances of war" could be punished with a three-month to three-year sentence and a fine of 1500 to 25,000 francs.[44]

The adultery law, despite the insistence of some members of the government on passing it, appears not to have been particularly effective. Toward the end of the war, the Famille du prisonnier referred to the adultery law as "widely unknown and rarely applied," and the Berlin SDPG complained to its Paris office that courts sanctioned prisoners' complaints of adultery in a ridiculously weak manner. Of the two hundred complaints that had gone through the SDPG, only one wife received a one-year jail sentence, two others received six months, and the rest had been given three months.[45]

In fact, the adultery law rested on an old principle, that a husband always had the right to prosecute his wife and her accomplice for adultery.[46] The law of 23 December 1942 only created a special case allowing the state to prosecute the accomplice to adultery with a prisoner's wife and disallowing attenuating circumstances for the wife. That the husbands were away in POW camps added another twist to the procedure.

Before the war, a husband who believed his wife was unfaithful lodged an adultery complaint with the police in order to establish a certified report. The commissioner of police then verified the flagrant offense (*flagrant délit*). A bailiff appointed by the presiding judge could also verify adultery, although this was not considered conclusive proof. If the prosecutor did not have sufficient documentary proof of adultery to convict, the court could order an investigation. Once proven, adultery constituted sufficient grounds for divorce.

Given his absence, how would a POW know if his wife had been unfaithful? Some wives wrote their husbands directly and asked for forgiveness or for a divorce. In these cases, the husband retained the prerogative either to forgive or to start the divorce procedure. Sometimes the POW received a letter from his parents, other relatives, or friends. Prisoners also received anonymous letters accusing their wives of misconduct. Having received such a letter, prisoners usually went to the camp prisoners' representative, who often had a legal advisor. The prisoners' representative notified the Berlin branch of the SDPG. Berlin sent the letters on to the Paris SDPG, which forwarded the materials on to the local authorities. As before the war, if the husband filed an adultery complaint, either the police, a bailiff, or the court conducted an investigation and questioned the wife, neighbors, and family.

Unfortunately, the general suspicion that fell on prisoners' wives meant that neighbors and family were not always accurate sources of information. People repeated gossip, possibly motivated by jealousy or malice. Even the immediate family could be inspired by unresolved rivalries. The Family Bureau of Stalag VII A warned about letters from parents. "We are, from experience, cautioned against this kind of notification. Unfortunately it happens that the alleged grievances have been greatly exaggerated. Relatives, disregarding their essential duties, cast doubts into the minds of their captive relative based on vague information, because often the daughter-in-law has not been accepted without reservations into the family."[47]

One testimony appeared in *Femmes d'absents . . . Témoignages* from a POW wife whose mother-in-law hated her. Married just fifteen days before the war broke out, she explained that her husband never considered her to be his wife, "always putting his mother before me. She's the one who has kept our furniture, our household utensils, who receives my husband's salary. Not only that, but she is also trying to ruin me in his esteem, and despite all the proof I can give him, my husband does not believe me." She remained faithful to her husband "out of duty although my husband has told me that he is no longer interested in me and is giving me my liberty."[48]

Many prisoners' representatives, who had seen unfounded or inaccurate accusations, worried that filing an adultery complaint if the wife had been unjustly accused could destroy the marriage. In Germany, unable to communicate openly, a prisoner could not evaluate the situation fairly. "A premature law suit could be dangerous"; therefore the lawyer for Stalag VI A counseled POWs requesting divorces based on denunciations to wait until they returned to France.[49]

Prisoners' representatives also found that the prisoners wanted more than accurate information about their wives' fidelity; they also wanted some way of winning their wives back and saving their marriages. Even the SDPG, so insistent on the need for swift and sure punishment of adulterous wives, admitted that the POWs "would prefer that first every measure be taken in their absence to bring wives who have gone astray back to their homes." The SDPG applauded the efforts of the prisoners' representative of Stalag VII A, who had taken to heart the moral interests of his comrades by not counseling divorce as "the only possible solution."[50]

Although the courts acted informally to save marriages, the complaint required to start an investigation was still the first step to divorce. Therefore, bypassing the courts, new agencies and bureaucracies began to investigate adultery of prisoners' wives. The SDPG requested that the Family Secretary devise a system "which would allow intervention with wives in order to avoid aggravating the misunderstandings that arise simply owing to the fact that their husbands are prisoners." The Family Secretary agreed, when notified of a case, that its departmental delegates would try to alleviate disputes, sidestepping judicial action that could "alarm families."[51]

The Famille du prisonnier, which took seriously its role of replacing the absent head of the family, also investigated wives' behavior and intervened with both husband and wife to prevent divorce. Famille du prisonnier social workers first attempted to have the wife end the affair and ask her husband's forgiveness. They then wrote the husband urging him to forgive his wife's misconduct, trying to "maintain as often as possible the integrity of the home."[52] In fact, a record number of public and semipublic agencies policed prisoners' wives. In addition to the courts, police, Family Secretary delegates, and Famille du prisonnier social workers, Maisons du prisonniers personnel conducted investigations of the wives and intervened with the husbands to prevent divorce. Even the Union des femmes de prisonniers felt it had the right to intervene with POW wives.[53]

No matter who conducted the investigation, mail not on official POW stationery could not be sent directly to the camps. Hence the Paris SDPG filtered most of the information before sending reports on to Berlin, which forwarded the information on to the prisoners' representative of the camp, who informed the POW. Occasionally, by the time it got to the prisoners' representative or the POW, information had been pruned. In one case, a wife told her husband she had been raped. The prisoner requested an investigation and prosecution of the guilty party. The investigation concluded that she had become pregnant as the result of an affair and fabricated the rape story to explain her pregnancy to her husband. But the SDPG told the prisoners' representative that the report was confidential and in no circumstances could he pass the details on to the POW.[54]

Because the prisoners remained in the service of the state while absent, adulterous prisoners' wives became a state problem. If husbands could not protect their own families, then the state, the ultimate patriarch, had an obligation to prevent adultery. Yet the Vichy regime had a second, equally important preoccupation. Vichy family policy defined divorce as a serious national problem, the primary cause of both the drop in the birthrate and the general moral decline of France leading to the defeat of 1940. Rebuilding the French family included preventing divorce. A somewhat ambiguous policy thus emerged, attempting both to punish adultery and to prevent divorce. The two goals were reconciled by the idea that if there were any way to convince the wife to stop seeing the other man and return to her home, someone should attempt it. If she refused, she and her accomplice should feel the full weight of the law.

The number of people and institutions meddling in the private sexual lives of POW wives, together with the tendency by the public to make quick judgments about the behavior of a woman alone, made it difficult if not impossible to ascertain the truth. One of the uglier aspects of French society during the German occupation compounded the general mistrust of women alone—the shocking and ever-increasing number of anonymous letters of denunciation, a trend noticed and condemned even by the Vichy administration.[55]

Prisoner of war wives became subjects of such anonymous letters. One prisoners' representative intercepted an anonymous letter meant for a POW in his camp. He refused to pass it on because of the "insane terminology" of the author, "who does not even have the courage to make himself known." The prefect's investigation found that the POW wife in question, "of good conduct and morality," ran a café with her mother-in-law. "The commercial affairs of this establishment being prosperous, there is room to conjecture that the author of the letter acted out of jealousy."[56]

In another case, the presiding judge informed the prisoners' representative that the POW had levied unjustified accusations. "We fear he has believed certain rumors circulated by people trying to break up the marriage." Deprived of the chance to answer when her husband stopped writing to her, the wife had been unable to defend herself.[57] In still another case, a signed denunciation by the prisoner's family turned out to be false. One POW filed an adultery complaint with his local prosecutor. His wife was living with a Mr. X, whose name and address he did not know. His mother, he wrote, would be happy to provide all the details. The investigation was unable to prove that the two lived together.[58]

Pierre Hautefort, journalist for *Notre Coeur,* wrote a full-page editorial describing prisoners' wives as unfortunate objects of harmful gossip. He received voluminous mail from POW wives, and he considered it unfortunate that, to the burden of their material difficulties, "they add these imaginary worries, these superfluous scruples. One wife scolds herself for going to the cinema once a week ... after listening, red-faced, to an old hag vituperate the harebrained wives who allow themselves little outings." (In the 1940s, even going to a movie indicated immorality. Nice girls did not go alone to the movies because films purveyed immoral and decadent attitudes and movie stars led indecent and debauched lives.) He tells of another wife worried about the "gossip stirred up in her workshop by her visits to the doctor. What affliction requires such regular treatment, if not a shameful, unmentionable disease, the punishment of her frivolity?" Although people gossiped freely, most neighbors did not go so far as to send letters to the camp with their observations. Official investigations, however, sometimes relied upon local gossip: one police report concluded, "In her neighborhood, she is said to have had several liaisons with soldiers from the occupation army."[59]

Neighborhood gossip also played a role when one POW received a letter from a man he did not even know accusing his wife of adultery. The prisoners' representative requested an investigation. The prefect's report concluded, "The confidential information collected about her allows us to say that she has a lover, a non-commissioned officer from the Army Service Corps, who cannot be identified. . . . This liaison has attracted public notice and is widely criticized." The SDPG wrote back to the prefect, angrily pointing out the shoddiness of the investigation. If the "liaison attracted public notice" why could the lover not be identified? The prisoners' representative refused to pass the report on to the POW, demanding a better investigation.

A second investigation revealed that the noncommissioned officer of the Army Service Corps was in fact the wife's brother, home on leave. The prefect admitted, "I was confused," for the NCO had often been seen going out with his sister.[60]

Some people made generalizations about all POW wives based on knowledge of one incident. One lawyer wrote to the local Famille du prisonnier asking it to award his client, a repatriated POW being treated at a military hospital, money to start divorce proceedings. Although unwilling to start the case without his fee, this lawyer exuded sympathy for the "poor boy" whose wife, "like many others, found the wait to be too long and sought consolation with soldiers from the occupation army." How many other wives had done the same? "If this is the first such case I have received, unfortunately, it will certainly not be the last."[61]

Prisoners' wives verify George Orwell's pronouncement that the sexual is political. Military propaganda frequently plays on soldiers' fears of their wives' misbehavior to demoralize enemy soldiers. The image of a prisoner's wife sleeping with a German soldier signified the ultimate insult to the French army. After the liberation of France, women who had slept with German soldiers, so-called horizontal collaborators, were punished by having their heads shaved and being paraded through town. Because the public deemed both adultery and sleeping with the enemy to be crimes against France committed by women using sex, not surprisingly, popular memory, both during and since the war, has equated the two.[62]

When the subject of infidelity of prisoners' wives arises, the issue of relations with German soldiers almost always follows, even when talking with former POW wives. Raymonde Moulin said, "There were cases where prisoners returned to find that someone had taken their place. There were even wives who had children by German soldiers." Another former POW wife wrote of "the wives (they had their excuses) who cheated on their husbands and had children (sometimes even with Germans)."[63]

As women alone, prisoners' wives lost respectability, became untrustworthy. People considered women unfaithful to their prisoner husbands equally as guilty of a crime against the state as women who slept with the German occupiers. The final scene in Aymé's book, in which Yvette kisses a German soldier, reflects precisely the widespread but distorted impression that emerges from documents of the time and from more recent conversations.

Reconciling Image and Reality:
Self-Image of POW Wives

Arlette and Yvette, the first two images of the prisoner of war wife, represent views from the outside. The third image, Madeleine of *La Guerre des captives,* represents the views that the wives had of themselves. As members of French society, prisoners' wives absorbed the same social norms as the rest of France. Living in France during World War II, they became objects of both the traditional, moralizing literature and of the less complimentary attitudes of the general public. They faced both the high standards of the Arlette model and the widespread cynicism and mistrust of the Yvette model. But as a group with a sense of separate identity, prisoners' wives surpassed being passive objects of propaganda or public opinion and eventually developed a collective self-image.

Prisoners' wives rejected the popular, cynical image of Yvette. Although they acknowledged that some prisoners' wives were unfaithful to their husbands, their response differed considerably from that of the general public. Prisoners' wives considered adultery wrong but did not attribute it to women's inherent weakness or love of luxury and ease. They saw themselves as only human and blamed the unfaithfulness of some wives on their misery, deprivation, isolation, and alienation. Prisoners' wives also accused unscrupulous men of taking advantage of the unhappiness, loneliness, and even powerlessness of women alone. One prisoner's wife, after receiving an indecent proposal from a neighbor who had helped her out occasionally, realized "that this man had sensed my weakness, that he had calculated on it, persuaded that it would be impossible for a prisoner's wife to hold on long enough, and that one day or another, without fail, I would fall."[64]

Knowing how it felt to face the emotional and physical hardships of life alone, prisoners' wives were more forgiving toward those of their sisters who "fell." Adultery was wrong but understandable under the circumstances; the blame did not fall entirely on the woman. A wife willing to make amends should be forgiven. In other words, POW wives substituted a single standard of morality for the prevalent double standard. Further, they rejected the idea that women fell due to inherent weakness or an inability to behave without the guidance of a man. Rather, prisoners' wives blamed infidelity on the magnitude of the hardships they endured—hardships that could overwhelm anyone of either sex. Their own writings, unlike the traditional, normative works, also offered a real way to deal with their hardships and avoid infidelity. Madeleine's story counseled prisoners' wives that lonely, empty lives would be filled not by meditating dreamily on their husbands but by developing supportive friendships with other prisoners' wives.

Although they rejected the Yvette model and the double standard that gave her meaning, prisoners' wives generally accepted the traditional social mores promoted by Vichy. They believed that women were destined for marriage and childbearing and that within the family husband and wife had separate roles to play. Prisoners' wives struggled, not only to survive in the world, but also to reconcile the general norms they accepted with the very different reality of their lives. The contradiction between perception and reality created internal turmoil. The increased independence these women gained from taking on new responsibilities ran counter to their own acceptance of a traditional family structure and resulted in an uncomfortable ambiguity which emerges in their writings about themselves and their new roles. They describe themselves contradictorily both as weak and emotional and as strengthened by this experience, as needing their husbands but gaining new so-called masculine qualities. Writings by prisoners' wives suggested resolving the internal conflict by thinking of themselves as temporary heads of families.

Maintaining a strong sense of the prisoner's presence in his absence allowed a wife to adjust successfully to the separation without changing the basic pattern of the relationship. Griot, in her article "The Rules of Happiness," recommended telling husbands everything. Most important, prisoners' wives should "act as if he were there. . . . Ask his advice, because he still is the Father and the Head." Eliane Clause recommended not idealizing their husbands. How to avoid this? "Live with him every day. . . . Do everything as if he were there." Living as if he were there, writing him all the details of daily life, and asking his advice before making major decisions were the most frequently offered, if not always the most practical, suggestions. Almost every prisoner's wife reserved a prominent place for her husband's photograph. One woman kept several jars of jam she and her husband had made together before the war for when he returned; another bought annual birthday gifts for her husband and kept them in a box. Madeleine wrote in one issue of *Femmes de prisonniers* that she kept everything ready for her husband. "The ties, the shirts are impeccable, the clothing is ready to be worn." Some wives reminded themselves of their husbands by cooking a favorite dish.[65]

Some families maintained the husbands' physical space in the family. One wife wrote, "For me he is still the head of the family. . . . Moreover, no one sits in his place; his empty armchair is there waiting for him, I never offer it." Another wife claimed, "At every meal, one or the other of the children sets their father's place at the table."[66]

Prisoners' wives stressed the importance of keeping the memory of the father alive in the children as well as in themselves. As Clause put it, "Make him live in their little hearts. Interest them in the letter received, in the packages." Making his presence vivid reminded children that the situation was temporary and would make the father's return easier. An article by Hélène and Maurice Bourel, "They Are Waiting for Him Too," advised mothers to prevent the father becoming a stranger or an idealized superman to his children. A child who forgot that his or her father was human would be disappointed when he returned, as "little by little, the hero of the early days becomes the tiresome and disappointing troublemaker." They recommended painting "a real portrait of Papa and not an idealized person. . . . Do not represent the captive as a distributor of indulgences and sweets."[67]

In addition, a photo of the father "should occupy a prominent place," to keep his features familiar to the children. In making major decisions about the children, "Do not hesitate to ask father's advice: Try in spite of the distance to resolve certain problems together."[68] Some advice went further, recommending that prisoners' wives let their children know "that no decisions are made at home without consulting him. He is informed about everything, foolishness or kindness." Children needed to remember that, "despite his absence, he is still the Head of the family, the loved and awaited Head of the family."[69] Involving the children in communication with the POW also maintained contact between father and child. Letters from the father could be read aloud to the children. Occasionally older children could write directly to their fathers.

Children also helped with packages for their fathers. Even for children, a little self-sacrifice was deemed healthy, and it also brought home the reality of the absent father. "At our house, a candy box is placed near the photo of Dad. The children, when they want, without any pressure, put in a little sweet. They know that whatever they put in the box will be sent off and will make Daddy happy, which unites them with him in a tangible way." Although many wives mentioned that their children contributed their own chocolate or candy to the packages, they admitted that at times children resented the sacrifice. Children also drew pictures or made things to include in packages. Because the father would return, it was crucial to "keep his place in the home as if he were going to take it back tomorrow."[70]

The contrast between such advice and real life problems left prisoners' wives in a dilemma. No matter how well they succeeded in reminding their children of the father's existence and ultimate authority, the mothers in the meantime were present and responsible on a daily basis for the children. The issue of raising children crystallized the contradiction between the way society and the wives saw themselves and what they needed to do to succeed.

According to the dominant social norms, mothers and fathers each played a specific, non-interchangeable role in raising children. The mother, emotionally closer to her children, provided love and support and educated them in human values and morality. The father represented the higher, more distant authority; he was responsible for judging his children's behavior and punishing misdeeds. How could mothers alone maintain the father's position as ultimate authority and yet discipline their children on a daily basis? How could a mother judge and punish her children and yet remain the soft and loving figure she was expected to be?

Some women had trouble asserting themselves with their children, like the wife who wrote, "The children give me a lot of trouble: neither willing to help nor obedient, especially the eldest whose character is very difficult and who does not help me at all. I lack the desirable authority." Nevertheless, most prisoners' wives with children managed to exert authority over their children. But the wives' confusion about child rearing emerges from the survey of prisoners' wives conducted in 1943. One woman wrote, "The big difficulty is raising my children alone." Although she admitted her children were "not very disobedient," still, "the father's authority is lacking." She herself had no trouble with her children, but in the abstract she believed the father's authority was necessary. In a still more contradictory paragraph another wife claimed, "The father's absence is detrimental to their education and their character," but "I don't have the impression that if the father had always been present, they would have evolved differently."[71]

Child rearing intensified POW wives' internal ambivalence about their proper role in the family because it compelled them to impose their will upon somebody else. Wives who felt uncomfortable being the head of the family could assume the role of father's delegate to assert authority over children. The title of one article, "His Children and Myself," expressed this view. This prisoner's wife insisted that she needed her husband in order "to be a good mother"; she stressed the importance of acting as if he were there and of letting the children know his authority was ultimate. She also described the struggle to overcome her own weakness in order to adopt the "virile qualities of the absent one." According to former POW Joseph Folliet, the prisoners themselves worried, "Is she succeeding in imposing herself on the children with the most difficult characters?" In his view, a prisoner's wife should "replace the father, . . . extend his will . . . make herself energetic and virile. . . . At every moment she will ask herself, 'What does my husband want? What would he do in my position?' "[72] He advised women not to become authoritative mothers but rather to adopt a masculine, fatherly role that the husband could resume when he returned.

Society considered the absence of paternal authority particularly troublesome for boys. Girls were thought to be softer, more malleable, and easier to discipline. Mothers understood them intuitively and prepared them by example to become wives and mothers. Sons, more aggressive, autonomous, harder to manage, needed their fathers for discipline and as role models. Clause worried about her two sons: "They are growing and they need the firmer hand of their father." A mother with boys ages ten and fourteen explained, "For boys, the father is necessary because mothers do not have the needed authority." The older boy concerned her in particular. "He would be nice if his father were here, because he's not a bad boy: he only thinks about games."[73]

In fact, the incidence of juvenile delinquency increased dramatically during the war years in France. The pattern of juvenile crime corresponded to a general rise in petty crime during the war years, both clearly resulting from the conditions of occupation, rationing, and severe shortages. Still, few contemporary observers made that connection, preferring to attribute juvenile crime to the absence of fathers. One expert on juvenile delinquency noted that the rising curve "coincided with the departure of fathers (prisoners of war, deportees, forced laborers)." Another expert similarly blamed the increase in delinquency during the war on the "*lack of paternal authority.*" He explained, "A mother almost never has over her daughters, much less her sons, a sufficient educational influence. Never will the sweetness of her affection replace the firm words of a father."[74]

One interesting phenomenon occurred primarily in prisoner of war households. Some prisoners' sons became "domestic dictators" (*bourreaux domestiques*). G. Heuyer described these "family tyrants" as adolescent boys "who, owing to the father's absence, remain in their mother's company. . . . They consider themselves to be the head of the household and refuse to obey; they take on the tone and the habit of command; they act like an authoritative, tyrannical, sometimes violent and brutal man; they refuse to go to school . . . ; they demand money; they do not give way to threats or blows. We have even seen some who made sexual demands." A similar case reported by Reubin Hill and Elise Boulding in their classic study of American servicemen's families during World War II furnishes a possible explanation as to why this happened. They came across one family whose oldest son kept careful watch over his mother, sending his father lengthy reports on her behavior. It turned out that the father, before he left, had taken his son aside and told him to be the man of the house and look after his mother.[75] Such extreme cases, although probably the exception, highlight the dilemma facing these mothers alone.

Widows and divorced mothers face similar problems, although with less ambiguity. If single parenthood is permanent, families adjust without reference to the father. But prisoners' wives lived in a temporary situation. Whatever adjustments they made to the separation during the war would presumably have to be unmade after the reunion. The lack of finality of their situation left them in a state of suspended animation, which gave rise to a recurring theme in writing by prisoners' wives; the wait. This theme had an undertone of expectation (the verb "to wait" [*attendre*] also means "to expect"). In addition to adjusting to separation and absence, these women focused on a return that would occur at some unknown time and that somehow seemed to depend on what the wives did.

The frequent use of the future tense in articles written by prisoners' wives indicates this mode of expectation. "He Will Return" was the title of Eliane Clause's article. She claimed that the return would be "what we will have made it every day of our wait." N. Ulrich, writing about the possible problems of the return, could give her fellow wives little specific advice. "But when the absence will have ended, when communal life will start again, when your mutual life . . . will have found again its great flame that enlightens and warms, the problems of the return will appear to you in their true light."[76]

Although offering only vague advice, the authors of these articles brought the wait into the range of more common female experiences by picturing it in images familiar to women. Clause compared it to the period of engagement before marriage. Ulrich compared it to the joy of a mother anticipating the birth of her first child. Waiting also took on explicitly Christian overtones. Just as the prisoners would be redeemed by the suffering of their exile, the wives and even the marriages would be strengthened by the wait. One wife wrote to her husband, "For both of us the ordeal will have ripened our love; it will be more beautiful, grander, more noble because it will have suffered." As a Catholic prepares for each sacrament, prisoners' wives prepared for the return. The booklet *Femmes d'absents,* published by Fêtes et Saisons, included a liturgy of waiting.[77]

Waiting and preparation directed POW wives' thinking beyond the present and on to the future return of the husband and what that might entail. The return theme appeared as often as the wait in writing by prisoner's wives. The possible problems that might arise after the return worried prisoners' wives as much as the absence itself, increasing the anxiety of waiting. Hence wives considered it crucial to prepare for the reunion. One article explained why wives bore full responsibility for the success or failure of the return. Marriage created a common flame, which separation divided into little "uncertain and flickering watch lights." Whether the flame would rekindle "depends for the most part on the wife, who by vocation is the guardian of the flame."[78] The role of guardian placed a heavy burden on prisoners' wives. One repatriated prisoner stated, "The future of the prisoners and of all of France is in the hands of their wives."[79]

Being prepared for the return meant having the proper expectations. "Let us not delude ourselves, the return will demand a huge effort of adaptation. The most loving and least complicated among us will not escape that law." Prisoners' wives warned each other not to idealize the return or the men. Articles by repatriated POWs alerted wives to some of the psychological reactions to captivity, such as "weariness, shock, bewilderment, resentment." Returned POWs would be irritable, easily angered, intolerant of noise, and perhaps even disinterested in sex.[80]

Prisoners' wives should not expect to return to normal life all at once. "Think about the patience and self-effacement that will be demanded of us." Wives would have to be understanding of their husbands' moods, forget their own years of suffering and hardship, and help their husbands re-adapt to civilian life. They might even have to mediate between their husbands and their children. "During this period of readaptation, be more than ever the supple and strong bond that holds together the members of a single body." The wife should explain her husband's mood to the children, quiet the children when the husband needed silence, and try to start up family conversations and activities. Wives also expected to buffer the prisoner from the rest of society, explaining to him gently how things worked in the greatly changed France of rationing, points, and lines; trying to keep him from being discouraged; and interpreting his actions for friends and neighbors.[81]

Most important, wives had to prepare themselves to let their husbands resume the position of head of the family. The first of the "Rules of Happiness" was, "Be ready to give him back the reins of the household." One prisoner's wife wrote in the survey, "When my prisoner returns, I will fully dedicate myself to him and to my child. . . . I do not plan on continuing to work because I consider that a woman's place is in the home. A family that works well requires a wife willing to devote herself entirely and unreservedly to it: Thus I will do everything I can to help my husband readapt and make my loved ones happy."[82]

Prisoner of war wives, in addition to running the household alone, dedicated their lives to preparing for their husbands' return. They had somehow to obtain enough money for their families to survive, decide how to spend it, maintain the house, discipline the children, but at the same time keep the husband's presence alive and ask his advice before acting. They had to replace the father and at the same time "prepare themselves to let him resume his responsibilities . . . because he is the head of the family."[83] Being a waiting wife, being in limbo, being a single parent and yet acting as though the other parent were still there was not simply an attitude imposed by a patriarchal society and government. The wives themselves shared these views, expressing the resulting anxieties in their writings and suggesting strategies to reduce the mental dissonance.

The study of prisoner of war wives' self-image reveals the extent to which they internalized dominant social norms. Although their families could not conform to the ideal family, they tried valiantly to reconcile their lives with that ideal. At the same time, the women rejected the double standard of morality and the prevalent popular attitude that, unable to behave without their husbands, they led fast and loose lives. All three strands of social thought played crucial roles during the war. The negative popular view of prisoners' wives catalyzed their development of a collective identity and their activism. Their acceptance of ideas about domesticity and family life that predated the war and remained strong during and after the war limited the impact on French society of the five-year experience of independence and responsibility.

Conclusion:
The Return

Life returned to normal with a
lot of patience.
—Louise Cadieu

For five years, prisoners' wives, with and without children, became heads
of their households. They paid bills, made decisions without consulting
their absent husbands, and disciplined their children. To survive, they took
on unfamiliar responsibilities, learned novel skills, and worked outside the
home, many for the first time. Prisoners' wives undoubtedly gained self-
confidence from their achievements and a new awareness of their own abilities; they realized that they could do things women supposedly were not
capable of doing.

But prisoners' wives filled this role as head of the household only temporarily. Wives and mothers were expected to rally for their families in a
time of crisis, even if doing so involved "unfeminine" actions. As often as
prisoners' wives were praised for saving their families, they were also reminded—by others as well as themselves—of the impermanence of their
status. When their husbands returned, life would go back to the way it was
before the war. Given the conflict between experience and expectation, did
prisoners' wives reject such sexual stereotypes and establish more egalitarian family relations as a result of the war?

Repatriated Prisoners of War

After the initial excitement faded, the period of reunion was difficult for many couples. The war and five years of captivity left their mark on the men. POW camps in Germany were not concentration camps; the German army neither worked to death nor systematically exterminated French POWs. However, in contrast to the media portrayal prevalent during the war in France, prison camps were hardly summer resorts or monastic retreats. Most POWs spent six days a week working long hours for scant pay and minimal food. Life was highly regimented, with little time for rest. For those still in Germany in 1945, the extreme trauma of the war's final months augmented the stress of four years of captivity.

France was liberated in September 1944, three months after the Allied invasion of Normandy. The fall of the Vichy government, retreat of the German armies, and liberation generated rejoicing in France, for prisoners' wives as well. Although Germany had not yet been defeated, the war was clearly coming to an end, and wives hoped their husbands would soon return. Unfortunately, although the trauma of war had ended for France, perhaps the worst period of captivity was in store for the prisoners of war. The collapse of the Vichy government disrupted the communications link with German prison camps, and many families lost contact with their prisoners for many months. Eventually mail and packages were exchanged via the International Red Cross in Geneva, Switzerland—a considerably slower process.

The rapid advance of the Allied armies ended in the fall and winter of 1944 as fighting bogged down in the Ardennes. Meanwhile, Allied planes bombed German urban, military, and industrial targets continuously. Despite the Geneva Convention prohibition, many prisoners of war worked in German military industries and were at risk of being killed by Allied bombing. Constant air raids, the breakdown of food distribution, and eventually the renewed fighting on German soil took many prisoners' lives in the last eight months of the war in Europe.[1]

Worse still, the German army, rather than leaving prisoners of war behind as they retreated, decided that prisoners might be useful bargaining chips of the last resort. Throughout the winter of 1944–45, prisoners in camps on both the eastern and the western fronts retreated on forced marches with German troops toward the center of Germany, experiencing the total collapse of the country from the inside. The constant bombing raids, forced marches, hunger, and lack of contact with home reminded more than one POW of the earlier trauma in France. "The routes take on the same physiognomy as ours did in May 1940. . . . When I think that I saw these things in France, maybe it made them laugh at the time, now the roles are reversed."[2]

Even liberation from the German army did not necessarily end the hardship for POWs. Unable to dedicate any resources to repatriating foreign nationals, the Soviet army marched the prisoners it liberated back through war-ravaged Germany to the east and away from the battle front. Although they were liberated earlier than POWs in the west, the men waited longer for repatriation. When the fighting finally ended, the Soviets took most French prisoners to the Allied contact point where they crossed from the Soviet zone to the West.[3] Prisoners in the western half of Germany remained captive much longer, but once liberated by British or American troops (the French army liberated one camp, Stalag V B), they were repatriated quickly by train or even by airplane.

Most of the nearly two million French nationals in Germany, including prisoners of war, deportees, and forced laborers, returned to France between March and July 1945. April and May were the peak months, with 313,000 and 900,000 repatriations, respectively. Some 940,000 prisoners of war returned to France almost exactly five years after they were captured, nearly six years after the initial mobilization, and eight months after the rest of France had been liberated.[4]

Military captivity entailed a blend of deprivation, physical hardship, and enormous psychological stress. Studies of groups of POWs from different countries and different wars report that repatriated prisoners of war are at high risk for a "staggering range of physical disabilities and symptoms that can be ascribed to the over-all captivity episode."[5] In the Paris region, medical examinations conducted four months to a year after repatriation disclosed that 17 percent of the prisoners had health problems ranging from tuberculosis and digestive disorders to dental problems.[6] Later studies of the French POWs confirmed certain long-range health problems related to captivity including pulmonary disorders (tuberculosis, bronchitis, emphysema), cardiovascular disorders (cardiac disturbance, arteriosclerosis), digestive disorders, chronic rheumatism, and lesions of the nervous system. In addition, former POWs often age prematurely (experience fatigue and loss of memory and concentration, take on an aged appearance in skin and gait) and have a higher morbidity than other men of the same age group.[7] Of the forty-nine women in my group for whom the information is available, twenty-four reported that their husbands returned in poor health. Some men were weakened, fatigued, or aged. Others suffered more serious problems such as ulcers, bronchitis, and asthma. Four men returned so ill that they died within a year of repatriation.

Although the captivity experience rarely led to true psychosis, it did have psychological repercussions.[8] Segal, Hunter, and Segal, in their summary of research on the consequences of captivity, listed depression, guilt, anxiety, insomnia, fatigue, and psychosomatic complaints as common psychological responses to captivity. A study of six hundred repatriated French POWs done between 1946 and 1950 documented a variety of emotional reactions, including melancholia, manic fits, hyperemotionality, anxiety attacks, nervous crises, crying fits, profuse sweating, and trembling. Both postwar studies and contemporary observations confirm short-term sexual dysfunction among repatriated prisoners of war.[9]

When questioned about the impact of captivity on their husbands, sixteen of the forty-nine women in my group described analogous psychological states. Most frequently, the women described the repatriated prisoners as bitter (*aigri*); other descriptions included hardened, uncommunicative (*renfermé*), irritable, and aggressive. Joelle Meliard's husband returned "bitter, bad tempered, very nervous, and did not put up with being contradicted." Evidence from the 1940s confirms these descriptions of recently repatriated prisoners. A woman whose husband returned in 1941 wrote in distress to *Marie-Claire*, "Since my husband has come back, his personality has changed a lot. He is somber, nervous. He flies into rages at the least little thing. Our children, for fear of being scolded, are developing terrible habits of deceit. My home is turning into a hell."[10]

While some men were aggressive and irritable, others fell into a state of depression and became somber and oversensitive. Josette Lorin's husband had nightmares and often woke up breathless and in a sweat. After the war he was "less cheerful and he rarely sang anymore, even though before the war he really liked to enliven gatherings of friends and family." Along with depression, Claudine Dages noted a "certain laxness about day to day problems" in her husband. Monique Roussel's husband seemed to have lost all his prewar ambitions. Some men returned "prematurely worn out," aged, tired, and having lost hair or teeth.[11]

Many of the symptoms described thus far pertain to any group of returning POWs. The specific experience of serving as a French soldier in 1939–40, being captured in 1940, and returning to France in 1945 gen-

erated another set of problems for the men. Although most soldiers experience shock and shame when they are captured by the enemy, the
crushing and humiliating defeat of France intensified these feelings for the
French prisoners of 1940. The speed with which French defenses were over-
run and the total chaos of June 1940 left the soldiers with the feeling that
their army was inferior not only to the German army but also to the once
great French army of 1914–18.[12]

In fact, many people in France reproached the army for the defeat and
wondered how so many men had been captured so quickly. The French still
had an almost mythical vision of their army based on romanticized memories of Napoleon's army. Further, a well-known maxim, usually attributed
to Napoleon, dictated that a good French soldier would die rather than
allow himself to be captured.[13] Although the prisoners may have had
doubts about themselves, they sorely resented the doubts expressed by people in France who had not risked their lives in battle. Former POW Raymond
Henri claims to have seen in an editorial, "The prisoners are France's
shame. They should have gotten themselves killed rather than accepting a
life of luxury [la vie de château] in Germany. It is a dishonor from which
they will never recover and which will follow them all their lives."[14] To one
editorialist's assertion that the prisoners represented "the shame of their
families and of France," a prisoner responded, "I would never have believed
that by doing my duty as a Frenchman, I could in the eyes of this great
journalist dishonor France and my family. Certainly this individual did his
duty by keeping his feet nice and warm in a parlor."[15]

Intensifying the prisoners' post-repatriation perception of public ingratitude, the Vichy regime had for four years sent propaganda to the camps
portraying the prisoners as future saviors of France, purified and strengthened by their suffering, expected to undertake the task of national renewal
when they returned. To believe Vichy was to expect to be greeted as a hero.
But in the France of 1945, the public viewed the resisters, and not the prisoners of war, as the heroes; resistance fighters had liberated France while
the POWs waited in their camps. Repatriated prisoners of war at a government meeting objected to the "anti-prisoner frame of mind [which] has
been observed particularly among fighters and other members of the Resistance." Jean Vedrine, POW representative, claimed that two resistance
journals conducted campaigns "to discredit the status of prisoner in the
eyes of the population."[16] Not only had prisoners been replaced as the heroes in 1945, but their suffering was also overshadowed by revelations of

the horror of concentration camps. The prison-camp experience paled in comparison to the suffering of the deportees.

After dreaming for five years of a triumphant return to France, the prisoners felt demoralized by "the unexpected coldness of the welcome, the ingratitude of certain people who had not experienced captivity."[17] Raymonde Moulin's husband was "disgusted by the reception. . . . [The POWs] were told that they were lucky to have been prisoners. . . . They were not welcomed home the way they thought they would be." The prisoners resented such callous popular attitudes and felt abused by a government that seemed to share in this assessment as well. The prisoners of war received neither the treatment nor the benefits to which they felt they were entitled. The Fédération national des prisonniers de guerre (FNPG), formed in 1945, waged a lengthy struggle in defense of prisoners' rights.[18]

Aside from officers, noncommissioned officers, and civil servants, most prisoners of war did not receive pay for their military service while in captivity. When they returned they received a "Welcome Bonus" of 1,000 francs and a "Demobilization Bonus" of 1,000 francs. They were given one month's average departmental salary to allow for a vacation before returning to work. The highest amount, for the Paris area, was set at 2,250 francs. They had been paid for the work they did in Germany not in regular German currency but in *Lagermarks,* camp money useful for purchasing cigarettes or candy but worthless outside the camp. The French government decreed that prisoners could exchange a maximum of 100 *Lagermarks* at 20 francs per mark, for a total of 2,000 additional francs. Thus, a repatriated non-officer POW living in Paris received a maximum of 6,250 francs after five years of military captivity ($212.50 in 1978 dollars). Many of the men were unaware of just how meager this compensation was until they tried to buy something and discovered how much prices had risen in six years—200 percent or more.[19]

The FNPG lobbied the government to pay POWs for their military service, but the issue was settled only in 1952. Prisoners received 400 francs per month of captivity. In comparison, Belgian prisoners of war received the equivalent of approximately 4,000 French francs per month of captivity during World War II, and American prisoners of war received the equivalent of 15,000 francs per month of captivity. Furthermore, the state dispensed the meager compensation not in a lump sum but over a five-year period. Former POWs received the last payment only in July 1958, thirteen years after they had returned. Officers and noncommissioned officers never received the remaining quarter to half of the military pay to which they were entitled.[20]

Emotions ran highest, however, over an issue not purely financial. From the beginning, some members of the Consultative Assembly wanted "a distinction to be made between those prisoners who actually saw combat and the rest." The FNPG informed the minister of prisoners, deportees, and refugees that it "does not acknowledge such a distinction."[21] At stake was eligibility for a veteran's card. Because men were called into service at various times of the year, some were captured after they had been mobilized but before they had been incorporated into a military unit. Sanitary personnel and other men not engaged in combat were also captured and held by Germany as enemy soldiers. Yet some people in the government believed that only those men in actual fighting units should be considered veterans.

François Mitterrand, a former POW who was appointed minister of prisoners, deportees, and refugees in 1947, passed a law authorizing the "Veteran of 1939–1945" card for all prisoners of war, rather than establishing a special "Prisoner of War" card or a "Veteran of 1939–1940" card.[22] At that point, the Fédération nationale des prisonniers de guerre became the Fédération nationale des *combattants* prisonniers de guerre (FNCPG), signaling that it considered every former POW a veteran.

The Union française des anciens combattants (UFAC), filled with World War I veterans, battled Mitterrand's law and in 1949 succeeded in including a condition of ninety days in a fighting unit in order to qualify as a veteran. The FNCPG waged its biggest struggle ever against the ninety-day condition, devoting all its energies to removing the restriction. The FNCPG considered it a moral issue, insisting that a prisoner of war should be considered a veteran not just for seeing combat but also by virtue of captivity. Although the law was never restored to its original version, the FNCPG succeeded in extending the legal category of veteran little by little until almost all its members qualified for a veteran's card. In 1955, summing up ten years of activity, the FNCPG stated, "The struggle for material compensation has always been on a par with the combat to defend our honor, which certain people have greatly offended by refusing to consider us veterans."[23]

Readjustment to Married Life

Family reunions involved more than the prisoners. The waiting wives' frame of mind presented another potential source of difficulty. Unquestionably, after five years of living without their husbands the women had developed new skills. Michelle Dupuy explained that before the war, "I had never even been to the post office for a money order! Oh, Mamma, he did everything!" Whatever ideas they held about normal life, the women had grown accustomed to acting without their husbands' advice or permission. One prisoner's wife described a "noticeable maturation" of her personality during her husband's absence. Some prisoners' wives came to enjoy their "independent existence." Nicolle Bouchard believes the years alone "accentuated my taste for responsibility."[24]

Prisoners' wives who took jobs outside the home or became active in outside organizations also gained experience in and were exposed to the world outside their own homes. For Bouchard, in charge of the Famille du prisonnier in her canton, "those years exposed me to many problems and facilitated my contacts with social strata that otherwise I may have had some difficulty coming to know." Florence Morin, active in the Service des femmes de prisonnier of the MPF, felt enriched by her activities and by the meetings and conferences she attended. Before the war she "lived a very simple life," but she gained a new self-awareness through her involvement with the Service.[25]

Prisoners' wives often became more assertive and accustomed to acting independently. Nevertheless, some wives were happy to give up their independence after their husbands' return. Elisabeth Doremus, when asked if she had "any desire to continue making decisions alone" after the war, responded, "No, not at all. And even now, before I do anything, I ask him. I would not go off and do something on my own, just like that, no."[26]

Whether wives willingly ceded their family leadership to their husbands, the five years of separation left the spouses unfamiliar with each other. Several prisoners' wives related having forgotten their husbands' faces, and undoubtedly the men had similar lapses of memory. The sense of unfamiliarity left at least one couple awkward in each other's presence. "We had come to be embarrassed with each other . . . a sort of modesty came over us."[27] There was also the possibility that one or the other of the spouses had been unfaithful.

Children, however, presented the greatest challenge in family reunions. Prisoners' wives with children were more likely to have become authoritative, as they had provided for and disciplined the children. The father's captivity and his return were also trying experiences for both children and fathers.[28] Many children of POWs either had never known or no longer remembered their fathers. Even if mothers were careful to hang a photo in a prominent place and to talk about the father frequently, the real person often came as a surprise. Dominica's husband went to find his daughter, who was watching the cows in a nearby pasture. "But when the little one saw a strange man advancing, she tried to chase him away. Her father was quite vexed about not being recognized." Marguerite's children were disappointed with their real father. "They only knew him through stories, which had nothing to do with reality." "I don't know that gentleman," one prisoner's son informed his mother. Children often resented the presence of a newcomer. "In short, they rejected this intruder." Estelle Sergent's daughter asked her mother, "Couldn't he go live in another apartment?"[29]

Sons appear to have been especially resentful and even jealous of the competition for their mother's attention. Marthe Jolliet's son was "used to not sharing my affection. . . . He did not want me to sleep with my husband." Germaine described perhaps a common situation. From the time he was born her son had slept in her bed. "He did not want to leave me. . . . When my husband returned home, our child did not accept him. 'What did he come here for . . . ? We were better off without him.' "[30]

Some older sons resented being replaced as the man of the house. Sons of farmers or shopkeepers often begrudged their loss of authority in the family business after the prisoners returned. Stéphanie Thibault's son had been a tremendous help to her on the farm, but when her husband returned, "he did not take well to being ordered at his work and especially in the overall organization of the farm." To escape and perhaps to get even, Thibault's son joined the French Forces of the Interior (FFI) in 1945. "For me, that was terrible," wrote Thibault.[31]

The fathers in turn had difficulty adjusting to their children. In particular, men whose first child was born while they were away and who had never experienced fatherhood found their own children to be a mystery. "He did not know what a child was," explained Anne Devron. "I remember one day when my husband was sitting here on this chair and our child was walking around and around it. I said to him, 'Can't you see that he wants you to hold him on your lap?' But no, it was not an idea that came to him!" With their second child, she never had to tell her husband, " 'Take him on your lap.' He knew." Repatriated prisoners had to rediscover their children and learn to put up with them, which was not always easy. "Their noise is tiresome. We are no longer accustomed to their childish reactions."[32]

Many people in France were concerned that the lengthy absence of so many fathers would create a massive problem of juvenile delinquency. One observer maintained in 1945 that "debauchery of minors and stealing by minors are acts whose frequency is incontestably higher when the father was a prisoner or a deportee." Henri Frenay, the first minister of prisoners, deportees, and refugees, reported to the Provisional Assembly that "alas, children of the prisoners of war made up a considerable proportion of juvenile delinquents."[33] Actual figures on the statistical relationship between prisoner of war fathers and juvenile delinquency have never been compiled.

Several testimonies indicate that relationships between the POW father and children born before the war never completely returned to normal. Françoise, the daughter of a POW, still shakes when she remembers her father's rages. Even forty years later, her father had "never recovered his good humor. The war . . . planted in me the roots of a profound anxiety that persists to this day." A rift could also develop between children born before the war and their postwar siblings. After a sister was born, Germaine's son "had the impression that his sister was preferred. Even now, he still says from time to time, 'My father didn't love me.' "[34]

Certainly, prisoner of war families faced serious problems. Every member of the family experienced particular stresses owing to the POW's captivity. Personalities and habits had adapted to the circumstances of separation, and reunion took an effort. Nevertheless, by far the majority of these families readjusted successfully. A widespread inability to readapt would have been reflected in a high divorce rate. Unfortunately, although contemporary observers speculated freely, the exact number of divorces among married prisoners of war has never been ascertained. The divorce rate among POW couples was probably higher than that of the general married population during peacetime, but I believe it was not as high as it could have been considering what these families had been through, and it was certainly nowhere near as high as people suspected at the time.[35]

As the POWs began to return in 1945, fears of massive family upheaval ran rampant. Reports estimated that 60 to 75 percent of the returning married POWs might begin divorce procedures after their return. Anticipating the mass repatriations about to occur, Frenay reported to the Provisional Assembly in March 1945, "It is to be feared—and unfortunately our experience of repatriation up to now has proven it—that numerous households will experience difficulty restoring harmony. If we believed certain, naturally debatable, indications I am afraid as many as 20 to 25 percent

TABLE 8.1   *Divorce in France, 1936–1951*

Number of Departments	Year	Divorces Granted	Divorces Registered
90	1936	21,403	22,135
	1937	25,000	23,926
	1938	26,300	24,318
	1939	——	21,833
87	1940	13,500	11,070
	1941	17,000	14,519
	1942	28,166	14,273
	1943	31,976	17,563
	1944	21,544	17,300
90	1945	37,718	24,359
	1946	64,064	51,985
	1947	56,292	57,413
	1948	45,903	47,015
	1949	40,335	39,502
	1950	34,663	32,732
	1951	33,420	29,611

Source: Louis Roussel, "Les Divorces et les séparations de corps en France (1936–1967)," 300.

could divorce."[36] *Le Monde* reported that, anticipating the problem of postwar divorce owing to lengthy separation, "Fantastic figures have been put forward: the talk is about 200,000 divorce cases in the Paris courts."[37]

Both the absolute number of divorces and the divorce rate in France did shoot up immediately after the war. In 1938, a total of 26,300 divorces were granted; in 1945, there were 37,718. The number of divorces peaked in 1946 with 64,064 (see table 8.1). From then on, the absolute number of divorces declined steadily until the mid-1950s, when it returned again to the 1930s annual figure of approximately 30,000 divorces every year.[38] Most demographers attributed the entire postwar increase in divorce to wartime captivity. Jacques Desforges asserted, "Here, we are measuring the ravages caused to the French family by circumstances born of the war which separated so many households." The many postwar studies on divorce, though meticulous in their statistical analysis, assumed a cause and

effect relationship between wartime separation and the divorce rate without ever directly proving it. One study done in 1969 of four cohorts, couples married in the years 1936, 1956, 1960, and 1964, seems to confirm
the disruptive impact of the war on family life. The 1936 cohort had the
highest divorce rate, 18 per 100.[39] This study sampled all couples married
in 1936, not just POW couples; hence the divorce rate specific to prisoner
of war families has yet to be determined. Nearly two million individual files
contain information about the marital status of former POWs, but neither
the government nor the two statistical agencies, the Institut national
d'études démographiques and the Institut national de la statistique et des
études économiques, have compiled them.

Undoubtedly, factors other than separation contributed to the huge increase in the postwar divorce rate. The divorce curve followed a typical
pattern. During periods of crisis, the divorce rate usually falls dramatically.
For example, the divorce rate declined in both France and the United States
during the Great Depression of the 1930s.[40] In France it also declined during both the first and the second world wars. Demographers and sociolo-
gists have speculated that the difficulty of survival at times of crisis induces
couples to overlook incompatibility and stay together. Furthermore, the
end of a crisis frequently leads to a dramatic increase in the number of
divorces. The post–World War I era in France and the post–World War II
era in the United States both conformed to this pattern.[41] In a sense, therefore, an increase in divorce after a crisis makes up for the crisis-era decline:
couples have not rejected but merely postponed the decision to divorce.

The hypothesis of suspended divorce also accounts for the fact that, although the divorce rate in France has increased steadily since divorce was
reintroduced in 1884, the rate after each war did not continue to increase
from the immediate postwar high but rather declined back to a rate close
to that of the prewar period and then began again to rise slowly from that
point. In other words, the divorce rate drops, jumps, and then returns to
normal (see table 8.2). Louis Roussel in 1970 ascertained that by 1956 the
divorce rate in France had returned to the 1935–38 rate of approximately
27 divorces per 10,000 married women, where it remained until 1964.
Roussel was struck by the fact that, aside from wartime perturbations, the
frequency of divorce in France had been remarkably constant.[42]

One demographer studying World War I calculated that, indeed, the
postwar increase represented a "recovery of suspended break-ups" during
the hostilities. In contrast, by 1947 the number of divorces had surpassed

TABLE 8.2   *Divorce Rates in France, 1926–1955*

Years	Divorces per thousand married couples	Divorces per thousand population
1926–30	2.38	—
1931–35	2.50	0.51
1936–37	2.63	0.56
1946–50	5.01	1.13
1951–55	3.18	0.72

Source: Institut national des statistiques et des études économiques, *Mouvement de la population*, 58. United Nations, *Demographic Yearbook 1958*, 468–69.

the number suspended during World War II, yet the divorce rate remained high for nine more years. The postwar increase may have been higher after the Second World War than after the first because far fewer French men were killed during World War II.[43]

Attempts by the Vichy government to curtail divorce also accounted in part for the precipitous decline in divorces in the 1940s. The law of 2 April 1941 prohibited divorce during the first three years of marriage and narrowed the judicial interpretation of the loosest of the three allowable grounds for divorce, cruelty and abuse (*sévices et injures graves*). This category, according to prevalent opinion, had become flexible enough almost to allow for divorce by mutual consent. In addition, during the war it would have been very difficult for prisoners' wives in France to obtain a divorce because, with their partners absent, none of the three allowable grounds for divorce could be invoked. In April 1945 the new government repealed the three-year prohibition, although it maintained the strict definition of cruelty and abuse.[44] Thus, legal changes explain at least a part of the wartime drop as well as the postwar jump in the divorce rate. Finally, the three departments lost and regained between 1939 and 1945 should also be considered a factor in the variation of the absolute number of divorces.[45]

In other words, based on national figures it is impossible to ascertain the frequency of divorce among repatriated POWs, for merely attributing the postwar increase in the divorce rate to prisoners' families overlooks the many other factors at play. Certainly there were more divorces among returned prisoner of war couples than the prewar national average. By December 1945 in the Paris area, approximately nineteen thousand new divorces were requested, ten thousand more than had been started in 1938. Of the total, ten thousand cases requested judicial assistance to help pay for the procedure; those requests came for the most part from prisoners. Ten thousand divorces among prisoners' families is a significantly large number, yet *Le Monde* pointed out, "It is far from the figure of two hundred thousand cited here and there." In the fall of 1945, after the prisoners had returned, Frenay's ministry revised its pre-repatriation prediction of a 25 percent divorce rate among returnees down to 10 percent.[46]

In the late 1970s, Yves Durand sent questionnaires to 1,801 former POWs. He found that 8 percent of those prisoners had divorced. Fifty-seven percent of the 1,801 were married before the war. Assuming the divorces applied only to prewar marriages, about 14 percent of Durand's married sample divorced.[47] Christophe Lewin estimated that a total of 50,000 POW couples separated between 1945 and 1948, which represents about 6 percent of the approximately 800,000 prisoners married before the war. A recent study of divorce calculated, based on prewar trends, that of the additional 125,000 divorces that occurred after World War II, 50,000 couples would have divorced in any case, leaving 75,000 divorces due to the specific traumas of the war.[48]

Thus Frenay's last estimate that 10 percent of the repatriated POWs would divorce was closest to the truth. Interestingly, in the 1930s, Sully Ledermann, a renowned French demographer, calculated that one in every twelve or thirteen marriages ultimately ended in divorce, an 8 percent rate. Consequently, the 10 percent divorce rate for POW marriages was only slightly higher than that of the population as a whole.[49] Certainly by current standards the number of divorces among repatriated POW families no longer seems very high.[50] In spite of the lengthy separation, personality changes, financial strains, and other potential difficulties, an estimated 90 percent of prisoner of war couples managed to stay together, testifying to the success of readaptation for POW families on a national level.

Although the statistics alone are not conclusive, evidence from testimonies confirms the prevalence of successful reunions. Fifty-two former prisoners' wives addressed the issue of readaptation after the return.[51] Thirty women described the reunion period as wonderful and trouble free. Marguerite wrote, "Seeing each other again was marvelous." Renée experienced her husband's return as "an immense joy that makes you shake from head to toe." For Raymond and Germaine Doucet, "It was as if the five years were erased. We started up almost exactly where we left off, the five years were completely forgotten." Some prisoners' wives even asserted that the experience strengthened their marriages. Suzanne Goupillat wrote, "Captivity tightened our mutual affection, we felt even closer to each other. . . . No problem at all returning to married life." Another prisoner's wife explained that after the return, both she and her husband concentrated on making each other happy: "Never have we been so happy and so united."[52]

Only ten of the fifty-two openly confessed that the return was difficult. Nelly wrote cryptically, "My husband's return did not produce the great joy I had hoped for." Joelle Meliard had become independent and used to making her own decisions, and her husband returned bitter and nervous. "There was a fair amount of friction; we had to learn how to live together again." Likewise, Catherine Michel, who had grown accustomed to running everything herself, described her husband as "very authoritarian." Michel accepted his authority when they were first married, "but I no longer accepted it when he returned after six years of absence." After several years of friction her husband "took the upper hand and strained at the leash because he wanted to make up for lost time. He died of cancer at age 56 in 1964."[53] For those families, life may never have been particularly happy, or they may have taken years to reestablish an equilibrium.

Finally, to my question, "Did you have any difficulty readjusting to married life?" there were twelve wives who answered, "No, but . . . ." "No but our characters were embittered," wrote Sylvie Crouet. "We were run down. . . . We had to help our six-year-old girl adapt to a new life that cut her off from the grandmother she adored." Although the women deny having difficulties readjusting, the reunions clearly presented problems. Martine Lombardi reported, "Our life as a couple itself was easy to take up again, but I had to bend to his unreasonable demands." Her husband insisted that she quit her job because he was angry that her employer refused to give her a month's vacation rather than the two-week "husband return" vacation mandated by law. "I believe it was my willingness to satisfy him that preserved our marriage," she admitted.[54]

Gilberte Voisin presented another contradictory response, beginning with a description of the problems she and her husband experienced. "At the time of his return, my husband had lost his sense of reality." He ran his business just as he had before the war, unable to adapt to the higher prices and new competition that had developed in his absence. "That is why for a while he set his fees at the 1939 rate. I had to turn myself into a nurse, an accountant, and a housekeeper, according to the hour of the day." Surprisingly, in her very next sentence she insists, "My family life was not upset."[55] Louise Cadieu, who also experienced difficulty readjusting to her husband's return, closed by stating, "Life returned to normal with a lot of patience."[56]

War and Social Change: The Case of Prisoner of War Wives

Patience provides the key to understanding why so many wives report having had no trouble or only temporary difficulties. Probably prisoners' wives, many of whom are now widows, were reluctant to admit or discuss marital discord. In addition, the forty-year time lapse has softened the memories of the year or so of hard times, which seem insignificant in comparison to a lifetime of happy marriage. The apparent contradiction between the women's descriptions of serious problems and assertions of successful readjustment was not a matter of lies or understatements but of expectations. Prisoners' wives expected and were willing to be patient, to put up with their husbands' moods, and to give in to their demands, however unreasonable. As guardians of the family, wives anticipated the need for patience to keep their families together.

After the collapse of Germany, with the return of the prisoners imminent, a flood of literature advised women about what to expect and how to treat the men. People from across the political spectrum alerted prisoners' wives about the serious role they would soon play in their families. In a women's newspaper associated with the Communist party, a repatriated prisoner of war requested of wives, "Do not judge us too harshly if we are somewhat bitter and if we have lost the language of love. . . . We ask you to show a great deal of understanding and kindness toward us." Folliet explained that the prisoner's wife needed "much understanding and self-effacement," because "even after the return, she remains more than ever guardian of the home."[57] The wives themselves agreed. A successful readjustment, one claimed, "is our duty, and it will be our victory over exile and separation."[58]

Expectations of womanly nurturing and self-effacement, then, accounted for the successful readaptation of most families. These expectations also reconcile the apparent contradiction of wives such as Gilberte Voisin and Martine Lombardi who, although they had to bend to their husband's demands, maintained that they had no trouble returning to married life. Most prisoners' wives never anticipated continuing to be heads of their households. Theoretically, the women counted on resuming domesticity and relinquishing authority, responsibility, and outside work, even though this may have been hard for them to do in reality.

Even the leaders of the FAFP, among the most active and nationally visible prisoners' wives, sharply curtailed or abandoned their public lives for their families. The statutes of the FAFP dictated that the federation would dissolve when the prisoners of war returned. Although the FNPG considered asking local associations of prisoners' wives to join, the wives' federation was true to its word and simply dissolved itself.[59] Jeanne Bajeux alone of the leaders of the prisoners' wives movement remained visible in the MPF; she was nominated in 1945 to its Central Committee. Andrée Aulas and her husband Robert continued to be active in their local MPF. Agnès Griot found that once the war ended, "It was over; I did not militate much after that because I had four children. I was thirty-two when I had my first. We were six years behind because of the captivity. . . . We wanted to raise a family." She did not drop out of the MPF entirely but took on only "minor responsibilities that I could reconcile with my work in the home."[60]

Griot's testimony evokes several factors that played a role in the postwar era. A strong desire to return to "normal" life and make up for lost time mitigated the short-term difficulties faced by prisoners' families. Second, many POW families had children shortly after the return. Lewin suggests that prisoners' families significantly raised the birthrate, thereby contributing to the postwar baby boom in France. Of the seventy-two cases for which this information is available, thirty-three families had children after the prisoner's return. From 1946 on, birth announcements filled local POW papers and bulletins. The POW community even designated such children "les enfants du retour" (children of the return).[61]

Although families usually returned to the prewar patriarchal structure and division of labor, the experience prisoners' wives had of running their homes, working outside, and making decisions was significant and contributed to reevaluation of women in postwar France. Similar to the participation of women in the Resistance, the role prisoners' wives played in their husbands' absence offered additional proof that women had earned full citizenship. On an individual basis as well, prisoners' wives often gained respect. One prisoner's wife wrote that her husband was "satisfied with all the decisions I made while he was gone. I even have the feeling that he discovered that his wife had more thoughtfulness, judgment, and wisdom than he thought before he left."[62]

Still, the case of French prisoner of war wives during World War II demonstrates that the experience of work or family responsibility alone is not enough to change deeply held beliefs and social norms. The perception of the experience and the way in which reality is interpreted can counteract the expected effects. In this instance, prisoners' wives expected their husbands to return. Therefore, whatever they did to survive during their husbands' absence was a temporary adjustment to a family crisis.

An interesting comparison can be made with American wives of POWs in Vietnam who developed qualities of independence and leadership at a time of rapid social change and pressure for women's rights. American soldiers left home in the mid-1960s, at the end of the postwar conservative era, missed the civil rights, women's liberation, antiwar, and youth movements of the late 1960s, and returned to a society that had developed drastically different social values in the mid-1970s. Within five years of their return, nearly one third of their marriages had ended in divorce.[63] The case of the wives of French prisoners during World War II demonstrates that although France had undergone tremendous upheavals owing to the war, occupation, and liberation, social values remained stable.

Prisoners' wives considered the war an era not of liberation and freedom but one of loneliness, hardship, and anxiety, and they greeted the end of this period with relief. The war had created an abnormal situation; peace and the return of the prisoners restored normalcy, defined as domesticity for women. As Gisèle Desbois explained, when her husband returned, "An equilibrium was reestablished."[64]

Postwar Progress
for Women in
France

Women of France, we are
counting heavily on you to
restore our humanity.
—*Femmes françaises* 39:3

One puzzling question remains. Why, if women's social status remained essentially unchanged as a result of the war, did French women win rights after the war they had been seeking unsuccessfully since before the turn of the century? Not only did women finally gain the right to vote, but the regulation of prostitution, a legal endorsement of the double standard, was abolished on 13 April 1946. The provisional government also endorsed the principle of equal pay for equal work. The French Economic Planning Commission even recommended recruiting female labor by providing more training facilities, access to higher positions, and day-care centers.[1]

Neither a shift in attitudes toward women nor pressure from women's groups produced the significant gains women made after the war. Women benefited from national imperatives and the peculiarities of postwar French politics. For example, the decision to recruit female labor and to endorse equal pay for equal work did not signal a new belief in women's right to work outside the home, nor was it a response to pressure from women's groups or unions. Rather, women were recruited into the labor force to compensate for the postwar shortage of male labor needed for reconstruction.[2]

The campaign against state-regulated prostitution succeeded largely be-

168

cause houses of prostitution in Paris were deeply compromised by collaboration with the German army. Prostitutes were not the only ones who had slept with the Germans. Likewise, the Vichy experience badly discredited conservatism and especially the traditional conservatism Vichy represented. Monarchism vanished from the French political scene, and the radical right lost legitimacy completely for the next forty years. The politics of the immediate postwar period in France witnessed the virtual temporary disappearance of right-wing parties.

Thus conservatives, without a voice, could not prevent female suffrage or progressive social legislation. Furthermore, the French Resistance, which took over the state after the war, promised women the vote to dissociate itself from Vichy. Even de Gaulle, in spite of his social conservatism, guaranteed women the right to vote. After the liberation of France, a constituent assembly was to be elected by "secret and direct ballot of all Frenchmen and women of legal age." The Committee of National Liberation went further, promising women complete equality of education and employment and even appointing two women to its assembly before the liberation.[3]

Moreover, the myth of "Forty Million Resisters" was powerful enough to benefit women. Women's notable contributions to the Resistance prompted the idea that women, politically immature and undeserving of the vote before the war, had proven themselves worthy of the vote through their resistance activities. Colonel Rol-Tanquy, commander-in-chief of the French Forces of the Interior, stated, "Women have proven their worth: they have demonstrated that they are capable of exercising all civil, economic, and political rights and a just society should put them, in every way, on the same level as men." Whether or not participation in the Resistance was truly a departure from a past of political inactivity for women, in the immediate postwar period the resistance experience was widely interpreted as the "rite of passage to full citizenship after the war."[4] Although this one form of political activity justified female suffrage, women in France did not win the vote as a result of pressure from the women's suffrage movement.

Even though the victory of female suffrage was guaranteed by the shift of postwar politics to the left, the participation of women in the municipal elections of 1945 generated strong reactions. The debates and commentary about women voting illustrate that the victory was only a small step for women in terms of changing social values.

Defenders of women's right to vote in 1944–45 used the same arguments heard in the 1920 debates. Certain areas of politics fell within the female domain of the family and children. An editorial vindicating female suffrage answered several hypothetical objections to women voting. "Should not women's roles be distinct from those of men?" Women had the right to speak on issues such as hygiene, education, and child welfare, but as for finance, economic policy, and labor law, should a woman not "give precedence to her companion?" The editorialist responded, "Precisely, hygiene, education, protection of children are regulated by *laws,* and it is those *laws* about which women must be able to have their say: which is why it is absolutely necessary for them *to vote.*"[5]

That women should vote not because they were equal but because they were different had its roots in nineteenth-century notions of women as social housekeepers. Women were experts at cleaning up their own homes, and a community was nothing more than a large home. The first female mayor in France explained, "Women in their homes have, on a small scale, the same concrete and urgent problems to resolve. You can be sure that they will contribute to public affairs the same common sense, the same realism, the same instinct for finding quick and effective solutions."[6] Also, because women are more moral and caring in nature, their influence in politics would mediate men's calculating and self-serving nature. "A harmonious and balanced society cannot allow the masculine to predominate, for then a mechanistic order will reign from which is excluded all sensitivity."[7] As in 1920, favoring female suffrage indicated altered perceptions, not about the nature of women, but about the nature of politics.

Prisoner of war wives provided additional proof of womankind's worthiness. Marcelle Mazeau described POW wives' five years of running their homes alone as "a tough education that made them in general into women who know what they want, women used to initiative and action." She found it "scandalous" that women had never before voted in France and felt that prisoners' wives in particular had to vote in 1945 because "they are replacing their absent husbands." The first election in France took place before the majority of the prisoners had been repatriated, creating some resentment among the prisoners. One man wrote from Germany that he was not surprised about the timing of the elections "because we know that we count for little in France."[8] Giving prisoners' wives the vote took some of the sting out of the prisoners' exclusion.

In contrast to the widespread repudiation of the leaders and policies of the Vichy regime, family policy promoting traditional family life and encouraging childbearing continued after the war: family allowances, single salary allowances, bonuses for the birth of a first child within two years of marriage, strict interpretation of divorce laws, and prohibition of abortion and distribution of contraceptives. Family policy was one of Vichy's least controversial programs, and postwar political parties quickly rescued it from association with Vichy. After the war, for example, the Radical Republican Party emphasized that a radical government had passed the Family Code in 1939. "Family policy is a republican tradition."[9]

In an indirect way, the war and captivity were instrumental in promoting social progress for women: by uprooting a large number of peasants, these two events sped up what French observers referred to with alarm as the "rural exodus." Despite attempts to stem the flood from countryside to city, France ultimately urbanized after the war. This slow but steady change contributed more over the course of the twentieth century to deep changes in French society, social norms, and women's status than did either of the two wars. World War II was not a turning point or a social revolution. Rather, it intensified an ongoing social evolution in France.

Thus, twenty years after the war ended women once again began to win significant improvements. Legal discrimination against married women in the Civil Code was addressed in 1965, owing in part to a 1963 opinion poll, commissioned by the minister of justice, on marriage law, the results of which clearly indicated that French people wanted a change in married women's legal status. For example, 64 percent of those polled felt that wives should control their own property.[10] The law of 13 July 1965 limited husbands' property rights, giving wives control over their personal property and a say in the disposition of community property. Still, husbands retained many legal prerogatives. Only in 1970 did the notion of parental authority replace that of paternal authority over children. Ten years after the 1965 marriage law reform, divorce by mutual consent was legalized.[11]

A left-wing resurgence in the 1965 elections, when Mitterrand forced de Gaulle into a run-off for the presidency, reintroduced feminist issues to the national political discourse. The spectacular postwar population growth and resolution of the German problem lowered French nationalist anxieties, allowing the left and feminists to press for women's rights to contraception and abortion without being labeled traitors. Contraception was legalized in 1967, and abortion in 1975, after a major political struggle by the women's movement.[12]

By 1985 women made up 42 percent of the labor force in France.[13] Still, employed women remained predominantly in "female" sectors. A 1983 study found 62 percent of the female work force in the sixteen most "female" occupations.[14] Women held only 14 percent of high-level managerial positions but 61 percent of all clerical jobs. Women made up 73 percent of the semiskilled work force and only 24 percent of the skilled work force. With the feminization of an economic sector the average pay declines, resulting in a salary differential for men and women that persists to this day. In 1981 the average monthly wages of women still fell at least 20 percent below those of men.[15] Ever-increasing numbers of women have pursued higher education and entered the professions since the war, yet both popular attitudes toward women's roles and government policies have been slow to change.

France of the late 1980s is very different politically, economically, and socially from the France of the 1940s. In individual terms, it was not the war generation but the following one whose lives reflected the social changes. The women who were prisoners' wives continue to live in traditional marriages and espouse traditional values, but their children often manifest very different values and expectations.[16] The women I interviewed often told me about their daughters and daughters-in-law, many of whom hold higher degrees or work in a variety of professions. Some of the younger generation have emigrated to the United States or Canada, some have postponed marriage or children for their careers, and some have divorced. Prisoners' wives seem proud of but also bewildered by the younger generation, aware that time has begun to erase the values instilled in them and that five years of separation failed to shake.

Questionnaire
for the Wives
of French
Prisoners of War

Nom—Prénoms:

Adresse:

Date de Mariage:

Date de Naissance des Enfants:

Pour vous laisser répondre le plus librement et le plus complètement possible, aucun emplacement de réponse n'a été inclus dans ce questionnaire. Pouvez-vous utiliser une feuille séparée? D'avance je vous remercie.

1. Quelle était la situation de votre mari (profession avant la guerre, date de mobilisation, grade militaire, camp de prison ou kommando, date du retour)?

2. Avez-vous travaillé en dehors de la maison avant, pendant, ou après la guerre?

3. Quelles étaient vos ressources pendant la guerre?

4. Avez-vous eu des difficultés matérielles pendant la captivité de votre mari? Lesquelles? Avez-vous déménagé—vous êtes-vous installée chez vos parents, par example?

173

5. Si vous aviez des enfants, croyez-vous que l'absence du père a changé leur évolution? Dans quel sens? Leur éducation a-t-elle souffert?

6. Quelles étaient les difficultés morales que vous avez éprouvées pendant l'absence de votre mari?

7. Est-ce que vous étiez active dans un groupement—par example, une oeuvre s'occupant des prisonniers de guerre, une amicale de femmes de prisonniers, un mouvement catholique? Quelles étaient vos activités?

8. Votre santé a-t-elle souffert pendant la guerre? Celle de vos enfants?

9. Les années de captivité ont-elles changé votre mari? Comment? Vous ont-elles changée?

10. Avez-vous eu du mal à reprendre une vie en commun?

*   *   *

Last Name—First Name:

Address:

Date of Marriage:

Date of Birth of Children:

To allow you to respond as freely and completely as possible, a response space has not been included on this questionnaire. Please use a separate sheet of paper. Thank you in advance.

1. What was your husband's situation (prewar profession, date of mobilization, military rank, prison camp or labor detachment, date of return)?

2. Did you work outside the home before, during, or after the war?

3. What were your financial resources during the war?

4. Did you have any material difficulties during your husband's captivity? What were they? Did you move—did you move back in with your parents, for example?

5. If you had children, do you believe that their father's absence changed their development? In what way? Did their education suffer?

6. What emotional difficulties did you experience during your husband's absence?

7. Were you active in any groups—for example, a charity that worked

to help the prisoners of war, a friendly society of prisoners' wives, a Catholic movement? What were your activities?

8. Did your health suffer during the war? That of your children?

9. Did the years of captivity change your husband? How? Did they change you?

10. Did you have any trouble resuming married life?

This project has been reviewed by the University of Houston Committee for the Protection of Human Subjects. 713-749-3412

INTRODUCTION

1 "Je vas toujours tenir ta soupe au chaud." "L'Ecuelle au coin du feu," *Femmes de prisonniers, Espoir* no. 6, p. 6.

2 Durand, *La Captivité,* 20–28.

3 Williams, *Home Fronts,* 217, 34.

4 Chafe, *American Woman,* 136. Many people have cut short the quotation, "The war marked a watershed in the history of women," in order to use Chafe as a straw man. In fact he is right about the magnitude of changes for women at work, which is the focus of the chapter. In subsequent chapters he examines the persistence of inequality and the paradoxes of change. His interpretation of the evidence may be overly optimistic but not so unreserved as it sounds when the citation is cut short.

5 Chafe claims that three-fourths of the women who took jobs during the war wanted to keep working. Ibid., 178.

6 See Elshtain, *Women and War*; Marcus, "Corpus, Corps/Corpse: Writing the Body in/at War," and Helen Cooper et al., "Arms and the Woman: The Con[tra]ception of the War Text," both in Cooper et al., *Arms and the Woman.*

7 Fussell, *Great War and Modern Memory,* 270–309; Sandra M. Gilbert, "Soldier's Heart: Literary Men, Literary Women and the Great War," and Susan Gubar, " 'This Is My Rifle, This is My Gun': World War II and the Blitz on Women," and Joan Scott, "Rewriting History," all three in Higonnet et al., *Behind the Lines.*

8 Arthur Marwick picked up on the sense of rampant immorality, writing of France during World War I, "Paris entered upon a new phase of hedonistic living: interruptions in normal family life; the billeting of vast numbers of soldiers, French and foreign, in rural areas; conditions of privation and heightened emotion: all these factors understandably had a direct effect on standards of moral behavior." *War and Social Change,* 56.

9 Durand, *La Captivité,* 21. For a breakdown of the 600,000 POWs repatriated or deceased between 1940 and 1944, see table 3.1.

10   A 1942 French government estimate that, of the 1.3 million POWs remaining in Germany, 760,000 were married confirms Durand's figures. Secrétariat général, Archives nationales (hereafter AN), F60:558.

CHAPTER 1: WOMEN IN FRANCE BEFORE THE WAR

1   Besides Paris, only two cities, Lyons and Marseilles, had populations of 500,000, and only fourteen cities had over 100,000 people; Mayeur and Rebérioux, *The Third Republic,* 334.

2   Michelle Perrot, "The New Eve and the Old Adam: Changes in French Women's Condition at the Turn of the Century," in Higonnet et al., *Behind the Lines,* 51–60; Sohn, "*La Garçonne,*" 3–27.

3   Cited in Albistur and Armogathe, *Histoire du féminisme,* 381.

4   The same deputies passed the restrictive law on birth control in 1920, in a chamber notoriously the "most right wing of any the Republic had known since 1875." Bernard and Dubief, *Decline of the Third Republic,* 89. By the 1920s, pro-suffrage could be combined with conservative views on marriage and family life; even the pronatalist Alliance Nationale newsmagazine, *La Mère et l'enfant,* advocated female suffrage. Huss, "Pronatalism," 43.

5   The Senate voted 156 against female suffrage to 134 in favor. The Chamber voted for female suffrage three more times, in 1925, 1932, and 1935; each time the Senate refused to bring the debate to the floor. Albistur and Armogathe, *Histoire du féminisme,* 382.

6   See Steven Hause, "More Minerva than Mars: The French Women's Rights Campaign and the First World War," in Higonnet et al., *Behind the Lines,* 99–113.

7   In 1898 women were given the right to vote for the *tribuneaux de commerce*; in 1900 they could both vote and run for seats on the *Conseil Supérieur du Travail* and, after 1907, for the *conseil des prudhommes.* Perrot, "New Eve and Old Adam," in Higonnet et al, *Behind the Lines,* 54.

8   Albistur and Armogathe, *Histoire du féminisme,* 382–83. Although Léon Blum appointed three women to secondary positions in his cabinet in 1936, female suffrage was not a major concern of the Popular Front. Clark, *Schooling the Daughters of Marianne,* 97.

9   Before Napoleon, universities in Europe taught ideal Roman law, as opposed to the actual laws which, reflecting the diversity of medieval systems, were not uniform throughout each state. Napoleon intended his Code to set down one uniform law to order all social relations for France, based on ideal Roman law. Legislation, the primary source of law, thus "plays the same role in France as judicial decisions play in common law countries." Fur-

thermore, there is no equivalent of the Supreme Court, only a Council which examines laws for their constitutionality before they are promulgated. The eight changes of government have had little impact on the Napoleonic Codes, still in effect, amended but intact. David, *French Law*, xiii, 124–25. See also Jacques Godechot, "Institutions," in Kafker and Laux, *Napoleon and His Times*, 278–95.

10 The legal experts were Tronchet, Portalis, Bigot de Préameneu and Maleville. Lefebvre, *Napoleon*, 151–54; Fisher, "The Codes," 154. See also Hutt, *Napoleon*, 49–50; Garaud and Szramkiewicz, "Women and the Family," in Kafker and Laux, *Napoleon and His Times*, 307–16.

11 Citations from Fisher, "The Codes," 155.

12 Both citations from Hutt, *Napoleon*, 50.

13 Goy, "Civil Code," 446.

14 Fisher, "The Codes," 155–57.

15 Berenson, "The Politics of Divorce," 39.

16 Ibid., 45. Interestingly, most proponents assumed divorce would benefit men more than women, since marriage supposedly bound men but protected women. Even feminists had serious reservations about divorce, fearing that women, economically vulnerable, could fall victim to men's lust and taste for variety. In fact, divorce gave women a way out of bad situations. For example, even before divorce was reinstituted, Michelle Perrot points out that women initiated 80 percent of all *séparations de corps*, predominantly due to violence and physical abuse. Perrot, "The New Eve and the Old Adam," in Higonnet et al., *Behind the Lines*, 53 n. 3.

17 Perrot, "The New Eve and the Old Adam," 53, and Hause, "More Minerva than Mars," 107, both in Higonnet et al., *Behind the Lines*.

18 Cazin, *Le Travail féminin*, 106. Although married women controlled their own wages as of 1907, they still needed their husband's prior permission to work.

19 The sea of military uniforms earned the postwar chamber its "chambre horizon bleu" designation. The 1920 law punished the dissemination of birth control information with fines up to 5000 francs; encouraging abortion carried a possible 100–3000 franc fine and six-month to three-year jail term. Note that this same Chamber voted for female suffrage, indicating that female suffrage no longer threatened traditional family values. Hause, "More Minerva than Mars," in Higonnet et al., *Behind the Lines*, 108. In 1967 the law authorized contraception; abortion was legalized in 1975. Sullerot, *Pour le meilleur et sans le pire*, 73; Larkin, *France since the Popular Front*, 341.

20 The double standard was also reinforced by state regulation of prostitution which gave men access to medically inspected, certified prostitutes. Men

were thereby able to have sex outside of marriage without fear of contaminating their wives.

21 Carré, Dubois, and Malinvaud, *French Economic Growth*, 54.

22 The number equals the percent of the working population that earns its living in agriculture. In 1980 that figure had fallen to 8 percent. Wright, *France in Modern Times*, 289, 456.

23 Carré, Dubois, and Malinvaud, *French Economic Growth*, 49–54.

24 Sullerot, *Travail féminin*, 230.

25 Daric, *L'Activité professionelle des femmes*, 94; Carré, Dubois, and Malinvaud, *French Economic Growth*, 53–54; Sullerot, *Travail féminin*, 232–34; United Nations, *Economic Role of Women*, 40.

26 Collinet, *L'Ouvrier français*, 45.

27 McMillan, *Housewife or Harlot*, 116–62.

28 Only in 1980 did the rate of female participation, 38 percent, surpass that of 1906, 36 percent, but the same number masks two very different realities. Wright, *France in Modern Times*, 463. In 1987 the female participation rate was 43 percent. Ibid., 4th ed., 456.

29 Mayeur and Réberioux, *The Third Republic*, 89.

30 Male illiteracy, 16 percent in 1880, also disappeared by 1914. Clark, *Schooling the Daughters of Marianne*, 13, 26.

31 The first girl to do so, Julie Daubié, studied Latin with her brothers and passed the examination in 1861 but was refused the diploma.

32 Clark, *Schooling the Daughters of Marianne*, 48; Guélaud-Leridon, *La Condition féminine*, 74–76.

33 There were 21,018 women enrolled in universities in 1939. Guélaud-Leridon, *La Condition féminine*, 73, 76.

34 McMillan, *Housewife or Harlot*, 120–22. Other than the one hundred women at the Paris bar, there were three in Lyons, one in Le Havre, and two in Caen. Nursing and social work also offered new opportunities for professional women but were considered incompatible with marriage and family life. Most nurses and many social workers remained single.

35 Clark, *Schooling the Daughters of Marianne*, 26–59, 81–101.

36 McLaren, *Sexuality and Social Order*. In 1854–55 the number of deaths exceeded the number of births. Pp. 9–12. McLaren also points out that a French man, Achille Guillard, coined the term *demography* in 1855. P. 9.

37 McMillan describes motherhood as "a crucial battleground in the struggle between republican anti-clericals and the Catholic Church." McMillan, *Housewife or Harlot*, 11.

38 Knibiehler and Fouquet, *L'Histoire des mères*, 247. In her study of women and the working class in Lyons, Laura Struminger concluded that the "bourgeois ideology broadcast by the schools, the church, and the media,

triumphed within the very heart of the socialist opposition—the Internationale." Struminger, *Women and the Making of the Working Class,* 110.

39 For example, Charles Fourier, the St. Simonian Church, and Flora Tristan: see Boxer, "Socialism Faces Feminism," 77.

40 Sowerwine, *Sisters or Citizens?* 1–47.

41 Boxer, "Socialism Faces Feminism," 86; Hilden, *Working Women,* 4. Madeleine Pelletier complained, "In its preoccupation with assuring an electoral clientele it dropped the cause of those who necessarily could not bring the party votes." Cited in Boxer, "Socialism Faces Feminism," 101. Guesde's evolution was particularly disappointing in the Lille-Roubaix-Tourcoing textile region, where the strong Guesdist POF included many active working-class women. Until the 1890s, the POF in the north advocated women's equality, included women in all levels of the movement, and encouraged local working-class women's groups. Hilden, *Working Women,* 4.

42 Hilden, *Working Women,* 265; Boxer, "Radical and Socialist Feminism," 60.

43 Hilden, *Working Women,* 241–44; McMillan, *Dreyfus to De Gaulle,* 81–82.

44 Boxer, "Radical and Socialist Feminism," 60; Knibiehler and Fouquet, *L'Histoire des mères,* 247–48. The CGT demanded improved working conditions for mothers.

45 Richer stated, "Woman will remain, by her own preference, the guardian of the family, the diligent hostess of the domestic home." Cited in Moses, *French Feminism,* 202.

46 Offen, "Depopulation, Nationalism, and Feminism," 654. Offen argues that this was an astute tactic given the atmosphere in France at the time.

47 In the end, Pelletier, who renounced political activism in favor of practicing her beliefs, was arrested for performing abortions and declared unfit to stand trial. She died in an asylum in 1940. Boxer, "Radical and Socialist Feminism," 67; Boxer, "Socialism Faces Feminism," 98–105; and McLaren, *Sexuality and Social Order,* 164. See also Ronsin, *La Grève de ventres.* All of the neo-Malthusian groups and papers were effectively silenced under the 1920 law. McLaren, *Sexuality and Social Order,* 181.

48 Berenson, "The Politics of Divorce," 41.

49 Ibid., 45–48.

50 Ibid., 35.

51 See Offen, "Depopulation, Nationalism, and Feminism," 648–76; Pedersen, "Reconstruction of the Family," 53–70, 479–550; Pollard, "*Femme, Famille, France,*" 10–78.

52 Offen, "Depopulation, Nationalism, and Feminism," 674. In spite of their familial orientation, opponents argued that feminists "take the feminine

mission lightly and in general do not take it into account" and that feminism itself destroyed the French family. Cazin, *Le Travail féminin,* 49.

53 Familialists splintered off from the Alliance nationale to form their own organizations: the Confédération générale des familles, open to all families; and the Fédération nationale des familles nombreuses, open only to fathers of large families. See Talmy, *Histoire du mouvement familial en France,* vol. 1. Pollard and I agree that it would be wrong to overemphasize the differences between pronatalism and familialism: "While familialists explicitly embraced natalism in defense of *familles nombreuses,* natalists exclusively envisaged population growth within the legitimate nuclear family." Pollard, "*Femme, Famille, France,*" 14 n. 13.

54 The opinion of those Offen categorized as "patriarchal patriots" (Bertillon, Boverat, Piot). Offen, "Depopulation, Nationalism, and Feminism," 669.

55 *Journal officiel,* 30 July 1939.

56 L'aggravation du péril extérieur." Ibid.

57 Ibid.

58 "Les enfants constituent la part la plus importante du patrimoine national; il est donc juste que chaque individu participe aux frais de leur entretien." Ibid.

59 Pedersen, "Social Policy and the Reconstruction of the Family," 286–373. The motives of its originators in the north were not just familial: industrialists used allowances to prevent general wage increases, defuse labor pressure, and augment management control.

60 *Journal officiel,* 30 July 1939.

61 The idea that peasants had large families contradicts the also widely held belief that the Napoleonic equal-inheritance law had caused peasant families to limit their size to prevent excessive subdivision of farmlands. Bailey Stone reminded me that partible inheritance existed in much of France well before Napoleon. In Old Regime France, the equal division of estates, in some cases excluding children receiving marriage portions, was preferred in areas of customary law: the west through Champagne, the Paris basin, and Flanders. In areas subject to written law, unequal inheritance was the custom. See Goy, "Civil Code," 439.

62 *Journal officiel,* 30 July 1939.

63 Typical of France, the evils of alcoholism were attributed principally to the production and consumption of alcohol of poor quality "circulant en fraud." Huss explains that pornography included "any kind of contraceptive practice as well as abortion, promiscuity and certain forms of public entertainment." "Pronatalism," 44. Among the suggested ways to finance the measures of the Family Code, Deladier proposed a special surtax on estates with childless inheritors over age thirty. *Journal officiel,* 30 July 1939.

64 On the Family Code in the historical context of the late 1930s, see Pollard, "*Femme, Famille, France,*" 39–49.

CHAPTER 2: THE TRAUMA OF SEPARATION

1 The words were Neville Chamberlain's, cited in Kitchen, *Europe between the Wars,* 306.
2 "J'ai jêté ce bouquet-là en disant, 'Bah oui, drôle de fête!' " Interview with Fernande Damart, conducted by Madeleine Blaire, December 1985.
3 For French military doctrine and its relation to defense spending and diplomacy, see Dutailly, *Les Problèmes de l'armée*; Frankenstein, *Le Prix du réarmement*; Doughty, *The Seeds of Disaster*; Schuker, "Remilitarization of the Rhineland," 299–338; Young, *In Command of France*; Posen, *Sources of Military Doctrine*; essays by René Girault, Maurice Vaïsse, Robert Frankenstein, and Anthony Adamthwaite in Mommsen and Kettenacher, *The Fascist Challenge*. On the phony war, see Rossi-Landi, *La Drôle de guerre*; Bédarida, *La Stratégie secrète*; Michel, *La Drôle de guerre*; and Fonvieille-Alquier, *The French and the Phoney War.*
4 Interview with Josette Garnier, 3 May 1985.
5 Interview with Germaine and Raymond Doucet, 20 November 1985.
6 Azéma, *From Munich to the Liberation,* 33, 217 n. 9.
7 On the Battle of France, see Duroselle, *L'Abîme*; Michel, *La Défaite de la France*; Durand, *La France dans la 2e guerre mondiale*; Horne, *To Lose a Battle*; Mysyrowicz, *Autopsie d'une défaite*; Osgood, *The Fall of France*; Daridan, *Le Chemin de la défaite*; and Leca, *La Rupture de 1940*. Cairns, "Along the Road Back to France," is still well worth reading. For a remarkable personal account, see Bloch, *Strange Defeat.*
8 Cited in Mason, "Women in Germany," 2:20. Göring, chief of the Four Year Plan, in a January 1939 directive to the OKW stipulated that, in the event of war, POWs would be employed in large numbers to keep the war economy going. Homze, *Foreign Labor,* 16. After the defeat, Göring viewed France as a source of "booty and loot." Milward, *The New Order,* 46.
9 On the exodus, see Vidalenc, *L'Exode de mai–juin 1940*; Ollier, *L'Exode sur les routes.* For a sharply perceptive personal account of the exodus, see Simone de Beauvoir, *The Prime of Life,* 348–59; also François Pakonyk, *1940–1945 Les Enfants de l'exode.*
10 Interview with Elisabeth Doremus, conducted by Madeleine Blaire, December 1985.
11 Azéma, *From Munich to the Liberation,* 39.
12 In Durand's sample of 1800 former POWs, 49.6 percent were captured between 17 and 25 June. *La Captivité,* 43.

13   Ferro's biography of Pétain includes a description of this crisis entitled "Les 'durs' et les 'mous' s'affrontent." Among the "durs" were Paul Reynaud, Charles de Gaulle, and Georges Mandel, minister of the interior; the "mous" included Pétain, Adrien Marquet, General Maxime Weygand, Yves Bouthillier, Paul Baudouin, and Pierre Laval. Ferro, *Pétain*, 60–63.

14   Paxton, *Vichy France*, 6–7; Azéma, *From Munich to the Liberation*, 42.

15   Although Pétain, Laval, and others were defeatist and believed England would fall quickly, few historians would argue that they accepted defeat in 1940 out of a pro-fascist sentiment. Some individual fascists, such as Lucien Rebatet, hoped for a German victory, but the fascists "were not the men who made the decisions of 1940." Paxton, *Vichy France*, 5; see also 228–33, 251–58. Bertram M. Gordon distinguishes fascist "collaborationists" from the Vichy regime, calling the one group the alter ego of the other. Gordon, *Collaborationism*, 19. Hitler knew that French fascists were unimportant and unpopular. He had no desire for a rival fascist regime in France, so he used them as a threat, a Damocles sword, to keep Vichy docile. See Milward, *The New Order*, 40–41; Gordon, *Collaborationism*, 24; Ory, *Les Collaborateurs*, 42–43. On the issue of fascism and Vichy, see the next chapter.

16   Jean Berthelot's expression, from a 1941 speech, cited in Paxton, *Vichy France*, 14.

17   Amouroux, *La Vie des français*, 268; Paxton, *Vichy France*, 52–54; Azéma, *From Munich to the Liberation*, 45–46.

18   Azéma claims that 100,000 soldiers were killed in the Battle of France, but most other estimates put the figure at approximately 92,000. Dyer, *Population and Society*, 127.

19   Deroy and Pineau, *Celles qui attendaient*, 27. The wives are referred to by first name only.

20   Letter from Hélène Noiret, 30 July 1985.

21   Beauvoir, *The Prime of Life*, 360. The POWs on their side shared the same anxieties. "L'une des pires souffrances des débuts de la captivité, ç'avait été de demeurer sans nouvelles des nôtres [One of the worst things we suffered from at the start of our captivity was being without news of our loved ones]." Ambrière, *Les Grandes Vacances*, 84.

22   Beauvoir, *The Prime of Life*, 363.

23   Correspondence between Hélène Jamon and her father, 26 July 1940, consulted with permission.

24   Letter from Marthe Jolliet, 5 August 1985.

25   Deroy and Pineau, *Celles qui attendaient*, 49.

26   *Le Temps*, 6 January 1941; ibid., 10 October 1941.

27   "C'est en tant que main d'oeuvre, indispensable à l'économie allemande,

que les dirigeants du Reich vont les [prisonniers de guerre] retenir pendant toute la guerre [It was as labor, indispensable to the German economy that the leaders of the Reich kept the prisoners of war during the entire war]." Durand, *La Captivité*, 111. See also Homze, *Foreign Labor*, 15–16, 45–49; Milward, *The New Order*, 23–44, 46, 78; and especially Billig, "Le Rôle des prisonniers de guerre," 53–76; Durand, *La France*, 56–58.

28 Interview with Evelyne Crinon, 4 April 1985.

29 Interview with Michelle Dupuy, 8 June 1985; interview with Josette Garnier, 3 May 1985; Deroy, *Celles qui attendaient*, 23.

30 Interview with Germaine Doucet, 20 November 1985.

31 Robert Paxton found "no good contemporary evidence of any Frenchman remaining in France in July 1940 who did not share the general expectation of an imminent peace treaty between France and Germany which would bind the two countries for many years to come." Paxton, *Parades and Politics at Vichy*, 68. It is striking how rarely government documents mention the war.

32 Interview with Marie-Hélène Corbel, conducted by Paula Schwartz, 21 March 1984. Raymonde Moulin, who worked during the war for the Ministère des anciens combattants claims she and her coworkers followed the war on maps, rejoicing at every Allied advance. Even so, "We had no idea it would last so long." Interview, 23 March 1985.

33 Interview with Anne Devron, 10 June 1985.

CHAPTER 3: THE VICHY REGIME, THE PRISONERS OF WAR, AND THEIR FAMILIES

1 *France during the German Occupation*, 204.

2 Ferro, *Pétain*, 285; see also my "Grand delusions."

3 Among the least happy were General Mittelhauser in the Near East and General Noguès, commander-in-chief of North Africa, who felt the North African option was too lightly dismissed. Noguès wrote, "The government, finding itself in an atmosphere of disorder, proved incapable of recognizing the important element of morale and strength that North Africa represented . . . it was bitterly to regret its failure to do so." Cited in Azéma, *From Munich to the Liberation*, 219 n. 44.

4 Paxton disagrees that Vichy policy in 1940 limited itself to a strict interpretation of the armistice, as Weygand asserted at his postwar trial. Paxton, *Vichy France*, 59. Weygand's reputation has been helped by his refusal to sign the Protocols of Paris in May 1941 and by the fact that he was considered unreliable by the Germans, forced out of the government, and eventually arrested and taken to Germany on 12 November 1942, as all of France

was being occupied. Rousso, *La Collaboration,* 152–53; Warner, *Pierre Laval,* 342–43.

5   On Pierre Laval, see Warner, *Pierre Laval,* as well as Kupferman, *Laval,* and Michel, *Pétain, Laval, Darlan.* Laval's belief in France's bargaining leverage did not change after November 1942, when France no longer had a fleet, an army, or the empire. Warner, *Pierre Laval,* 311, 351–52. Laval also maintained his belief in a German victory long after the tide had turned against Germany. Ory, *Les Collaborateurs,* 39. Warner asserts that Laval maintained it up to D-Day and concludes that Laval's ideas were remarkably consistent over his career. Warner, *Pierre Laval,* 291–302, 391, 422. Ferro's biography of Pétain sheds new light on the stormy relationship between Pétain and Laval. Ferro, *Pétain,* 114–32, 168–69, 471–526, 645–47. See also Rousso, *La Collaboration,* 114–17.

6   On the particularly enigmatic figure of Darlan, who negotiated the Paris protocols with Germany in May 1941, became head of state after Laval and Flandin, and then negotiated a cease-fire with the Americans in Algiers on 10 November 1942 (the "Darlan Deal") before being assassinated in December 1942, see Coutau-Bégarie and Huan, *Darlan;* Michel, *Pétain, Laval, Darlan;* Melka, "Darlan between Britain and Germany 1940–1941," and Funk, "Negotiating the 'Deal with Darlan,'" both in the *Journal of Contemporary History* 8, no. 2 (April 1973): 57–80, 81–117; Tompkins, *The Murder of Admiral Darlan;* Warner, *Pierre Laval,* 249–53; Paxton, *Vichy France,* 101–35; Ory, *Les Collaborateurs,* 39; and Rousso, *La Collaboration,* 79–81. Darlan, *L'Amiral Darlan parle,* includes some of Darlan's notes and personal papers. The most complete treatment of Huntziger is in Paxton, *Parades and Politics.* There has yet to be a biography of Huntziger, the first Vichy representative to the Armistice Commission at Wiesbaden and then chief of the Armistice Army. Huntziger, who died in an airplane crash on 12 November 1941, is best remembered for his comment "Il faut chasser les Anglais [We must drive out the English]," made to General von Rundstedt on 31 October 1940, in response to British attacks on French colonies. Cited in Warner, *Pierre Laval,* 228. Paxton insists, however, that Huntziger wanted neutrality rather than war against England. Paxton, *Parades and Politics,* 87–88. See also Warner, *Pierre Laval,* 249–53; Paxton, *Vichy France,* 51–135; Rousso, *La Collaboration,* 63.

7   Scapini, although blinded in World War I, became a partisan of Franco-German entente in the interwar years. Even after the Nazi takeover in 1933, Scapini did not abandon hope for reconciliation and met in Berlin with Joachim von Ribbentrop. Durand, *La Captivité,* 315. See also Scapini, *Mission sans gloire.*

8   Scapini, "Prisoners," 204–05, quote on 208.

9   Scapini learned his lesson from this episode and opposed its eventual re-
    alization in June 1942, the *Relève*. Durand, *La Captivité*, 321.

10 "La convention était largement dépassée puisqu'aussi bien le gouvernement
    allemand avait accordé des conditions de traitement et des libérations qui
    n'étaient pas prévues par la convention visée. Qu'au surplus, l'orientation
    de la politique française et les négociations en cours donnaient aux rapports
    des vues beaucoup plus larges en fonction du travail en commun pour une
    reconstruction de l'Europe." Durand, *La Captivité*, 323.

11 Ibid., 324.

12 Jewish prisoners of war were segregated into separate barracks within the
    camps. Interview with Jules Braunshwig, July 1985; correspondence with
    Bernard Lisik, 1985. After the war, the Grand Rabbi Julien Weill wrote a
    letter on behalf of Scapini, published in *France during the German Occu-
    pation*, 208.

13 *Le Temps*, 22 August 1941.

14 Ibid., 28 October 1941. The same assassinations led the Germans to shoot
    over one hundred French hostages. See Paxton, *Vichy France*, 223–24.

15 Cover of *L'Illustration*, 19 September 1942. Durand provides photographic
    evidence that the slogans were not on the train cars but were added to the
    photos later for effect. Durand, *La Captivité*, 326–27. See also Denis Ma-
    réchal's photo essay on the Relève in *Images de la France de Vichy*, 249–
    53.

16 *Le Temps*, 20 November 1940 and 6 July 1941.

17 *L'Illustration*, 5 July 1941.

18 Most of the men in this situation were mobilized before the fourth child
    was born.

19 Hoffmann, "Collaborationism in France during World War II," 379.

20 Durand, *La Captivité*, 228.

21 CGPGR, AN, F9: 3028.

22 Laval announced the ratio in a speech of August 12, 1942, though censors
    told the press, "Il ne devra pas être fait mention par ces titres de l'indication
    relative aux chiffres de 150,000 et 50,000 concernant les specialistes et les
    prisonniers [You must not mention in the headline the relative figures of
    150,000 and 50,000 concerning skilled workers and prisoners]." Rather,
    the figures were to be left buried in the speech. *Censure Vichy*, Dossier
    BDIC Fol. Rés. 75 I; Présidence du Conseil, "Consignes de censure, 14e
    région, Lyon, October 1941, no. 158, and 12 August 1942, no. 598.

23 "Je souhaite la victoire de l'Allemagne." *Le Temps*, 24 June 1942.

24 Information, AN, F41: 300.

25 Ibid. One woman who did so wrote her memoirs. The disbelief she en-

countered from the authorities indicates that few wives took up this offer. Dailly, *La Femme du prisonnier.*

26 *Le Temps,* 29 June 1942. Clearly a manufactured account of prison camp reactions as, based on the date of the article, these prisoners were repatriated before the Relève.

27 *Le Temps,* 5 October 1942.

28 "La désignation des bénéficiaires de la Relève suscite toujours de vives critiques." Chef de l'état, AN, AG2: 27, Service des contrôles techniques, Rapport statistique, Annexe, Etat d'esprit des prisonniers de guerre, January 1944. See also Durand, *La Captivité,* 331, 456–57.

29 Chef de l'état, AN, AG2: 608, cm23, December 1943; see also cm24b; cm22a, 30 August 1943; cm22b, 6 October 1943.

30 Ibid., cm24, 26 March 1944 and cm22a, August 1943.

31 Ibid., cm23b, 19 November 1943 and cm22b, 1 October 1943.

32 Ibid., cm23, 26 December 1943 and cm22b, 6 October 1943. Some historians disagree that there was still strong support for Pétain as late as 1943. Based on the Contrôle postale's weekly summaries of popular opinions from thousands of letters, I maintain that although most of the French were probably hostile to the Vichy regime and Laval by 1943, Pétain continued to be a popular figure to many people. For example, the report of 2–8 June 1944 lists 681 expressions of "veneration, confidence, and faith in the Marshall" and only 2 "anti-Pétain" allusions. Even in August of 1944, there were 230 expressions of veneration, confidence, and faith, 160 expressions of compassion, and only 20 expressions of hostility, compared to 29 mentions of Laval—26 hostile, 3 favorable. These opinions were not taken from letters written directly to Pétain, and although wisdom dictated discretion about antigovernmental opinions, it did not require expressions of fidelity to Pétain. Contrôles techniques, AN, F7: 14927.

33 Chef de l'état, AN, AG2: 608, cm23, 6 January 1944.

34 A law of 4 September 1942 made every French man between eighteen and fifty and all unmarried French women from twenty-one to thirty-five liable "to carry out any work which the government judges useful in the higher interest of the nation." *Journal officiel,* 13 September 1942, following Sauckel's decree of 30 August 1942, which rendered all men and women liable for labor service in Germany. See also Warner, *Pierre Laval,* 308. John Sweets found that in October 1942 in Clermont-Ferrand, when volunteers were not forthcoming, businesses were given quotas of workers to supply the Relève. In response, a flurry of strikes broke out at the train stations, and workers were arrested and forcibly put on trains. Sweets, *Choices in Vichy France,* 24–25.

35 The equivalent of two army divisions. Gascar, *Histoire de la captivité,* 272.

36 *L'Illustration,* 8 May 1943.
37 Robert Paxton, throughout *Vichy France,* argues this point decisively.
38 Roderick Kedward, "The Vichy of the Other Philippe," in Hirschfeld and Marsh, *Collaboration in France,* 3.
39 On collaboration, see Azéma, *La Collaboration;* Defrasne, *Histoire de la collaboration;* Duroselle, *L'Abîme;* Gordon, *Collaborationism;* Hirschfeld and Marsh, *Collaboration in France;* Hoffmann, "Collaborationism in France during World War II," 375–95; Jäckel, *La France dans l'Europe de Hitler;* Kedward, *Occupied France;* Lévy, *Les Nouveau Temps;* Ory, *Les Collaborateurs;* Paxton, *Vichy France;* Sweets, *Choices in Vichy France;* Veillon, *La Collaboration.*
40 The phrase was first used by Stanley Hoffmann, in "Aspects du régime de Vichy," 47–48. Paxton uses the phrase as a chapter subtitle in *Vichy France,* 249.
41 Although the first two groups were both represented at Vichy from the start, only a few members of the last group (Darnand, Henriot, Déat) gained a foothold in 1944, at the very end of the war. See Paxton, *Vichy France,* 228–33; Ory, *Les Collaborateurs,* 40–43; Durand, *La France,* 60–64; Gordon, *Collaborationism,* 19–20, 24; Ferro, *Pétain,* 162–68; Paul J. Kingston, "The Ideologists: Vichy France, 1940–1944," in Hirschfeld and Marsh, *Collaboration in France,* 47–71; Cointet-Labrousse, *Vichy et le fascisme;* Chalas, *Vichy et l'imaginaire totalitaire.* A tiny group of prewar leftists, including syndicalist René Belin, also improbably joined Vichy.
42 *Le Temps,* 12 October 1940.
43 Ferro's recent biography of Pétain is by far the most comprehensive and even-handed work on Pétain. See also Lottman, *Pétain.*
44 *Le Temps,* 12 October 1940. On Vichy's agricultural programs, see Pierre Barral and Isabel Boussard, "La Politique Agrarienne," in *Le Gouvernement de Vichy,* 211–39; Cépède, *Agriculture et alimentation,* 43–204; Paxton, *Vichy France,* 200–10.
45 For a discussion of Vichy's economic policies, see Jones, "Illusions of Sovereignty," 1–31; Jacques Julliard, "La Charte du travail," in *Le Gouvernement de Vichy,* 157–210; Kuisel, *Capitalism and the State,* 128–56; Zdatny, *The Politics of Survival,* 128–53; Paxton, *Vichy France,* 210–20.
46 Paxton, *Vichy France,* 271.
47 Cited in Duquesne, *Les Catholiques français,* 18. On the Catholic church see also De Montclos et al., *Eglises et chrétiens;* Bédarida, *Les Armes de l'esprit;* Bolle and Godel, *Spiritualité, théologie et résistance;* Dansette, *Destin du catholicisme français;* W. D. Halls, "Catholicism under Vichy: A Study in Diversity and Ambiguity," in Kedward and Austin, *Vichy France and the Resistance,* 133–46; Louis Allen, "Jews and Catholics," in the same collection, 73–87; and Pierrard, *Juifs et catholiques français.*

48   John Sweets's careful study of Clermont-Ferrand, *Choices in Vichy France,* 33–42, 80–81, indicates that actual purges at the local level were not particularly thorough. On the purges of schoolteachers, see Ferro, *Pétain,* 265, and especially Halls, *The Youth of Vichy France,* 112–17. Pollard discusses the purge issue as well as the additional threat to female schoolteachers of the 10 October 1940 law against married women's work. *"Femme, Famille France,"* 192–93, 244–46. On Free Masons, see Rossignol, *Vichy et les Francs-maçons,* 133–43.

49   Both Paxton and Azéma cover in detail the controversy surrounding Pétain's firing of Laval on 13 December 1940. Paxton, *Vichy France,* 92–101; Azéma, *From Munich to the Liberation,* 56–57. Most historians agree that Pétain's firing of Laval was not a rejection of collaboration but a combination of Pétain's personal dislike of Laval with anger at his secretive tactics and irritation at his lack of success. Durand, *La France,* 54; Ferro, *Pétain,* 200–15; Warner, *Pierre Laval,* 256–60. On Darlan's technocratic orientation see Gordon, *Collaborationism,* 19; Ferro, *Pétain,* 306. On French technocracy, see Brun, *Technocrates et technocratie.*

50   Ferro cites German interpreter Stehlin's 1964 reconstruction of the 25 December 1940 conversation between Darlan and Hitler. Darlan hoped that Germany would "nous réserver une place dans l'oeuvre de reconstruction européenne [save a place for us in the work of European reconstruction]." Ferro, *Pétain,* 307–08. See also Rousso, *La Collaboration,* 40–42.

51   In spite of being freed of parliamentary meddling, Vichy did not run efficiently, as the rest of this chapter illustrates. The conditions of war and occupation and the fact that German plans took little heed of French technocratic ambitions made for chaos. Recent historical work has even broken down the myth of Nazi efficiency, also undermined by the chaos of competing bureaucratic structures and absence of rules other than the Führer's favor. (See Broszat, *The Hitler State*). For a study of the real economic structures in France, see Jones, "Illusions of Sovereignty"; Kuisel, *Capitalism and the State*; Milward, *The New Order*; Sauvy, *La Vie économique*; Cépède, *Agriculture et alimentation*; and Sweets, *Choices in Vichy France.* For a complete and up-to-date survey of work on economic issues, see Rousso, "L'Activité industrielle," 25–68.

52   The exceptions to the general historical consensus on this point are Bourderon, "Le Régime de Vichy"; and Sternhell, *Ni droite ni gauche,* 299–300. Sternhell argues, based on an extremely broad definition of fascism and an overly optimistic view of the national revolution's actual accomplishments, that the Vichy regime, far from being reactionary, was a modern "totalitarian" new order with traditionalist window dressing. Sternhell's analysis is highly problematic and oriented primarily toward the prewar era.

53 On French fascism, see in particular Soucy, *French Fascism,* and "French Fascist Intellectuals," 445–58, as well as his biographies of Maurice Barrès and Drieu La Rochelle; Milza, *Fascismes et idéologies réactionnaires;* Nolte, *The Three Faces of Fascism;* Remond, *La Droite en France;* Sternhell, *La Droite révolutionnaire,* and especially his *Ni droite ni gauche;* Weber, *Action française,* and "Nationalism, Socialism and National-Socialism in France," 273–307. For the conservative right and its evolving relations to the new radical right in the 1930s, see Irvine, *French Conservatism in Crisis.* For the relation between fascism and the Vichy regime, see Ory, *Les Collaborateurs;* Gordon, *Collaborationism;* Kingston, "The Ideologists," in Hirschfeld and Marsh, *Collaboration;* and Cointet-Labrousse, *Vichy et le fascisme.*

54 The traditionalists not only made up the top layer of government leaders, they controlled the press, radio, and propaganda at Vichy, although they did not control the Parisian media. On the continued popularity of Pétain despite the tarnishing of the early mystique, see footnote 32 above and Ferro, *Pétain,* 227–30, 259–61, 466, 545–46.

55 By far the best and most thorough work on Vichy family policy is Pollard, "*Femme, Famille, France.*" See also her article, "Women and the National Revolution," in Kedward and Austin, *Vichy France and the Resistance,* 36–47; and Aline Coutrot, "La Politique familiale," in *Le Gouvernement de Vichy,* 245–62.

56 Paxton, *Vichy France,* 21; Pétain, *Paroles aux français,* 128, 168.

57 On the personnel of Vichy family policy, see Pollard, "*Femme, Famille, France,*" 90–112.

58 Chef de l'état, AN, AG2: 498, "Concours Référendum national sur les causes de la dénatalité française"; Cazin, *Le Travail féminin,* 36.

59 Varenne, *La Femme dans la France nouvelle,* 5, 14.

60 Secrétariat général, AN, F60: 628, 7 March 1941.

61 *Journal officiel,* 27 October 1940.

62 Ibid. Pollard argues that the law embodied Vichy's vision of labor hierarchies in which women's access to employment was mitigated by male workers' needs, with its corollary that all women have a "foyer" in which they belong and to which they could be returned. For the genesis and the outcome of this law, see Pollard, "*Femme, Famille, France,*" 209–59.

63 The law of 4 September 1942 warned all single women between the ages of twenty-one and thirty-five that they "peuvent être assujetties à effectuer tous travaux que le Gouvernement jugera utiles dans l'intérêt supérieur de la nation [can be compelled to carry out any work that the government deems to be in the national interest]." *Journal officiel,* 13 September 1942.

64 Pollard points out the irony that despite its profamily rhetoric, Vichy pro-

gressively demoted the family ministry, which became the Secrétariat d'état à la famille et à la santé, and then was further broken up in September 1940, with the Famille et santé section placed under the Ministère de l'intérieur, effectively demoting family policymakers. In September 1941 the Direction de la famille became the Commissariat général à la famille to raise the profile of family policy. On the structures of Vichy's family politics, see Pollard, "*Femme, Famille, France,*" 79–141.

65   The report of November 1941 on family propaganda achievements lists 150,000 copies of a brochure, "L'Instituteur et son role dans la restauration de la famille française," sent to all public primary school teachers; 25,000 of each of two posters sent to city halls, chambers of commerce, police stations, hospitals, and others; 500 newspapers running the propaganda campaign entitled "Alerte à la Famille," and so on. Chef de l'état, AN, AG2: 459. Pollard concludes that the vigorous family propaganda campaign of the CGF in 1941 was its "most successful public intervention" as well as "one of its more coherent and conspicuous initiatives." Pollard, "*Femme, Famille, France,*" 113.

66   The Commissariat général à la famille held a series of conferences entitled *Propagande "Journée des Mères"*; in 1941 the leaders of all the Chantiers de la jeunesse were sent a "Note relative à la Fête des Mères" with suggestions that the groups do something nice for a mother who lived nearby, recite poems about motherhood around the campfire, and so on. Information, AN, F41: 291.

67   Guerrand, *La Libre Maternité*, 110. During the war several nurses and midwives were given sentences of twenty years to life for performing abortions. The number of convictions increased from 1225 in 1940, which was already double the 1938 figure, to 3701 in 1944. One midwife was executed on 30 July 1943 for performing abortions. Szpiner, *Une Affaire de femmes*, 28.

68   One of the more intriguing puzzles about the Vichy era is not only the increase in the birthrate, from an all-time low of 13.1 births per 1000 in 1941 up to 14.5 births per 1000 in 1942, but its sustained increase through the war. In 1945 it was up to 16.6 per 1000. In other words, the baby boom in France began during the war. Alfred Sauvy credits the increase to family legislation, but other demographers are not so sure, as the birthrate has varied widely under the same family laws. If Vichy legislation did influence the birthrate, I suggest that it did so more by restricting divorce and repressing abortion than by granting family allowances, given the ever-increasing lag of base salaries against inflation during the occupation. An argument for psychological motives could be made in conjunction with some of the other interesting social trends of the occupation years, such as the

drop in suicide rate, slight increase in marriage rate, and 20 percent increase in illegitimacy. See Sauvy, *La Vie économique,* 194–96; Paxton, *Vichy France,* 168; Azéma, *From Munich to the Liberation,* 102, 235 nn. 42, 43.

69 Homze, *Foreign Labor,* 200. Frenay claimed there were 200,000 deportees in Germany; 75,000 were Jewish, of whom 2500 survived. Frenay, *Bilan d'un effort,* 9. Marrus and Paxton, in *Vichy France and the Jews,* 343, also give a figure of 75,000 deported Jews. Azéma gives a figure of 63,000 nonracial deportees together with 75,000 Jews for a total of 138,000 people deported from France. Azéma, *From Munich to the Liberation,* 115.

70 *Documentation à l'usage des responsables,* 39–40; *Journal officiel,* 1 September 1939. The measures were also extended to families of POWs who had not been members of a military formation—men who had been mobilized and were captured while reporting for duty but before actually being incorporated into a unit. Ibid., 12 June 1941.

71 *Documentation à l'usage des responsables,* 59; *Le Temps,* 18 March 1941, 28 August 1942, 18–19 October 1941, 29 February 1942, 1 June 1942, and 2 September 1942.

72 Chef de l'état, AN, AG2: 459, Chevalier, letter of 10 July 1941.

73 In May 1941, a prisoner's wife living in Paris received 5.50 francs a day for the first child; in March 1942 the amount was 10.50.

74 *Journal officiel,* 15 May 1942.

75 Chef de l'état, AN, AG2: 459.

76 Caisses d'allocations familiales, AN, F22: 1536.

77 Secrétariat général, AN, F60: 558, P2Bsd10, 2 July 1941.

78 Centre national d'information, AN, F9: 2828, 30 July 1941.

79 Labor secretary Belin responded to this request with a circular to the caisses d'allocations familiales praising those caisses that had continued voluntarily to pay family allowances to prisoners' wives without salaried jobs, and recommending that the caisses pay higher allowances to salaried prisoners' wives than those to which they were legally entitled, contradicting his earlier order of 18 November 1940 not to pay allowances above the amounts fixed by regulation. Chef de l'état, AN, AG2: 497, 11 August 1941.

80 A parallel and equally futile effort had been instigated in May 1941 by delegations from Dunkirk and Pas de Calais. Their area, which experienced much of the fighting in 1940, suffered from extremely difficult circumstances. They requested an increase in all forms of government assistance, and in particular they wanted military allowances for POW wives raised to the level set for Paris and the Seine (14 francs a day). Darlan approved these suggestions but the minister of finance refused, proposing instead either stricter control of prices and of the border with Belgium to prevent smuggling, supplementary rations, and aid in kind, or soup kitchens pro-

vided by the Secours national. Secrétariat général, AN, F60: 390 D1D9D, 10 October 1941, 6 November 1941.

81   Ibid., F60: 390 D1D9D, 16 December 1941.

82   Ibid., F60: 558 P2Bsd10, 2 January 1942, and 9 June 1942.

83   Schieber, *Un Fléau social*, 61. The law of 24 December 1940 gave official recognition to maisons de tolérance, and prostitution eventually became an authorized commerce incorporated in an organization committee and submitted to state sanitary surveillance to control venereal disease. See Corbin, *Les Filles de noces*, 499–505; Van der Meersch, *Femmes à l'encan*; Schieber, *Un Fléaux social*; and Romi, *Maisons closes*. Vichy policy of toleration toward prostitution seems to contradict its moralism. In fact, as Pollard astutely points out, the traditional gender ideology of masculinity included toleration of unfortunate but unavoidable male "drives." Pollard, *"Femme, Famille, France,"* 319–25. Sweets found a vigorous campaign against prostitution instituted in Clermont-Ferrand which failed owing to lack of police manpower. Sweets, *Choices in Vichy France*, 43.

84   Schieber, *Un Fléau social*, 60.

85   CGPGR, AN, F9: 3093, 7 January 1943.

86   Secrétariat général, AN, F60: 390 D1D9D, 18 December 1941.

87   Ibid., 16 December 1941.

88   Ibid., 18 December 1941.

89   CGPGR, AN, F9: 3027, 29 December 1941, and 21 January 1942.

90   Secrétariat général, AN, F60: 558 P2Bsd10, 2 January 1942.

91   If a prisoner's wife refused to accept the first job offer, her salary would be reduced; the second time, she would lose the salary altogether. Wives without skills could be required to accept apprenticeships in certain industries, with exceptions granted to disabled women or those with three or more children. Working POW wives would continue to receive a reduced POW salary to remove the disincentive of having allowances cut off if they earned a salary. The Secours national proposal was explicitly class based, as the wife's salary depended on her husband's profession, and the work the Secours national expected a prisoner's wife to accept depended on her "standing normal de vie." SDPG, AN, F9: 2326, 20 May 1942.

92   Secrétariat général, AN, F60: 558 P2Bsd10.

93   Ibid., Conférence, 9 June 1942.

94   Ibid.

95   *Journal officiel*, 25 July 1942.

96   CGPGR, AN, F9: 3025, 1.1, 25 February 1943; ibid., 25 February 1943; ibid., 1.1, 25 February 1943.

97   Chef de l'état, AN, AG2: 608 cm23, 15 December 1943; cm24, 14 April 1944.

98   CGPGR, AN, F9: 3025, 1.1, 4 May 1943; SN, *Bulletin de liaison,* 17: 4; CGPGR, AN, F9: 3025, 4 June 1943; *Guide pratique,* 31; CGPGR, AN, F9: 3025, 30 March 1944; Marwick, *War and Social Change,* 193; Sauvy, *La Vie économique,* 165–66.

99   France paid Germany a total of 631,866 million francs. Paxton, *Vichy France,* 53, 144.

100   Kedward, "The Vichy of the Other Philippe," in Hirschberg and Marsh, *Collaboration in France,* 34.

CHAPTER 4: THE DAILY LIFE OF PRISONER OF WAR WIVES

1   Gilbert, "Soldier's Heart," 447.

2   Chef de l'état, AN, AG2: 608, cm23b, 14 November 1943.

3   "Le Journal de Laure," Deroy and Pineau, *Celles qui attendaient,* 59.

4   Madeleine Cazin reports that female salaries were 60 to 80 percent lower than male salaries. Cazin, *Le Travail féminin,* 14.

5   Thirteenth arrondissement and Vitry-sur-Seine. Secrétariat général, AN, F60: 390, D1D9D.

6   In my group, 55 percent worked for wages, as did 59 percent of the 1943 group. The 1936 female employment rate was 30.5 percent; in 1946 it was 32 percent. Carré, Dubois, and Malinvaud, *French Economic Growth,* 49.

7   Questionnaire from Agnès Minot, 1985; interview with Fernande Damart, conducted by Madeleine Blaire, December 1985. Interestingly, although all twelve of the farmers' wives in my group continued to run their family farms, many of them responded as Gabrielle Coadelot did to the question, "Did you work outside the home?" "No, work on the farm" (questionnaire from Coadelot, 1985).

8   Questionnaire from Nicolle Bouchard, 1985.

9   Questionnaires from Monique Peletier and Francine Louvet, both 1985.

10   Interview with Estelle Sergent, 28 June 1985.

11   Interview with Anne Devron, 10 June 1985.

12   *Femmes de prisonniers,* "Pour Notre Dignité."

13   Prices taken from *S.O.S. des familles ouvrières,* 12. Black market prices were much higher: bread, for example, officially 3.7 francs, could cost as much as 13 francs in early 1944. Chef de l'état, AN, AG2: 612, cm29B.

14   Chef de l'état, AN, AG2: 612 cm29B, Comité d'organisation de l'industrie textile, 25 August 1943. The Geneva Convention of 1929 stipulated that the German army provide food and clothing equal to what its own soldiers received, but this rarely happened. Durand, *La Captivité,* 200.

15   *Femmes de prisonniers,* "Pour notre dignité." Twenty percent of the wives

reported costs of 150–300 francs a month; 80 percent spent 400 francs a month.

16   CGPGR, AN, F9: 3027, 20 January 1942. The Organisation d'hygiène of the League of Nations in 1936 estimated that adults need 2,400 to 2,800 calories a day. *Renseignements généraux,* 7–8. The bread ration in 1942 was 1,925 grams a week; meat ranged from 125 to 180 grams a week. Marwick, *War and Social Change,* 193; Amouroux, *La Vie des français,* 131–51.

17   Questionnaire from Catherine Michel, 1985; letter from Jeanne Capel, 4 October 1985.

18   *Femmes d'absents,* 43; questionnaire from Martine Lombardi, 1985; *Marie-Claire,* 10 May 1943.

19   "Moi qui aime à être assez élégante, je ne peux plus l'être," *Pour elle* 18 (December 11, 1940): 26.

20   Interview with Germaine Doucet, 20 November 1984. On fashion during the war, see Dominique Veillon's excellent book, *La Mode sous l'occupation.* Veillon points out, "Le vêtement comme révélateur d'identité peut devenir celui d'une approbation comme d'une résistance. En ce cas, la mode dépasse son cadre ... elle est façon d'être dans l'air du temps subi ou approuvé. Parfois synonyme de courage, elle est aussi le sursaut d'une dignité blessé qui ne veut pas abdiquer. . . . En certains cas, la coquetterie s'avère une arme psychologique efficace contre les agressions extérieures [Clothing, as something that reveals identity, can be a statement of approval or of resistance. In this case, fashion goes beyond its limits ... it is a way of being in an atmosphere submitted to or approved. At times, synonym of courage, it is also a leap of wounded dignity refusing to abdicate. . . . In some cases, stylishness proves to be an effective psychological weapon]." P. 8.

21   Pierre Join-Lambert Papers, BDIC, uncataloged; Commission des prisonniers agricoles, Ministère de l'agriculture, 1ᵉʳ sous-commission des prisonniers, 8 February 1943; questionnaire from Dominique Filasto, 1985.

22   Letter from Hélène Noiret, 30 July 1985; Chef de l'état, AN, AG2: 608.

23   Six to eight million quintals of grain annually by 1944, and 135,000 to 270,000 tons of meat annually. Paxton, *Vichy France,* 144.

24   Letter from Hélène Noiret, 30 July 1985.

25   Pierre Join-Lambert Papers, BDIC, uncataloged, Ministère de l'agriculture, "Les Prisonniers agriculteurs et leurs familles, Compte-rendu d'activité de la Commission de prisonniers agricoles et des familles des prisonniers agricoles," 1942; Corporation paysanne, "La Situation des familles d'agriculteurs prisonniers," 12 February 1943, p. 4; Ministère de l'agriculture, "Annexe, Compte-rendu des travaux de la Commission des prisonniers agricoles et des Familles des Prisonniers Agricoles," n.d.

26 Paxton, *Vichy France,* 201–09.

27 Laws of 9 June 1941 and 1 August 1942, *Journal officiel.*

28 Join-Lambert Papers, Corporation paysanne, "La Situation des familles d'a-griculteurs prisonniers," 12 February 1943, p. 5; ibid., "Réunion du 11 janvier 1943," 11 January 1943, p. 10.

29 Ibid., "Réunion du 11 janvier 1943," 11 January 1943, p. 5; ibid. "La Situation des familles d'agriculteurs prisonniers," 12 February 1943, p. 2.

30 See Laurence Wylie for a discussion of the term *fatigué,* which the French use rather than *malade.* Wylie, *Village in the Vaucluse,* 187–88.

31 Juillet and Moutin, *Psychiatre militaire*; Lewin, *Le Retour des prisonniers,* 67–70; Segal, Hunter, and Segal, "Universal Consequences of Captivity," 594–97.

32 *Femmes d'absents,* 54; questionnaires from Martine Lombardi and Odette Bondois, both 1985.

33 Questionnaires from Louise Cadieu, Camille Cassan, Josette Lorin, and Nicolle Bouchard, all 1985. A prisoner's mother wrote to the government during the war, "I know that my son is ill. He has not written this to me, but for a long time I have understood it." Secrétariat général, AN, F60: 558 P2Bsd10, *Pour nos prisonniers: Conseils et renseignements extraits de la revue Radio nationale,* 2.

34 Questionnaire from Madeleine Capot, 1985.

35 *Femmes d'absents,* 34. Isabelle Dreux used the word *ennui.* Questionnaires from Anne-Marie Perrin, Isabelle Dreux, and Nicolle Bouchard, all 1985.

36 Questionnaires from Stéphanie Thibault and Agnès Minot, both 1985.

37 *Femmes d'absents,* 54; questionnaire from Sylvie Crouet, 1985; letter from Marthe Jolliet, 5 August 1985; questionnaire from Lucette Nauman, 1985; Chef de l'état, AN, AG2: 608.

38 Deroy, *Celles qui attendaient,* 33 and 28.

39 Questionnaire from Sarah Lisik, 1985; interview with Annick Kasmer, 25 March 1985; questionnaire from Monique Becht, 1985.

40 Interview with Marie-Louise Mercier, January 1985.

41 Interviews with Michelle Dupuy, Patricia Longet, Arièle Chevalier, and Suzette Emile, 8 June 1985.

42 Questionnaire from Catherine Michel, 1985.

43 Ambrière, *Les Grandes Vacances,* 84.

44 Interview with Raymond and Germaine Doucet, 20 November 1984; interview with Jean and Elisabeth Doremus, conducted by Madeleine Blaire, December 1985. The Germans probably understood the double meaning of "no writing between the lines." Interview with Florence Morin, 17 June 1985.

45   Interviews with Raymonde Moulin, 23 March 1985, and Anne Devron, 10 June 1985.
46   Letter from Jeanne Capel, 4 October 1985.
47   Both Jacqueline Ariel and Patricia Longet mention this.
48   Interviews with Jean and Elisabeth Doremus, conducted by Madeleine Blaire, December 1985; interview with Michelle Dupuy, 8 June 1985.
49   Deroy and Pineau, *Celles qui attendaient,* 33; conversation with Roger Ariel, 10 April 1985.
50   Interview with Jean and Elisabeth Doremus, conducted by Madeleine Blaire, December 1985; letter from Christiane Motte, 3 August 1985; interview with Jacqueline Ariel, April 1985.
51   Interview with Jean and Elisabeth Doremus, conducted by Madeleine Blaire, December 1985; letter from Christiane Motte, 3 August 1985; *Lettre aux femmes et mamans de prisonniers,* "La Visite de Mme Aulas au Maréchal," March 1942.
52   Interviews with Raymonde Moulin, 23 March 1985, and Patricia Longet, 8 June 1985.
53   Ambrière, *Les Grandes Vacances,* 85.
54   Cited by Bellanger and Debouzy, *La Presse des barbelés,* 70.
55   "C'est curieux, mais il y avait une grande pudeur de ce côté là. . . . On était déluré, mal poli, grossier, mal élevé comme on peut l'être . . . mais il y avait un autre côté pudique. . . . Jamais je n'ai vu quoi que ce soit à l'époque qui pourrait faire douter de la bonne tenue. *Jamais.*" Interview with Raymond Doucet, 20 November 1984.
56   René Dubois, cited in Bellanger and Debouzy, *La Presse des barbelés,* 70.
57   Interview with Elisabeth Doremus, conducted by Madeleine Blaire, December 1985; Deroy and Pineau, *Celles qui attendaient,* 14; interview with Estelle Sergent, 28 June 1985.
58   "Il fallait se défendre pour rester digne et fidèle." Letter from Madeleine Capot, 24 August 1985.
59   Interview with Yvette Giraud, 4 November 1984.
60   *Femmes d'absents,* 38, 63–64; Deroy and Pineau, *Celles qui attendaient,* 34.
61   Interview with Fernande Damart, conducted by Madeleine Blaire, December 1985.
62   Interview with Patricia Longet, 8 June 1985; *Femmes d'absents,* 60; *Avec lui, entre nous* 14, n.p.
63   Deroy and Pineau, *Celles qui attendaient,* 15; *Femmes d'absents,* 38; questionnaire from Catherine Michel, 1985; interview with Gisèle Desbois, 21 March 1985; *Femmes d'absents,* 24.

64 Deroy and Pineau, *Celles qui attendaient,* 34; *Femmes d'absents,* 23, 20; questionnaire from Nicolle Bouchard, 1985.

65 Questionnaires from Martine Lombardi, Dominique Filasto, and Francine Louvet, all 1985; interview with Anne Devron, 10 June 1985; questionnaire from Annette Regnier, 1985. She believes the disturbances were brought on because she used to bring him to Resistance meetings and because her town suffered heavy bombing.

66 "L'autorité désirable me manque." *Femmes d'absents,* 22; Chef de l'état, AN, AG2: 608, cm23, 16 January 1944; *Femmes d'absents,* 35.

67 *Femmes d'absents,* 20. Another wife wrote, "C'est toujours ma fille aînée qui me donne le plus de mal. Elle est d'une nature volontaire, désobéissante, indomptable. L'absence de son papa lui a été très préjudiciable en ce sens qu'elle le craignait plus que moi [It is always my oldest daughter who gives me the most trouble. She has a headstrong, disobedient, uncontrollable character. Her father's absence has been very detrimental to her in the sense that she feared him more than me]." Ibid., 35.

68 Questionnaire from Sylvie Crouet, 1985; interview with Jean and Elisabeth Doremus, conducted by Madeleine Blaire, December 1985; interview with Estelle Sergent, 28 June 1985; questionnaire from Sarah Lisik, 1985.

69 "C'est là papa, ça maman?" Interview with Anne Devron, 10 June 1985.

70 *Femmes d'absents,* 32; interview with Fernande Damart, conducted by Madeleine Blaire, December 1985.

71 Interview with Michelle Dupuy, 8 June 1985.

72 Chef de l'état, AN, AG2: 608, cm23, December 1943; cm23, 26 December 1943; cm24, 9 March 1944; cm23, 1 January 1944.

73 Questionnaires from Nicolle Bouchard and Gilberte Voisin, both 1985.

74 Deroy and Pineau, *Celles qui attendaient,* 23; letter from Jeanne Capel, 4 October 1985; interview with Raymonde Moulin, 23 March 1985.

75 Interview with Raymonde Moulin, 23 March 1985; *Femmes d'absents,* 19.

76 This testimony concludes that society "se moque royalement des femmes de prisonniers [doesn't give a royal damn about prisoners' wives]." *Femmes d'absents,* 56.

77 Interviews with Raymonde Moulin, 23 March 1985, and Anne Devron, 10 June 1985.

78 Interview with Michelle Dupuy, 8 June 1985; letter from Hélène Noiret, 30 July 1985; interview with Fernande Damart, conducted by Madeleine Blaire, December 1985. John Sweets also found evidence in the provincial archives of public surveillance of prisoners' wives. Sweets, letter to author, 28 June 1990.

79 Interview with Raymonde Moulin, 23 March 1985; "J'avais l'impression d'être une fille mère. . . . On ne me recevait pas quand on recevait les

ménages." Interview with Estelle Sergent, 28 June 1985. American wives of prisoners in Vietnam experienced something remarkably similar: "They were politely dropped from the military's informal social rolls. . . . Other wives considered them 'on the prowl.' Any social contact with an adult man was viewed with suspicion." Hall and Simmons, "The POW Wife," 693.

80   Interview with Patricia Longet, 8 June 1985. Nineteen of the prisoners' wives in my group were members of either an Association des femmes de prisonniers (nine) or some other more or less formal, POW-related group.

81   Interview with Gisèle Desbois, 21 March 1985.

82   *Femmes de prisonniers,* "Notre libération . . . et la leur?" 1.

CHAPTER 5: POWER, CLASS, AND GENDER

1   CGPGR, AN, F9: 3027, 4 October 1941.

2   In addition to archival information about the Famille du prisonnier, the agency's monthly internal bulletin for its delegates and social workers includes directives, articles explaining its aims and policies, helpful suggestions, examples of what could be done, and reprints of relevant laws and agreements with other groups. In November 1943, the Famille held a national congress in Limoges with speeches by each of the national leaders of the Famille du prisonnier, the SN, and leaders of other organizations such as the Red Cross. The booklet contains the speeches and resolutions of the congress and summarizes the open discussion.

3   SN, *Premier Congrès,* 12.

4   SN, *Bulletin de liaison* 1:1.

5   John W. Bennet, "Paternalism," in *International Encyclopedia of Social Science,* ed. David L. Sills, vol. 11 (MacMillan, 1968), 472–76.

6   Dubreuil, *A l'image de la mère,* 1–8, 15–18, 36, 28.

7   SN, *Bulletin de liaison* 2:3.

8   SN, *Premier Congrès,* 41, 42.

9   SN, *Bulletin de liaison* 27:2.

10   Ibid., 29:2.

11   Ibid., 22:2.

12   *Salon du prisonnier,* 53.

13   "C'est à nous peut-être plus encore qu'aux femmes et aux mères, qu'il appartient d'essayer de remplacer le père absent." SN, *Premier Congrès,* 15.

14   SN, *Bulletin de liaison* 7:1.

15   SN, *Premier Congrès,* 5, 14.

16   According to Edmond Goblot, a wife who does not work outside the home is part of the very definition of being bourgeois. Goblot, *La Barrière et le niveau,* 34–35.

17 SN, *Bulletin de liaison* 5:3.

18 Centre national d'information, AN, F9: 2811, 10 October 1941; SN, *Bulletin de liaison* 3:1; CGPGR, AN, F9: 3027, 28 August 1941; SN, *Bulletin de liaison* 1:1.

19 CGPGR, AN, F9: 3027, 1 October 1942; SN, *Premier Congrès*, 14.

20 SN, *Bulletin de liaison* 7:1. In its defense, the Famille du prisonnier would not countenance using its funds to make up for underpaying POW wives in other workplaces. It fired one delegate after discovering that she used Famille du prisonnier funds to appease the salary demands of POW wives who worked in her husband's factory. Ibid. 27:1.

21 SN, *Premier Congrès*, 5; *L'Illustration*, 25 September 1943; SN, *Bulletin de liaison* 5:1, 2.

22 Secrétariat général, AN, F60: 558, P2Bsd10, "Etude No. 5, Préparation du Retour des Prisonniers," Comité d'etudes pour la France, November 1940.

23 Law of 23 September 1941, *Journal officiel*; CGPGR, AN, F9: 3027, 12 September 1942.

24 *Le Temps*, 19 February 1942.

25 Ministère de la population, Secrétariat général des prisonniers, déportés et refugiés, *Dispositions*, 9–46.

26 "Témoignage de Maurice Pinot," in Vedrine, *Dossier*, 2:625; law of 20 July 1942, *Journal officiel*.

27 Pinot claims he went to the SN to avoid asking Vichy for money. "Témoignage de Maurice Pinot," in Vedrine, *Dossier*, 2:629: CGPGR, AN, F9: 3027, 5 December 1941; SN, Circular, 31 December 1941. After the liberation of France, the Maisons became Maisons du prisonnier et du déporté. Ministère des prisonniers, déportés et réfugiés, *Bilan d'un effort*, 66.

28 The legion from the start had been frustrated by its inability to attract many "1939–40" veterans. It undertook many activities for the prisoners, sponsoring fund raisers and sending packages to the prison camps, and had no desire to see a rival organization siphon off repatriated POWs. See Sweets, *Choices in Vichy France*, 67, 69. The legion hoped to control the Maisons, but Pinot managed to hold it off. "Témoignage de Maurice Pinot," in Vedrine, *Dossier*, 2:631.

29 CGPGR, AN, F9: 3028, 6 July 1942.

30 In the entry of a Maison du prisonnier hung this inscription: "Le Maréchal s'efforce d'adoucir les rigeurs de leur sort et hâter leur retour, mais, en attendant, il faut que cette Maison du Prisonnier soit aussi la vôtre [The Marshall is doing his best to ease the rigors of their fate and to hasten their return but, meanwhile, this Maison du prisonnier must also be your home]." *L'Illustration*, 31 July 1943, 80.

31 CGPGR, AN, F9: 3025, 14 April 1943; F9: 3028, 15 April 1943.

32 There were complaints from the Maison director in Nevers and the directors in Carcasonne, Toulouse, and Poitiers. Ibid., F9: 3028, 25 June 1943; F9 3034, 19 October 1943.

33 SN, *Premier Congrès*, 31.

34 "La Famille du Prisonnier," in Vedrine, *Dossier*, 1:175; CGPGR, AN, F9: 3028, 8 October 1942.

35 SN, *Premier Congrès*, 22, speech by Jean-Pierre Maxence, director, Social Services, CGPGR.

36 The departmental delegate from Chalons-sur-Marne, though not foreseeing any problems with having members of the CEA visit newly liberated POWs, objected to having them visit wives, "and you must understand why." CGPGR, AN, F9: 3028, 28 September 1942.

37 SN, *Bulletin de liaison* 6:1; CGPGR, AN, F9: 3028, 20 July 1943.

38 Dominique Veillon's insight helped me understand what was at stake.

39 CGPGR, AN, F9: 3028, 20 July 1943 and 25 August 1942.

40 *Journal officiel*, 24 November 1941 and 20 July 1942.

41 Secrétariat général, AN, F60: 558 P2Bsd10, 27 October 1942.

42 CGPGR, AN, F9: 3027, 18 November 1942 and 12 December 1942. The CGPGR disliked the widespread use of POWs as a fund-raising theme. They complained that often POWs were used to "dissimuler sous les apparences de manifestation de charité . . . des entreprises commerciales [conceal commercial enterprises under the facade of . . . manifestations of charity]." Gouvernement provisoire, AN, F1A: 3680, circular no. 169, 6 August 1942. The SDPG added its voice to these complaints; most of the galas, concerts, and sports events for the POWs seemed to be an "excuse for festivities." Secrétariat général, an, F60: 558 P2Bsd10, 13 June 1942.

43 CGPGR, AN, F9: 3028, 18 June 1942.

44 The Famille du prisonnier stated as a proviso that if a CEA had its own funds, it still had to consult the Famille du prisonnier before giving away money. SN, *Bulletin de liaison* 10:2; CGPGR, AN, F9: 3027, 3 November 1942. Exceptionally, a CEA could organize its own fund raiser, but only to make up for the insufficiency of a particular local charity and only if it had the approval of the departmental Commission des manifestations. A local SN representative was to be informed of all money given to families deemed needy. CGPGR, AN, F9: 3034, 18 February 1943.

45 Ibid., F9: 3028, 1 July 1943 and 10 September 1943; DSPG, AN, F9: 2828, 6 October 1943.

46 CGPGR, AN, F9: 3025, 16 October 1943.

47 SN, *Premier Congrès*, 19.

48 When the Maisons were transformed, the SN complained, probably accu-

rately, that "la réforme ait pour objet d'assurer la direction totale de l'activité sociale, aussi bien du Secours National que des oeuvres privées [the aim of the reform was to take over entirely the direction of all social activity, that of the Secours national as well as of private charities]." CGPGR, AN, F9: 3027, September 1942.

49   SN, *Premier Congrès,* 3.

50   CGPGR, AN, F9: 3027, 17 September 1942, F9: 3028, 19 June 1943, F9: 3025, 26 June 1944.

51   *Le Temps,* 19 October 1942; SN, *Premier Congrès,* 1.

52   Forty years later Pinot claimed, "Les références au Maréchal relevaient du rituel sans importance [the references to the Marshall fall under the category of unimportant ritual]" and that it would have been impossible to avoid statements which risked becoming Vichy propaganda. In retrospect he realized he had not avoided that trap. After the war, Pinot claimed that he personally disapproved of granting full powers to Pétain and even of the existence of the Vichy government and its policies. Yet he asserted, "il est méprisable de traiter en bouc emissaire le vieillard notoirement diminué. . . . Entre les mains de Laval, le Maréchal n'était qu'un mythe [it is despicable to treat the notably diminished old man as a scapegoat. . . . In Laval's hands, the Marshall was nothing more than a myth]." "Témoignage de Maurice Pinot," in Vedrine, *Dossier,* 2:728, 727. Pinot also stated, "Leur [POWs] retour est un problème de politique générale. Il dépend donc du comportement de ce pays devant la défaite et ses conséquences [their return is a problem of general policy. It thus depends on the behavior of our country in the face of the defeat and its consequences]." Pinot, "Appel aux rapatriés," in *Salon du Prisonnier,* 7.

53   "Témoignage de Maurice Pinot," in Vedrine, *Dossier,* 2:676–78.

54   Ibid., 678. Whether he was one of the four POWs liberated for a "propaganda mission" is unclear. (See chap. 3, table 3.1.)

55   Durand, *La Captivité,* 347–48. "Feuille dactylographiée remise à Scapini par des Prisonniers de guerre français," 28 January 1943, BDIC Q. Pièce 723 Res.

56   Commissariat aux prisonniers, AN, F9: 3116, 29 November 1943.

57   Currently president of the Republic, Mitterrand was a POW. On his third attempt he escaped from prison camp and returned to France on 24 December 1941. He worked for the CGPGR until Pinot left, and then joined the Resistance. In November 1943 he traveled to London to contact the Free French, where he and de Gaulle took an instant dislike to each other. On POW resistance, see Durand, *La Captivité,* 382–83; Lewin, *Le Retour des prisonniers,* 37–57; and Bugeaud, *Militant Prisonnier de guerre,* 36–48. Uniting the Pin-Mitt group and the Gaullist and Communist POW

groups took some work, given the friction that persists to this day in the repatriated POW community. During the war, a common enemy pulled them together; since the war a common sense of needing to protect their interests has kept tensions at bay.

58   *L'Illustration,* 3 July 1943; Hulot, "Le Mouvement 'Prisonnier,'" *L'Illustration,* 3 July 1943; *Le Mouvement prisonnier,* n.p.; Commissariat aux prisonniers, AN, F9: 3105, 28 January 1943.

59   CGPGR, AN, F9: 3092, 5 April 1943.

60   SN, *Premier Congrès,* 31. Union members did visit homes and hospitals, raise money for POWs, distribute toys to children, and help families obtain clothing for returning POWs. The union had some success attracting members in Paris and the north, especially after May 1944 when it cut its affiliation from the Mouvement "Prisonniers" and joined the CEAS as the Centres d'entr'aide féminins (CEAF). CGPGR, AN, F9: 3092, 5 August 1944.

61   CGPGR, AN, F9: 3034, 20 February 1943, F9: 3034, 27 February 1943.

62   Ibid., F9: 3034, 27 February 1943, F9: 3025, 14 October 1943.

63   Ibid., F9: 3028, 2 August 1943.

64   Ibid., F9: 3025, 4 March 1944; Commissariat aux prisonniers, AN, F9: 3105, 8 January 1944.

65   Commissariat aux prisonniers, AN, F9: 3116, 29 November 1943; SN, *Premier Congrès,* 22.

66   SN, *Premier Congrès,* 8. That loyalty to Pétain was not considered a political position reveals that the Famille had not learned the lesson of the CGPGR.

67   CGPGR, AN, F9: 3028, 13 March 1942. The CGPGR responded that it was putting together just such a brochure for returning POWs. Ibid., 20 March 1942.

68   Ibid., 29 March and 15 June 1943.

CHAPTER 6: PRISONERS' WIVES UNITED

1   FAFP, *Compte-Rendu des associations,* 3.

2   Ibid., 2; Andrée Aulas, "Rapport," in FAFP, *Journeée des présidentes; Femmes de prisonniers,* "Notre Combat."

3   Aulas, "Les Débuts d'une Association de femmes de prisonniers, Roanne, Octobre 1940," in Vedrine, *Dossier,* 1:182; FAFP, "But des associations," 3; Jean Vedrine, Papers, Mini-dossier, "Femmes de prisonniers," BDIC; Interview with Andrée Aulas, 10 April 1985.

4   Interview with Andrée Aulas, 10 April 1985.

5   Interview with Agnès Griot, 3 May 1985.

6   *Femmes d'absents, Causerie,* 8; interviews with Andrée Aulas, 10 April 1985, Estelle Sergent, 28 June 1985, Anne Devron, 10 June 1985, and

Raymonde Moulin, 23 March 1985; "Pour les familles de prisonniers et les prisonniers libérés," in *La Spiritualité des prisonniers,* 6.

7   *Femmes d'absents, Causerie,* 8.

8   Suzanne LaPierre, "L'Esprit des Associations," in FAFP, *Compte-Rendu des associations,* 4; FAFP, "But des associations," 1.

9   *Femmes d'absents,* "Fêtes et Saisons," 18. Although "Fêtes et Saisons" is a series published by Les Editions du cerf, I will refer to this paper throughout as *Femmes d'absents,* "Fêtes et Saisons" to differentiate it from other works with similar titles.

10   "Entre nous, Par nous, Pour nous." The similarity to the close of Lincoln's Gettysburg address was, according to Aulas, purely accidental. *Femmes de prisonniers, Vos Associations vous attendent,* n.p.

11   FAFP, *Compte-Rendu des associations,* 2; FAFP, "But des Associations," 5.

12   *Compte-Rendu des associations,* 5.

13   "La note 'foyer.'" FAFP, Griot, "Responsables."

14   *Lettre aux femmes et mamans de prisonniers,* "La Visite de Madame Aulas au Maréchal," March 1942, 2; "Que font-ils de leurs loisirs?" *Femmes de prisonniers,* "Loisirs 44."

15   Griot, "Le Rôle de la présidente," in FAFP, *Journée des présidentes.* "Qu'est-ce qu'être responsable? Une responsable, c'est celle qui répond de quelque chose." FAFP, Griot, "Responsables."

16   See Hoffmann, "Paradoxes," 11–12.

17   "En route," *Page des responsables,* n.p.; Griot, in FAFP, *Journée des présidentes.*

18   FAFP, *Compte-Rendu des associations,* 2.

19   FAFP, *Journée des présidentes;* "Le don de soi," *Page des Responsables,* n.p.

20   Aulas, "Rapport," in FAFP, *Journeée des présidentes.*

21   FAFP, *Compte-Rendu des associations,* 7, 4.

22   "Nous les voulons toutes . . . les chics, les moins chics, celles qui ont fait une bêtise, celles qui se sont compromises, celles qui ont abandonné leurs petits. . . . Les envieuses, les aigries, les égoistes, celles qui ont perdu toute espèce de goût, les plus misérables, les malpropres, les negligées." FAFP, *Compte-Rendu des associations,* 5.

23   Ibid., 7; *Femmes d'absents, Causerie,* 12–13.

24   Interview with Agnès Griot, 3 May 1985. "Pour nous, aider à enrichir notre journal, écrivez-nous . . . Merci!" appeared in one of the papers. *Femmes de prisonniers, Lettre de la FAFP,* "Fidèles!"

25   Given the apolitical nature of the subject matter, the regional censor in Lyons rarely removed anything from the articles (for example, the exact location of a factory where POWs worked). The federation had time on the national radio, although I found no trace of those broadcasts.

26   *Lettre aux femmes et mamans de prisonniers,* 25 September 1941; Andrée Aulas, in FAFP, *Journée des présidentes.*

27   "Le don de soi," *Page des responsables,* n.p.

28   Ibid.; "Pour préparer le retour," *Page des responsables,* May 1944, n.p.

29   "Pour préparer le retour," *Page des responsables,* May 1944, n.p. Joseph Folliet, "Le droit de vivre," *Femmes de prisonniers,* "Loisirs 44."

30   "Pour préparer le retour," *Page des responsables,* May 1944, n.p.

31   Folliet, "Le droit de vivre," *Femmes de prisonniers,* "Loisirs 44"; "Pour préparer le retour," *Page des responsables,* May 1944, n.p.

32   Folliet, "Le droit de vivre," *Femmes de prisonniers,* "Loisirs 44."

33   "Que font-ils de leurs loisirs?" *Femmes de prisonniers,* "Loisirs 44."

34   *Compte-Rendu des associations,* 6.

35   Ibid., 4.

36   *Femmes de prisonniers,* "il y a d'autres souffrances."

37   *Entr'aide fraternelle, Les Associations de femmes de prisonniers,* 1941, 4.

38   DSPG, AN, F9: 2962, 9 March and 19 March 1941.

39   Ibid., 16 December 1940; *Journal officiel,* 23 May 1941. In August 1943, the director of the Centres d'entr'aide again suggested a special ration card for POW families. The CGPGR responded that it was negotiating for such a card. CGPGR, AN, F9: 3035, 19 August 1943.

40   "La Gerbe de leurs lettres," *Femmes de Prisonniers,* "Mon Amie de captivité."

41   Interview with Andrée Aulas, 10 April 1985; *Lettre aux femmes et mamans de prisonniers,* "La Visite de Madame Aulas au Maréchal," March 1942. In addition to addressing the issue of packages, the federation helped obtain an exemption for POW wives to the labor requisition law in 1944.

42   FAFP, "But des associations," 3.

43   *Lettre aux femmes et mamans de prisonniers,* "La Visite de Madame Aulas au Maréchal," March 1942.

44   FAFP, *Compte-Rendu des associations,* 2.

45   *Femmes de prisonniers,* "Pour notre dignité, nous revendiquons," 1.

46   Ibid., p. 1.

47   Interview with Jeanne Bajeux, 29 May 1985.

48   Institut d'histoire du temps présent, *Répertoire des archives centrales; Culture et liberté,* 17; MPF, *Travaux-1943,* 93.

49   The division led to the postwar power shift within the MPF, when resistance members took over from those leaders discredited by their links with Vichy. "Les Mouvements familiaux," 44–46.

50   Ibid., 37.

51   Interview with Agnès Griot, 3 May 1985.

52 Geneviève Dermenjian, "La Mixité et ses implications dans le Mouvement populaire des familles 1935–1949," *Pénélope* 11 (Autumn 1984): 47–52.

53 "Pris les habitudes de militant." Interview with Andrée Aulas, 10 April 1985.

54 Mazioux, *Entre vos mains,* 90.

55 FAFP, *Compte-Rendu des associations,* 4; Mazioux, *Entre vous mains,* 90.

56 Celebrating these holidays in France did not necessarily indicate deeply felt Christian beliefs. Laurence Wylie found that the people in the village he studied "go to Midnight Mass as they go to Prize Day exercises at the school." Wylie, *Village in the Vaucluse,* 284.

57 Agnès Fargeix, "Mon Amie de captivité," *Femmes de prisonniers,* "Mon Amie de captivité," 1.

58 FAFP, *Compte-Rendu des associations,* 5.

59 Join-Lambert, "Les Groupements de femmes de prisonniers," 1944, p. 1, Jean Vedrine Papers, BDIC.

60 Ibid.

61 FAFP, *Compte-Rendu des associations,* 5.

62 Ibid.; interviews with Andrée Aulas, 10 April 1985, and Michelle Dupuy, 8 June 1985.

63 Simone Demargne, in FAFP, *Journée des présidentes.*

64 As a result, officers in Oflags and the 5 percent of the regular troops who remained in the Stalags founded camp universities with lectures, study groups, language classes, and orchestras.

65 FAFP, *Journée des présidentes.*

66 Marie-Louise Sévénier, "L'Association, c'est une amitié!" *Femmes de prisonniers,* "Mon Amie de captivité," 8.

67 Join-Lambert's wife, Jacqueline, was a member of *Femmes d'absents,* which explains his awareness of both groups and their different class backgrounds —more pronounced in Paris than in the rest of France. Interview with Jacqueline Join-Lambert, 16 March 1985.

68 FAFP, *Compte-Rendu des associations,* 2. Simone Demargne, "Conclusions générales," in FAFP, *Journée des présidentes.*

69 FAFP, "But des associations," 2.

70 Although the federation stressed similarly the need for regeneration and restoration of traditional family and religious values, it never took part in the national self-castigation about the defeat—a sensitive area for the wives of the very soldiers defeated in the field.

71 *Lettre aux femmes et mamans de prisonniers,* "La Visite de Madame Aulas au Maréchal," March 1942.

72 "Il faisait vraiment vieillard; Il n'avait peut-être pas été mal dans son temps,

mais . . . il n'était plus lui-même." Interview with Andrée Aulas, 10 April 1985.

73 "Je n'ai pas du tout l'impression que c'est un grand Chef d'Etat qui vient de me recevoir." *Lettre aux femmes et mamans de prisonniers*, "La Visite de Madame Aulas au Maréchal," March 1942. Juxtaposing the 1985 interview with the 1942 public record reveals a certain ambiguity and possible double meaning in her 1942 article. Whether it was intended at the time cannot be known. Her testimony is one of the few that I could check against written sources from the war, and the accuracy of her memory for specific detail was astonishing. President Mitterrand recently awarded Aulas a medal for her wartime role as president of the federation.

74 FAFP, "But des associations," 3; Simone Demargne, "Conclusions générales," in FAFP, *Journée des présidentes*.

75 "La Légion doit être en quelque sorte la protectrice des familles de prisonniers." Secrétariat général, AN, F60: 558 P2Bsd10, 30 July 1941.

76 Interview with Andrée Aulas, 10 April 1985; FAFP, *Compte-Rendu des associations*, 4.

77 Interview with Michelle Dupuy, Patricia Longet, Suzette Emile, and Arièle Chevalier, 8 June 1985.

78 Commissariat aux prisonniers, AN, F9: 3116, 29 November 1943; *Un de la Résistance*.

79 *Lettre aux femmes et mamans de prisonniers*, 25 September 1941.

80 The Oflag-Stalag segregation divided men along class lines; many POWs worked in isolation, returning to the camp for a few days only before being sent on new labor detachments; Jewish POWs lived in separate barracks, and so on.

81 Jean Vedrine and G. Saurel, "Rectificatif à l'instruction commune no. 2 concernant les F. de P.G.," Paris, 26 December 1944, Jean Vedrine Papers, BDIC.

82 The recent book *Celles qui attendaient . . . témoignent aujourd'hui*, by Jacqueline Deroy and Françoise Pineau, is the exception. Durand's book, in other ways remarkably comprehensive, includes a discussion of prisoners' wives but does not mention the federation. See Durand, *La Captivité*, 228–32.

CHAPTER 7: WAITING WIVES

1 Claire Droze and Line Droze, "Après trois ans d'absence," *Dimanches de la femme* 301 (November 15, 1943): 6.

2 Aymé, *The Transient Hour*, 32. In 1959 Michel Boisrond directed a film based on the book, then in its 112th printing. Aymé, *Le Chemin des écoliers*.

3 Roche, *La Guerre des captives*. Note that the name Madeleine derives from Magdalen.

4 Père Villain, "La famille," *Manuel d'éducation civique*, 36, Chef de l'état, AN, AG2: 27; Equipes et cadres de la France nouvelle, *Appui mutuel des époux; Chef du foyer, aux jeunes gens*.

5 Père Villain, "La famille," *Manuel d'éducation civique*, Chef de l'état, AN, AG2: 27, 36; *Sauvons nos foyers!* 8; *La famille que nous voulons*, 58; *Gardienne du foyer, aux jeunnes filles*.

6 Boverat, *Conseils aux jeunes pour être heureux*, 6; Chef de l'état, AN, AG2: 497; *Marie-Claire* 185 (February 8, 1941): 2.

7 Philippe Pétain, *Le Temps*, 11 October 1940; *Les Prisonniers et la famille*, 66.

8 *Le Temps*, 3 July 1943; Liénart, Suhard, and Gerlier, *Message des cardinaux et évêques de France aux prisonniers*.

9 Duhamel et al., *Spiritualité de la famille*, 137.

10 During the war, popular culture applied the idea of *débrouillardise* (resourcefulness) to the black market, often referred to as the Système D (from *débrouiller*).

11 *Dimanches de la femme* 289 (November 15, 1942): 17.

12 *Pour elle* 45 (June 18, 1941): 4–5; ibid., 69 (December 3, 1941): 3.

13 *Dimanches de la femme* 295 (May 15, 1943): 8; Henry Bordeaux, *Marie-Claire* 248 (June 10, 1942): 3.

14 Monique Beaulieu, *Notre Coeur* 83 (December 1942): 13; *Pour elle* 69 (December 3, 1941): 10–11.

15 *Marie-Claire* 287 (July 20, 1943): 14; Claude Renaudy, "Aux fiancées de prisonniers," *Pages d'eaux-vives* 2 (1942): 9.

16 Marie Savinien, "Attendre," *Pour elle* 62 (October 15, 1941): 3; Pierre Hautefort, "Attendre . . . ," *Notre Coeur* 97 (February 1944): 2.

17 *Petit Echo de la Ligue française d'action catholique* 494 (April 1943): 1; Violette Leduc, *Pour elle* 46 (June 25, 1941): 3; Paulette Yves, *Notre Coeur* 70 (January 16, 1942): 20; *Pour elle* 14 (November 13, 1940): 27. See Clorinda Costantini, "La Presse féminine d'occupation," 387–88.

18 Claude Renaudy, "Aux fiancées de prisonniers," *Pages d'eaux-vives* 2 (1942): 8; *Marie-Claire* 190 (March 15, 1941): 2.

19 For examples of literature, see Aymé's writings about the war and also Roger-Ferdinand, *Les "J3" ou la nouvelle école*. Dutourd, *Au bon beurre*, vividly portrays the wartime *cremier roi* in all his hypocrisy. On wartime fashion, see Veillon, *La Mode sous l'occupation*. On the youth counterculture, see Rioux, "Les Zazous." For popular humor, see Galtier-Boissière, *Mon Journal pendant l'occupation*.

20 French Institute of Public Opinion, *Patterns of Sex and Love*, 194.

21 Proudhon, *Contradictions économiques. La Propriété* 2 (1846): 197.

James F. McMillan used Proudhon's phrase for the title of his book on women in French society during the Third Republic, *Housewife or Harlot*.

22   Michel Audiard, in *Patterns of Sex and Love,* 192.

23   Biot, *Ton Corps et ton coeur,* 10. See Keith Thomas, "The Double Standard," 195; and Zeldin, *France 1848–1945.* Zeldin reported (p. 307) that a recent study of the sexual habits of married men "reveals that adultery is maintained precisely by the survival of traditional moral doctrines."

24   *Notre Coeur* 58 (October 17, 1941): 20.

25   *Patterns of Sex and Love,* 182, 190, 187, 189.

26   Monique Beaulieu, *Notre Coeur* 45 (July 18, 1941): 2; *Notre Coeur* 35 (May 9, 1941): 2.

27   *Pour elle* 34 (April 2, 1941): 24; ibid. 47 (July 2, 1941): 25.

28   *Pour elle* 8 (October 2, 1940): 24; ibid. 32 (March 19, 1941): 24. A prisoner's wife who wrote to Pétain confessing her infidelity told him, "I live in the countryside and I hear from people distressing words, worse than if I had committed a crime." Chef de l'état, AN, AG2: 608, cm22a.

29   *Notre Coeur* 38 (May 30, 1941): 20; ibid. 90 (July 1943): 15.

30   Deroy and Pineau, *Celles qui attendaient,* 28; interview with Patricia Longet, 8 June 1985; *Femmes d'absents,* 6; "Vive la Famille," *Le Coq enchaîné* (June 26, 1942).

31   "Divorce des P.G.: Deuxième Note sur les divorces des prisonniers," Pierre Join-Lambert, Papers, uncataloged, BDIC.

32   Rouast and Bour, *Adultère, divorce et union libre,* 42. The authors do not give their sources.

33   Ministère de la santé publique, *Le Contrôle des rapatriés,* 53. On 1 July 1944 there were 119,000 POWs from the Seine and 34,100 from Seine-et-Oise. Durand, *La Captivité,* 23.

34   Of the 205,905 repatriated Parisians, 140,528 were POWs. Of the 115,475 who responded, 86,006, or 74 percent, were POWs; therefore, 61 percent of the repatriated POWs in Paris turned up for the examination. Ministère de la santé publique, *Le Contrôle des rapatriés,* 54, 57. Even if all 3,600 abandoned homes were from the 86,006 POW households, the percentage would be 4.18; if we add to that the 4,000 homes experiencing undefined "family trouble," assume that all involved adultery and that all 7,600 cases involved only POW homes, the percentage would be 8.8. This is a maximum figure, as the above assumptions are not likely to be true. Further, the 61 percent who showed up for the exam were more likely to be experiencing difficulties of all kinds than the 39 percent who did not show up.

35   "Les enfants adultérins nés aux foyers de prisonniers ou de déportés en l'absence du chef de famille," *L'Enfance et la Croix-Rouge française,* 32.

36   SDPG, AN, F9: 2183 H93, Stalag VIII C, 3 November 1941.

37   Under article 43 of the Geneva Convention of 1929, a prisoner was designated to represent each national group of POWs before the detaining authorities and the protecting power. The prisoners' representative also saw to the physical, moral, and spiritual well-being of the prisoners in the camp. Usually, the prisoners' representative set up an office with legal advisers, counselors, and so on. Although the first representatives were appointed by Germany, most prisoners' representatives from 1941 on were elected by the prisoners themselves.

38   SDPG, AN, F9: 2183 H93, Stalag VIII C, 7 November 1941. The Berlin delegation of the SDPG sent both letters to the Minister of Justice for action; meanwhile, the SDPG asked the Minister of Justice to instruct public prosecutors to apply the existing laws strictly in cases of adultery involving prisoners' wives. Ibid., 19 June 1942.

39   Ibid., 29 May 1942.

40   The adultery law was the one area of family policy that Vichy explicitly compared to Nazi policy. Prisoners were aware of German policy because they often lived and worked in close proximity to German civilians and could not help comparing their wives' situation to that of German soldiers' wives. The SDPG even requested copies of German legislation on the matter for purposes of comparison. *France Politique,* report no. 30510, Commissariat aux prisonniers, AN, F9: 3105, 25 April 1942, 11; SDPG, AN, F9: 2183 H93, 3 October and 19 March 1942.

41   SDPG, AN, F9: 2183 H93, 2 February and 18 February 1942. The two agencies disagreed about who could file a complaint because they had different concerns. The SDPG was preoccupied with reassuring the POWs in Germany that their families were being watched over, while the CFG hoped to lower the divorce rate in France; thus preventing infidelity took a back seat to preventing the breakup of marriages. Revers shared the CGF's concern about third-party prosecutions, "because many cases of adultery would become public knowledge, cases which, had they not been publicized, could have been resolved." He considered allowing close relatives to start procedures but worried about denunciations inspired by malice. Ibid., 19 March 1942. Although the SDPG denied it wanted an outside council to take the initiative, not only had it proposed exactly that, but it did so again on 15 June 1942 and on 4 January 1944. Ibid., 15 June 1942 and 4 January 1944.

42   The CGPGR insisted, "We refuse to allow a prisoner to return from captivity to find, without having been informed, his wife imprisoned for adultery." "Divorce des prisonniers de guerre," Pierre Join-Lambert, Papers, uncataloged, BDIC.

43   "Le Garde des Sceaux a persisté dans l'attitude qu'il avait déjà eue avec M. Pinot et avec M. Ariès. Il estime que les mesures que nous proposons ne

tiennent pas compte du fait que, d'une manière générale, les femmes ne valent rien et que nous voulons agir avec un sabre de bois." CGPGR, AN, F9: 3027, 28 and 29 August 1942.

44 *Journal officiel,* 26 December 1942.

45 SN, *Bulletin de liaison,* 27: 2; SDPG, AN, F9: 2183 H93, 3 April 1944. Join-Lambert wrote in January 1943 that the law was one "autour de laquelle une malheureuse publicité, d'ailleurs, a été faite." Commission nationale des prisonniers agricoles de la corporation paysanne, familles, 11 January 1943, p. 5, Pierre Join-Lambert, Papers, BDIC.

46 Articles 229 and 234 of the Civil Code.

47 SDPG, AN, F9: 2193 H93 Stalag VII A, 6 July 1942.

48 *Femmes d'absents,* 61.

49 SDPG, AN, F9: 2183 H93, Stalag VII A, July 1942; ibid., F9: 2183 H93, Stalag VI A, 17 August 1942.

50 Ibid., F9: 2183 H93, Stalag VII A, 11 March 1943; ibid., 8 March 1943. This particular prisoners' representative praised prosecutors in France who went beyond official investigations to intervene with wives: "Some prosecutors have been able to instill again in wives the correct notion of their duty (we have examples of homes that have been saved this way)." Besides, the prisoners' representative defined public prosecutors as the ultimate "guardians of order and protectors of the family." Ibid., Stalag VII A, 6 July 1942.

51 SDPG, AN, F9: 2183 H93, 30 July 1942.

52 Ibid., 8 May 1944. The Famille du prisonnier thought it should be the only agency to conduct investigations. That way, a minimum of people intervened, and investigations would be conducted "par une Assistante Sociale qui est tenue au secret professionnel [by a social worker bound by professional confidentiality]." Ibid.

53 SDPG, AN, F9: 2183 H93, 15 May 1943; CGPGR, AN, F9: 3034, 17 September 1943.

54 SDPG, AN, F9: 2183 H93, 3 December 1941.

55 "La Répression des dénonciations anonymes," *Le Temps,* 28 February–1 March 1942, p. 2.

56 SDPG, AN, F9: 2183 H93, 24 October 1942 and 22 February 1943.

57 DSPG, AN, F9: 2993, Divorces, 20 June 1943. The Germans gave POWs special stationery that looked like a double airgram. The POWs would write on one side of the paper and return letters came to them on the second half. With the exception of letters from the office of the prisoners' representative, only letters sent on this special stationery were delivered to the camps. The POW's wife could not write to her husband, therefore, since he did not write to her first.

58 DSPG, AN, F9: 2993, Divorces, Stalag 325, 2 April and 10 May 1943.

59 Hautefort recommended following the adage "see no evil, hear no evil, speak no evil." *Notre Coeur* 39 (June 6, 1941): 3; CGPGR, AN, F9: 3093, Stalag X B, 10 July 1944.

60 SDPG, AN, F9: 2183 H93, 15 June 1942 and 5 September 1942.

61 The Famille du prisonnier did not see fit to honor his request. CGPGR, AN, F9: 3028, 18 June 1942.

62 See Susan Gubar, "This is My Rifle, This Is My Gun," in Higonnet et al., *Behind the Lines,* 238–40. In the context of discussing POW wives, many people told me that the women whose heads were shaved after the war were prisoners' wives who had slept with Germans. In a different context, people stated with equal certitude that the "horizontal collaborators" were prostitutes. See Pollard, *"Femme, Famille, France,"* 319.

63 Interview with Raymonde Moulin, 23 March 1985; letter from Anne Barat, 22 December 1985. See also chapter 3, Chevalier's letter about the misery of POW wives leading to relations with Germans, and the police report and the lawyer's letter in this chapter.

64 *Femmes d'absents, Causerie,* 67.

65 Agnès Griot, "Les Règles du bonheur," and Eliane Clause, "Il reviendra," both in *Femmes de prisonniers,* "Espoir"; Madeleine, "Le Plus Féminin des loisirs," ibid., "Loisirs 44"; *Femmes d'absents,* 71.

66 *Femmes d'absents,* 69; Chef de l'état, AN, AG2: 608 cm24, 3 March 1944.

67 Eliane Clause, "Il reviendra," and Hélène Bourel and Maurice Bourel, "Ils l'attendent, eux aussi," both in *Femmes de prisonniers,* "Espoir."

68 Deux Mamans de Thurins, "Comment élever nos enfants?" *Femmes de prisonniers,* "Notre santé"; Agnès Fargeix, "Espérance," *Femmes de prisonniers,* "Notre combat," 5.

69 Deux Mamans de Thurins, "Comment élever nos enfants?" *Femmes de prisonniers,* "Notre santé."

70 Ibid.

71 *Femmes d'absents,* 21, 19–20, 30–31.

72 "Ses Enfants et moi," *Femmes d'absents,* "Fêtes et Saisons," 12; Joseph Folliet, "Comment élève-t-elle nos petits?" *Femmes de prisonniers,* "Ceux qui sont revenus," 3–4.

73 Eliane Clause, "Ma Lettre," *Femmes de prisonniers,* "Il y a d'autres souffrances"; *Femmes d'absents,* 20–21.

74 In 1938, the Juvenile Court of the Seine department saw 4,790 cases; in 1941, there were 10,784 cases. Cremieux, Schachter, and Cotte, *L'Enfant devenu délinquant,* 153–54. Scholars who have studied rationing during the war agree that adolescents were among the hardest hit by it: "Les privations alimentaires sont mieux supportées par les personnes d'un certain

âge [nutritional deprivation is better tolerated by middle-aged people]."
Sauvy, *La Vie économique*, 194. Joubrel and Joubrel, *L'Enfance dite "coupable,"* 21. The figures they give (p. 9) are 12,000 delinquent minors in all France in 1938; over 30,000 in 1945.

75 Heuyer, "Psychopathologie," 16; Hill and Boulding, *Families under Stress*, 62–63.

76 Eliane Clause, "Il reviendra," and N. Ulrich, "Les Problèmes du retour," both in *Femmes de prisonniers*, "Espoir."

77 Eliane Clause, "Il reviendra," and N. Ulrich, "Les Problèmes du retour," both in *Femmes de prisonniers*, "Espoir"; "Elles leur écrivent" and "Liturgie de l'attente," both in *Femmes d'absents*, "Fêtes et Saisons," 20, 4–5.

78 "Le Feu qui reprend mal," *Femmes d'absents*, "Fêtes et Saisons," 27.

79 Cited in Andrée Aulas, "Ceux qui sont revenus," *Femmes de prisonniers*, "Ceux qui sont revenus."

80 Simone Demargne, "Nous 'reconstruirons' notre foyer," *Femmes de prisonniers*, "Mon Amie de captivité"; Folliet, *La Psychologie du rapatrié*, 1–7.

81 Simone Demargne, "Nous 'reconstruirons' notre foyer," Hélène Bourel and Maurice Bourel, "Ils l'attendent, eux aussi," and N. Ulrich, "Les Problèmes du retour," all in *Femmes de prisonniers*, "Espoir."

82 Agnès Griot, "Les Règles du bonheur," *Femmes de prisonniers*, "Espoir"; *Femmes d'absents*, 74.

83 "Simples Conseils," *Femmes d'absents*, "Fêtes et Saisons," 28.

CHAPTER 8: CONCLUSION

1 Pierre Gascar claims that of the prisoners of war who died in captivity, 50 percent died between August 1944 and May 1945—a total of 24,600 men. Gascar, *Histoire*, 276.

2 Contrôle postale from Stalag III A, cited in Durand, *La Captivité*, 474.

3 Durand, *La Captivité*, 501–02. The Red Army marched nineteen thousand French POWs to Odessa, where they were eventually sent to Marseilles by boat.

4 Lewin, *Le Retour des prisonniers*, 63–76; Durand, *La Captivité*, 21.

5 Segal, Hunter, and Segal, "Universal Consequences," 595. See also Robert J. Ursano, "Viet Nam Era Prisoners of War: Studies of U.S. Air Force Prisoners of War," in Stephen M. Sonnenberg et al., eds., *The Trauma of War: Stress and Recovery in Viet Nam Veterans* (Washington, DC: American Psychiatric Press, 1985), 339–57.

6 Of 86,000 repatriated prisoners examined, 14,260 were "reconnus malades

[acknowledged to be ill]." Ministère de la santé publique, *Le Contrôle des rapatriés,* 57.

7 Lewin, *Le Retour des prisonniers,* 69; Segal, Hunter, and Segal, "Universal Consequences," 595–97. Nearly 50 percent of the eighteen hundred POWs who responded to Durand's questionnaire said their health suffered as a result of captivity. Durand, *La Captivité,* 519.

8 Ministère de la santé publique, *Le Contrôle des rapatriés,* 56. Of the 86,000 examined in 1945, only 38 were "severely disturbed."

9 Segal, Hunter, and Segal, "Universal Consequences," 599. Juillet and Moutin, *Psychiatre militaire,* 210. Psychiatrists currently label such reactions Post-Traumatic Stress Disorder. See also "Divorce des P.G." Pierre Join-Lambert, Papers, uncataloged, BDIC; Folliet, *La Psychologie du rapatrié,* 7; and Matsakis, *Vietnam Wives,* 53.

10 Interview with Ariel Chevalier, 8 June 1985, and Yvette Giraud, 13 November 1984; questionnaires from Elisabeth Manceau, Huguette Lagadec, and Joelle Meliard, all 1985; *Marie-Claire* 188 (March 1, 1941): 2.

11 Questionnaires from Josette Lorin and Claudine Dages, 1985; interview with Monique Roussel, 15 June 1985; questionnaire from Catherine Michel, 1985; interview with Yvette Giraud, 13 November 1984.

12 Vuillemin, *Le Problème prisonnier,* 6.

13 Alfred de Vigny attributed the statement, "I don't like POWs, one gets oneself killed," to Napoleon, cited in *Le Temps* 20 November 1941. Leonard Smith, who points out that Napoleon himself surrendered twice, suggests that the maxim probably derived from the motto of the Imperial Guard: "La Garde ne se rend jamais!" Mitterrand complained after the war about the feeling that "un pg ne mérite pas l'estime . . . on se fait tuer sur place [a POW does not deserve esteem . . . one gets oneself killed on the spot]!" Mitterrand, *Les Prisonniers de guerre devant la politique,* 9.

14 Henry, *Oflags VI D—VI A.* The original citation appeared in *Je suis partout* 549 (February 7, 1942): 2. Jerome and Jean Tharaud denied having said, "Nos prisonniers ne méritaient aucun intérêt et qu'ils avaient préféré à la mort mener la vie de château en Allemagne," which another journalist reportedly overheard in a restaurant. *Figaro,* 7 July 1942. DSPG, AN, F9: 2923.20, RadioDiffusion.

15 Commissariat aux prisonniers, AN, F9: 3105, *France Politique,* "Les Prisonniers."

16 Ministère des prisonniers, AN, F9: 3184, 8 August 1945.

17 Letter from Sophie Aimé, 19 March 1985. An interesting comparison could be made with Vietnam veterans who, for different reasons, also faced apathy or hostility when they returned to the United States. Matsakis, *Vietnam Wives,* 20–21.

18   Interview with Raymonde Moulin, 23 March 1985. The MNPGD, a POW resistance movement, merged with the CEAS to form the FNPG. See Lewin, *Le Retour des prisonniers,* 55–57.

19   *Journal officiel,* 12 May 1945; Vuillemin, *Le Problème prisonnier,* 21–22; Marwick, *War and Social Change,* 193; Cépède, *Agriculture et alimentation,* 350; Sauvy, *La Vie économique,* 242.

20   Lewin, *Le Retour des prisonniers,* 192–96; *Journal officiel,* law of 19 June 1952; *Front des Barbelés* 244, Supplement, "Du Barbelé à la liberté, Servir," 131.

21   Ministère des prisonniers, AN, F9: 3184, 4 July 1945.

22   Mitterrand, elected to the Chamber in 1946, was thirty when appointed, making him one of the youngest cabinet ministers ever. The next year he became minister of information.

23   *Dixième Anniversaire du retour,* 10.

24   Interview with Michelle Dupuy, 8 June 1985; *Femmes d'absents,* 95; Durand, *La Captivité,* 231, interview with Mme. Paumier; questionnaire from Nicolle Bouchard, 1985. Both during and after the war, Bouchard and her late husband were extremely active in their small community. She founded the town's public library in addition to raising six children, four born after the return.

25   Questionnaire from Nicolle Bouchard, 1985; interview with Florence Morin, 17 June 1985.

26   Interview with Elisabeth Doremus, conducted by Madeleine Blaire, December 1985.

27   "On était arrivé à être gêné l'un ou l'autre . . . il y avait une espèce de pudeur qui s'est installée." Interview with Raymonde Moulin, 23 March 1985.

28   An expert on juvenile delinquency pointed out after the war that, although the father's absence was traumatic for children, the return created just as many difficulties. Heuyer, "Psychopathologie," 17.

29   Deroy and Pineau, *Celles qui attendaient,* 13, 34, 46; interview with Estelle Sergent, 28 June 1985. Elisabeth Manceau's son "had some difficulty accepting his father's intervention in his habits and education" (questionnaire from Manceau, 1985).

30   Questionnaire from Marthe Jolliet, 1985; Deroy and Pineau, *Celles qui attendaient,* 46.

31   Questionnaire from Stéphanie Thibault, 1985. There was also the phenomenon of "domestic dictators" described in chapter 7.

32   Interview with Anne Devron, 10 June 1985; "Il nous faut redécouvrir nos enfants et faire leur conquête," *Femmes de prisonniers rapatriés,* n.s., no. 3, p. 2.

33 Vuillemin, *Le Problème prisonnier,* 19; *Journal officiel-Débats,* Assemblée consultative provisoire, 22 March 1945, 683.

34 Deroy and Pineau, *Celles qui attendaient,* 45–46.

35 Karl Ittmann's careful reading of this chapter helped me refine the analysis of divorce.

36 "Divorce des P.G.: Deuxième Note sur le divorce des prisonniers," Pierre Join-Lambert, Papers, uncataloged, BDIC; MPF *Travaux 45, 35; Journal officiel-Débats,* Assemblée consultative provisoire, 22 March 1945, 683. Note that the large majority of POWs returned in April and May, after this report.

37 *Le Monde,* 20 December 1945. The minister of justice, when asked about the estimate of 200,000 divorces among repatriated POWs, responded, "That's ridiculous!" There were 205,905 repatriated POWs, deportees, and laborers in the Paris area. Ministère de la santé publique, *Le Contrôle des rapatriés,* 54.

38 Roussel, "Les Divorces," 300. Lewin's figures, considerably higher, are taken from the Compte général de l'administration de la justice criminelle, which includes all divorces pronounced, some 10 percent of which were never transcribed because of death, reconciliation, or attorney negligence. Lewin, *Le Retour des prisonniers,* 71; Ledermann, "Les Divorces," 315–17.

39 Desforges, *Le Divorce en France,* 31; Françoise Vallot, "Mariages et divorces," 86.

40 In the United States the number of divorces dropped steadily between 1929 and 1933; the divorce rate per thousand married women declined 14 percent in 1932. U.S. Department of Health and Human Services, *Vital Statistics,* sec. 2, p. 5.

41 Louis Henry, "Mesure de la fréquence des divorces," 282. Although the divorce rate never dropped during World War II in the United States, it jumped dramatically just after the war: up 20 percent in 1945 and 24 percent in 1946 and 1947. The decline began in 1948, but the divorce rate per thousand couples only returned to the 1942 rate in 1954, where it stabilized until 1964. U.S. Department of Health and Human Services, *Vital Statistics,* sec. 2, p. 5.

42 Roussel, "Les Divorces," 279. For comparison, the 1956 divorce rate in the United States was ninety-two divorces per ten thousand married women. U.S. Department of Health and Human Services, *Vital Statistics,* sec. 2, p. 5.

43 Ledermann, "Les Divorces," 327–28; Henry, "Mesure de la fréquence des divorces," 281. Henry also points out that the Depression acted as a brake on divorce as well, possibly increasing the post-1945 jump.

44 *Journal officiel,* law of 2 April 1941; *Le Monde,* 11 April 1945. Although, as mentioned in chapter 7, POWs could institute divorce proceedings if their wives committed adultery, legally the divorce could only be *prononcé,* not *transcrit,* until the husband's return.

45 Not in the rate per thousand.

46 *Le Monde,* 20 December 1945. Ten thousand divorces would be 7 percent of the repatriated POWs in the area; Lewin, *Le Retour des prisonniers,* 71.

47 Many POWs married after they returned; some of those marriages also ended in divorce. I only make the assumption to obtain the highest possible estimate. Durand, *La Captivité,* 519.

48 Lewin, *Le Retour des prisonniers,* 71; "Seizième Rapport," 630.

49 Based on annual rates of 27 divorces and 4 separations per 10,000 married couples. Ledermann, "Les Divorces," 325. The 1936 marriage cohort of Vallot's study makes an interesting comparison. After 33 years, 18 percent of the 1936 cohort had divorced. However, Vallot's study, done in 1969, could not compare a 33-year span for each cohort. After 12 years, the 1936 cohort had 10.3 divorces per 100 couples, and the 1956 cohort had 9.3 divorces. Although the pattern of divorces for the 1936 cohort varied greatly, showing many fewer divorces in the early years of marriage and many more after 10 years, in the long run the divorce rate for the 1936 cohort probably will not differ that much from the rate for other generations. Vallot, "Mariages et divorces," 84–87. See also chapter 7 for a discussion of divorce rates and adultery.

50 In 1984 there were 103,700 divorces in France, a crude rate (per 1,000 population, not per 1,000 married couples) of 1.89. United Nations, *1985 Demographic Yearbook,* 350. For purposes of comparison, see table 8.2, column 3. In the United States, the 1984 crude divorce rate was 5.0 per 1,000 population. U.S. Department of Health and Human Services, *Vital Statistics,* sec. 2, p. 5.

51 Using the wives I interviewed or sent questionnaires to, Deroy and Pineau's collection, and *Femmes d'absents . . . Témoignages.* This is hardly a random sample, because it is nearly impossible to find divorced prisoners' wives to interview. In all my interview trips to France, I came across one divorced POW wife and two POWs whose wives had left them during the war.

52 Deroy and Pineau, *Celles qui attendaient,* 34; interview with Raymond and Germaine Doucet, 20 November 1984; questionnaire from Suzanne Goupillat, 1985; *Femmes d'absents,* 93.

53 Deroy and Pineau, *Celles qui attendaient,* 14; questionnaires from Joelle Meliard and Catherine Michel, both 1985.

54 Questionaire from Sylvie Crouet, 1985. "Notre vie de couple par elle-même a été facile à reprendre, mais j'ai dû me plier à ses exigences." Questionnaire from Martine Lombardi, 1985.

55 "J'ai dû me transformer en infirmière, en comptable, et en ménagère, suivant les heures de la journée. Mon ménage n'a pas été perturbé." Questionnaire from Gilberte Voisin, 1985.

56 Questionnaire from Louise Cadieu, 1985.

57 *Femmes françaises* 39 (June 21, 1945): 3; Folliet, "Reprendre place dans la vie." *Femmes françaises* was a woman's resistance newspaper during the occupation, connected in the northern zone with the Union des femmes françaises, a resistance movement affiliated with the French Communist party but not limited to party members. Léon Leloir, a deportee, counseled wives, "Do not begrudge us anything. . . . Be good and resuscitate love in us—love for the whole world." Leloir, *Les Paradoxes du retour,* 47–48.

58 Henriette, "Préparons leur retour," *La défense de prisonniers* 3 (April 3, 1944).

59 Jean Vedrine and G. Saurel, Rectificatif à l'instruction commune no. 2 concernant les Femmes de Prisonniers de Guerre, 26 December 1944, Jean Vedrine, papers, BDIC. Chapter 6 covers the attempt to create a group, Foyers de Rapatriés, consisting of repatriated POWs and their wives.

60 MPF, *Travaux 45,* 51; interview with Agnès Griot, 3 May 1985.

61 Lewin, *Le Retour des prisonniers,* 76.

62 *Femmes d'absents,* 96.

63 Thirty-two percent of the sample of sixty Navy POW families had divorced by 1977 (28 percent of them after the first year of reunion), compared to 11–12 percent of a control group of sixty non-POW Vietnam veterans' families. Hunter, "Treating the Military Captive's Family," 191.

64 Interview with Gisèle Desbois, 21 March 1985.

EPILOGUE

1 "Employment of Women in France," *International Labor Review* 55, no. 6 (June 1947): 549–55; *Premier Rapport de la commission de la main-d'oeuvre,* 28–29.

2 *Premier Rapport de la commission de la main-d'oeuvre,* 28–29.

3 *French Women in the War,* 1:2.

4 Henri-Georges Rol-Tanquy, in *Femmes françaises* 1 (September 1944): 1; Paula Schwartz, "Precedents for Politics," 2.

5 "Les femmes doivent voter," *Femmes françaises* 8 (November 2, 1944): 2.

6 H. Porte, "Ce que femme veut, Raymonde Fiolet, Maire de Soissons," *Femmes françaises* 20 (January 25, 1945): 5.

7 Marcelle Mazeau, "La Femme dans la cité," *Femmes de prisonniers, Espoir,* vol. 3.

8 Ibid.; Durand, *La Captivité,* 471.

9   Marianne Verger, "La Politique sociale," 25.

10 "La Réforme des régimes matrimoniaux," *Sondages* 29, no. 1 (1967): 38. Of the women polled, 74 percent felt it was "souhaitable que la femme administre ses biens propres [desirable that the wife administer her own property]," but only 54 percent of the men agreed.

11 Albistur and Armogathe, *Histoire du féminisme français,* 438–39.

12 Anne Batiot, "The Political Construction of Sexuality: Contraception and Abortion 1965–1975," in Cerny, *Social Movements and Protest.*

13 Compared to 44 percent in the United States. Thirty-five percent of the total female population of France was employed, compared to 42 percent in the United States. Organization for Economic Co-operation and Development, *Historical Statistics 1960–1985,* 33–34.

14 Organization for Economic Co-operation and Development, *The Integration of Women into the Economy,* 49.

15 This figure excludes agriculture, mining, quarrying, public utilities, the public sector, and private domestic service. Because a large percentage of public-sector clerical employees and domestic service workers are women with low wages, the real gap is probably significantly wider. Ibid., 70. Interestingly, the wage gap in France is considerably lower than in the United States, where in 1983 it averaged 36 percent. Sullerot, *Histoire et sociologie du travail féminin,* 315–17; Andrée Michel, "France," in Farley, ed., *Women Workers in Fifteen Countries,* 114–15; Smith and Ward, *Women's Wages,* 23.

16 For additional evidence of the changing attitudes of the postwar generation, see Roussel, "L'Attitude de diverses générations."

ARCHIVAL AND MANUSCRIPT COLLECTIONS

Archives Nationales, Paris, France

Caisses d'allocations familiales.
    F22: 1536.
Centre national d'information sur les prisonniers de guerre.
    F9: 2811.
Chef de l'état.
    AG2: 27, 459, 497, 498, 543, 605, 608, 612, 618, 654.
Commissariat aux prisonniers, déportés et refugiés du Comité français de la
    Libération nationale.
    F9: 3105, 3116, 3117.
Commissariat général aux prisonniers de guerre rapatriés et aux famillies de pri-
    sonniers de guerre.
    F9: 3025, 3027, 3028, 3034, 3092, 3093.
Contrôles techniques.
    F7: 14927, 14934, 14936.
Direction du service des prisonniers de guerre.
    F9: 2828, 2858, 2923, 2938, 2956, 2962, 2989, 2993.
Gouvernement provisoire de la république française: Commissariat à l'intérieur.
    F1A: 3797, 3778.
Ministère des prisonniers, déportés et réfugiés.
    F9: 3184.
Secrétariat général du gouvernement.
    F60: 390, 558, 628.
Service diplomatique des prisonniers de guerre.
    F9: 2107, 2151, 2183, 2195, 2325, 2326, 2581.
Services de l'information.
    F41: 226, 291, 300, 304, 353.

Bibliothèque de Documentation Internationale
Contemporaine, Nanterre, France

"Feuille dactylographiée remise à Scapini par des prisonniers de guerre français."
28 January 1943. Q Pièce 723 Reserve.

Join-Lambert, Pierre. Papers. Uncataloged. The papers of Pierre Join-Lambert, member of the Conseil d'Etat and founding member of the CGPGR who quit when Maurice Pinot was fired. One file contains reports on divorce. The rest of the papers are reports of three study groups on agrarian POWs.

Les Ménagères et le ravitaillement durant l'occupation allemande. Tracts 1942–43. 4°Δ 241 Reserve.

Ministre de l'information, direction de la censure. "Consignes permanentes de la censure à la date du 1 juin 1943." 4°Δ 168 Reserve A: La Censure pendant l'occupation allemande en France.

Présidence du conseil. "Consignes de censure 14e région, Lyon." Fol. Δ Reserve 75: 1 and 2, Censure Vichy.

Propagande pour le travail en Allemagne. 4°Δ 190 Reserve A and B.

Vedrine, Jean. Papers. Mini-dossier "Femmes de Prisonniers." F° D R5, donation 67239. Vedrine was the original director of the Centre d'entr'aide; he quit when Maurice Pinot was fired. His papers from the war years include huge quantities of material on almost every POW organization that existed.

PERSONAL NARRATIVES

Ambrière, Francis. *Les Grandes Vacances 1939–1945*. Paris: Seuil, 1956.

Beauvoir, Simone de. *The Prime of Life*. Trans. Peter Green. New York: World Publishing, 1962.

Betz, Maurice. *Dialogues des prisonniers, 1940*. Paris: Emile-Paul frères, 1940.

Bochot, Pierre. *Chez Eux*. Paris: René Julliard, 1946.

Bugeaud, Pierre. *Militant Prisonnier de guerre*. Paris: Harmattan, 1990.

Corday, Pauline. *J'ai vécu dans Paris occupé*. Montreal: L'Arbre, 1943.

Cormand, Reine. *La Vie d'une famille face à la Gestapo dans la France occupée novembre 1943–juin 1945*. Amoudriez-Thonon, 1972.

Dailly, Fernande. *La Femme du prisonnier*. Paris: La Pensée universelle, 1974.

Deroy, Jacqueline, and Françoise Pineau. *Celles qui attendaient . . . témoignent aujourd'hui*. Melun: ANRPAPG, 1985.

Dujardin, André. *Convalescence, précédé de Les Huits Derniers Mois de l'Oflag II B*. Paris: L'Amicale de l'Oflag II-B, II-D, 1961.

Escure, Karl et al. *Hirschberg, des P.G. se souviennent . . .* Paris: Peuples amis, 1978.

Femmes d'absents . . . Témoignages. Collected by the Associations de femmes de prisonniers and the Mouvement populaire des familles. Paris: Les Editions du cerf, 1945.

Galtier-Boissière, Jean. *Mon Journal pendant l'occupation.* Paris: La Jeune parque, 1945.

Guerlain, Robert. *A Prisoner in Germany.* London: Macmillan, 1944.

Henry, Raymond. *Oflags VI D—VI A, La Vie de chateau!* Paris: Charles-Lavauzelle, n.d.

Lavabre, Célestin. *Ceux de l'an 40.* Rodez: Editions Subervie-Rodez, 1981.

Livre d'or de l'exil français. Paris: Fédération nationale des prisonniers et déportés, 1946.

Loisy, George. *27— . . /37179 = notre jeunesse.* Reims: Coulon, 1975.

Martin-Chauffier, Simone. *A bientôt quand même . . .* Calmann-Lévy, 1976.

Mitterrand, François. *Leçons de choses de la captivité.* Paris: Les Grandes Editions françaises, 1947.

Mort, Noël de la. *Vie des prisonniers du frontstalag 210 au Stalag XII.* Paris: Grasset, 1941.

Pakonyk, François. *1940–1945, Les Enfants de l'exode.* Paris: La Pensée universelle, 1984.

Plessy, Jean et al. *Oflags, Récit photographique de la vie des prisonniers dans les camps allemands 1940–1945.* 1946.

Reuter, François. *Le Chemin du Stalag.* Marseilles: Editions Jean Vigneau, 1943.

Vedrine, Jean. *Dossier PG-Rapatriés 1940–1945.* 2d ed. 2 vols. Asnières: Imprimerie Daniel, 1987.

Vegh, Claudine. *Je ne lui ai pas dit au revoir.* Paris: Gallimard, 1979.

PRIMARY SOURCES

L'Ame des camps, Exposition de la vie intellectuelle, spirituelle et social dans les camps de prisonniers. Paris: Imprimerie Lamy, 1944.

L'Appel de la J.O.C. Paris: Librairie de la jeunesse ouvrière, 1938.

Aymé, Marcel. *The Transient Hour.* Trans. Eric Sutton. London: The Bodley Head, 1948 (*Le Chemin des écoliers.* Paris: Gallimard, 1959).

Bachelier, A. "Vos Responsabilités." *Pages d'eaux vives* 9 (1943): n.p.

Barrès, Philippe. *Sauvons nos prisonniers.* New York: Didier, 1943.

Binder, R. *Nos Prisonniers de guerre et leurs familles.* Paris: Dubois et Bauer, 1942.

Biot, René. *Ton Corps et ton coeur, Fidelité conjugale.* Lyons: Chronique sociale de France, 1940.

Boverat, Fernand. *Conseils aux jeunes pour être heureux.* Lyons: Alliance nationale contre la dépopulation, n.d.

Captivité. Paris: Editions Jacques Vautrain, 1946.

Cazin, Madeleine. *Le Travail féminin*. Rennes: Faculté de droit, 1943.

Centre d'entr'aide de l'Oflag IV D. *Extraits des bulletins de liaison décembre 1942 à juillet 1943*, 1943.

Chaumet, André. *Les Buts secrets de la Relève et du "S.T.O."* Paris: Editions CEA, n.d.

Chef du foyer, aux jeunes gens. Paris: Editions familiales de France, 1942.

Comment débuter dans un cercle d'études jociste. Paris: Librairie de la jeunesse ouvrière, n.d.

Commissariat général à la famille. *La Journée des mères*.

———. *Les Prisonniers et la famille*. Paris: L'Office de propagande générale, 1943.

Commissariat général aux prisonniers de guerre rapatriés et aux familles de prisonniers de guerre. *Dès votre libération vous devez retrouver votre métier*. Paris: Imprimerie de Montsouris, n.d.

———. *Quand ils reviendront*. Paris: Imprimerie E. Desfossé-Néogravure, 1942.

Commissariat général du plan de modernisation et d'équipement. *Premier Rapport de la commission de la main d'oeuvre*. October 1946.

Comptes-Rendus du 11ᵉ congrès des assistantes sociales du Secours National (zone occupée). Paris: Secours national, 1942.

Une Date, Une rélève, une étape. Montrouge: Editions "Toute la France," 1943.

Dillard, Victor. *Lettres du prisonnier inconnu*. Ste. Foy-les-Lyon: Editions du monde ouvrier, 1941.

Direction des services des prisonniers de guerre. *Les Camps de prisonniers de guerre en Allemagne*. N.d.

———. *Communiqués officiels de la Direction des prisonniers de guerre*. December 1942.

———. *Documentation sur les camps de prisonniers de guerre*. N.d.

———. *Guide du prisonnier*. 1943.

———. *Le Service des prisonniers de guerre en zone occupée*. Paris: Imprimerie nationale, 1942.

Documentation à l'usage des responsables des centres d'entr'aide, Maison du prisonnier de la Seine, 1 mai 1942. Paris: Reboul et fils, 1942.

Dubreuil, Hyacinthe. *A l'image de la mère. Essai sur la mission de l'assistante sociale*. Paris: Edition sociale française, 1941.

Duhamel, Bernard et al. *Spiritualité de la famille*. Lyons: Les Editions de l'abeille, 1942.

L'Enfance et la Croix-Rouge française. Paris: Service de documentation, Croix-Rouge française, 1946.

Entr'aide française. *Renseignements généraux sur la France après 4 ans d'occupation ennemie*. Paris: Société industrielle d'imprimerie, 1945.

Equipes et Cadres de la France nouvelle, Tract. *Appui mutuel des époux.* N.p, n.d.

Exposition "Prisonniers." Reims: Imprimerie du nord-est, 1944.

La Famille que nous voulons, Compte-Rendu de la semaine d'études des dirigeants nationaux de la J.O.C. Lyons: Imprimerie du salut public, 1943.

Femmes d'absents. "Fêtes et Saisons" series. Paris: Les Editions du cerf, 1943.

Femmes d'absents, Causerie faite à des prêtres rapatriés. Lyons: Imprimerie du salut public, 1944.

Fidelité. Pour les femmes de prisonniers. Paris: Durassié, 1943.

Folliet, Joseph. *Pour nous préparer à leur retour.* Paris: Seuil, 1944.

———. *La Psychologie du rapatrié.* Paris: Imprimerie du salut public, 1945.

———. "Reprendre place dans la vie." In *Regain, hors les barbélés.* Lyons: Service des foyers rapatriés du mouvement populaire des familles, 1944.

France during the German Occupation 1940–1944, trans. Philip Whitcomb. Stanford: The Hoover Institution on War, Revolution, and Peace, 1957.

French Women in the War. 2 vols. French Press and Information Service, Committee of National Liberation, April 1944.

Gardienne du foyer, aux jeunes filles. Paris: Editions familiales de France, 1942.

The Geneva Convention Relative to the Treatment of Prisoners of War. Ed. Jean de Preux et al. Trans. A. P. de Heney. Geneva: International Committee of the Red Cross, 1960.

Giraud, Ludovic. *La Fidelité à nos prisonniers.* Marseilles: Direction général des oeuvres, 1944.

———. *La Vie de nos prisonniers dans un oflag.* Marseilles: Imprimerie Moullot, 1941.

Guide à l'usage des prisonniers de guerre et de leur familles. Clermont-Ferrand: L'Association des prisonniers de guerre du Puy-de-Dôme, 1945.

Guide pratique des familles de prisonniers de guerre et des prisonniers rapatriés: Droits et avantages. Paris: Charles-Lavauzelle, 1944.

Guitton, Jean. *Les Fondaments de la communauté française.* Lyons: Les Cahiers des captifs, 1942.

Habault, Léon. *Pour nos prisonniers.* Blois: Grande imprimerie de Blois, 1941.

Ils reviendront . . . Aux femmes et aux mères de prisonniers. Paris: Durassié, 1941.

Institut national de la statistique et des études économiques. *Statistique du mouvement de la population. Part 1: Mariages, divorces, naissances, décès.* Paris: Imprimerie nationale, 1946–56.

Journal officiel.

Journal officiel: Débats. Assemblée consultative provisoire, 1944–45.

Leloir, Léon. *Les Paradoxes du retour.* Brussels: Editions universitaires, 1945.

Liénart, Achille, Emmanuel Suhard, and Pierre Gerlier. *Message des cardinaux et évêques de France aux prisonniers.* N.p. November 1942.

Ligue française d'action catholique féminin. *Sauvons nos foyers!* Paris: Durassié, 1943.

Ligue ouvrière chrétienne—Mouvement populaire des familles. *Travaux 42.* Paris: Imprimerie "Pax et Labor." N.d.

Masson, André. *Entre deux mondes.* Paris: Pierre Lagrange, n.d.

———. *M.P.* Paris: Curial-Archereau, 1943.

———. *Vous et nous, Deux messages des camps.* Paris: Librairie Plon, 1942.

Maziou, J. *Entre vos mains.* 6th ed. St. Etienne: Imprimerie Theolier, 1946.

Ministère de la santé publique. *Le Contrôle des rapatriés dans le département de la Seine: Bilan sanitaire et social.* Paris: Louis Arnette, 1947.

Ministère des prisonniers, déportés et réfugiés. *Bilan d'un effort.* Paris: Busson, 1945.

Mitterrand, François. *Les Prisonniers de guerre devant la politique.* Paris: Editions du Rond-Point, 1945.

Moreau, Robert. "Repatriated Prisoners and the Families of Prisoners." In *France During the German Occupation 1940–1944,* trans. Philip Whitcomb, 209–30. Stanford: The Hoover Institution on War, Revolution and Peace, 1957.

Mouvement populaire des familles. *Travaux 43.* Paris: Imprimerie "Pax et Labor." N.d.

———. *Travaux 45.* St. Etienne: Imprimerie Bringuier, 1945.

———. *Travaux 46.* St. Etienne: Imprimerie Bringuiere, 1946.

Le Mouvement prisonnier: Ses Équipes civiques, aux ordres du maréchal. Montrouge: Ste. Nelle-la-Platinogravure, 1943.

Nos Prisonniers. "Fêtes et Saisons" series. Paris: Les Editions du cerf, 1942.

Ophuls, Marcel. *The Sorrow and the Pity.* Trans. Mireille Johnston. New York: Outerbridge and Lazard, 1972.

Paris, Fernande. *Le Travail des femmes et le retour de la mère au foyer.* Paris: Librairie du receuil Sirey, 1943.

Pétain, Philippe. *Le Maréchal parle aux prisonniers.* Le Mans: Editions "CEP," 1942.

———. *Paroles aux français.* Lardanchet, 1941. N.p.

Les Prisonniers attendent . . . Paris: IPR, n.d.

Proudhon, Pierre-Joseph. *Contradictions économiques.* Vol. 2: *La Propriété.* 1846.

Radiguet, Raymond. *The Devil in the Flesh.* Trans. A. M. Sheridan. London: Calder and Boyars, 1968.

Radio nationale. *Pour nos prisonniers,* advice and information taken from the *Radio nationale revue.* N.d.

Regain. Hors les barbelés. Lyons: Services des foyers rapatriés du mouvement populaire des familles, 1944.

Renaudy, Claude. "Aux fiancées de prisonniers, son attente." *Pages d'eaux-vives* 2 (1942), n.p.

Revivre . . . Orientations spirituelles pour foyers de rapatriés. La Chapelle Montligeon: Imprimerie de Montligeon, 1945.

Roche, Sylvain. *La Guerre des captives.* Lyons: Imprimerie du salut public, 1944.

Roger-Ferdinand. *Les "J3" ou la nouvelle école.* Imprimerie de sceaux, 1944.

Salon du prisonnier, Musée Galliéra 12 décembre 1941–12 janvier 1942. Fontenay-aux-Roses: Imprimerie Louis Bellemand, 1941.

Savarit, Renaud. *Le Droit des prisonniers de guerre, Action et législation en faveur des prisonniers de guerre et de leurs familles.* Paris: Imprimerie Lavergne, 1943.

Scapini, Georges. *Mission sans gloire.* Paris: Morgan, 1960.

———. "Prisoners." In *France During the German Occupation 1940–1944,* trans. Philip Whitcomb, 203–08. Stanford: The Hoover Institution on War, Revolution, and Peace, 1957.

Secours national. *Premier Congrès national de "La Famille du prisonnier de guerre."* Vanves: Imprimerie de Kapp, 1944.

Secrétariat général de l'information. *Aux agriculteurs prisonniers de guerre libérés.* Lyons: Giraud Rivoire, n.d.

———. *Aux ouvriers prisonniers de guerre libérés.* Cannes: Robaudy, n.d.

Secrétariat général des prisonniers, déportés et réfugiés. *Dispositions prises en faveur des chefs d'entreprise rapatriés.* Paris: Imprimerie nationale, 1946.

———. *Textes concernant les agriculteurs rapatriés.* Paris: Imprimerie nationale, 1945.

Un Seul Coeur, Des Universités de France aux camps de prisonniers. N.p. Union nationale des étudiants de France, 1944.

S.O.S. des familles ouvrières, Pour une réforme profonde des allocations familiales, Propositions du Mouvement populaire des familles. Paris: Les Editions ouvrières, 1946.

Tallet, Xavier. *Les Délits contre la natalité: Avortement et propagande anticonceptionelle.* Avignon: Imprimerie Barthélemy, 1938.

Tinayre, Marcelle. "La Femme doit-elle travailler?" *L'Illustration,* 28 March 1942, 215–16.

———. "Le Problème de la natalité: Le Point de vue féminin." *L'Illustration,* 8 November 1941, 255–57.

Tournier, Michel. *The Ogre.* Trans. Barbara Bray. New York: Doubleday, 1972.

Triolet, Elsa. *A Fine of 200 Francs.* New York: Reynal and Hitchcock, 1947.

Les Unions des femmes de prisonniers. Paris: Union central des Femmes de P.G., 1943.

Van der Meersch, M. *Femmes à l'encan.* Paris: Michel, 1945.

Varenne, Georgette. *La Femme dans la France nouvelle*. Clermont-Ferrand: Mont-Louis, 1940.

Vercors. *Le Silence de la mer et autre récits*. Paris: Albin Michel, 1951.

Verger, Marianne. "La Politique sociale." *Parti Républicaine-Radicale et Radical-Socialiste, 36ème congrès*. Paris: Editions du Parti Républicain-Radical et Radical-Socialist, 1945.

26 mars 1944, Au profit des prisonniers de l'Imprimerie Praeger. Montrouge.

Vous leur avez dit: Compter sur moi . . . Montrouge: Ste. Nelle-La-Platinogravure, 1943.

Zousmann, Alexis, "L'Opinion des prisonniers, la vermine." Article intended for *Libération Sud* and not published following the assassination of Verdier—leader of the south-west Resistance. N.d.

Newspapers and Periodicals

Avec lui, entre nous
Bulletin de liaison de la Famille du prisonnier de guerre
Le Coq enchainé
La Défense des prisonniers
Dimanches de la femme
Espoir
Femmes françaises
Foyers de rapatriés
Front des barbelés
L'Illustration
International Labour Review
Marie-Claire
Le Monde
Monde ouvrier
Notre Coeur
Petit Echo de la Ligue française d'action catholique
Pour elle
Quelque-unes parmi nous . . .
Le Temps

Publications of the Fédération des associations de femmes de prisonniers (FAFP)

"But des associations."

Compte-rendu de la journée des présidentes. 23 May 1943.

Compte-rendu de la session des associations de femmes de prisonniers des 14 et 15 mars 1942.

Griot, Agnès. "Responsables." 12 May 1943. Handwritten speech. Tamburini. Private Collection.

Reconstruire, son esprit, son organisation. Scenic Tableau.

Travaux du congrès national de la Fédération des associations de femmes de prisonniers des 14 et 15 avril 1945 à Paris.

The federation papers have no volume numbers and often no publication date. The only way to indicate a specific issue is by referring to the article on the front page. The following list is in chronological order, with dates included when available.

Pages des responsables, 1941–1944.

Lettre aux femmes et mamans de prisonniers, September 1941.

Lettres de Noël aux femmes et aux mamans de prisonniers.

Lettre aux femmes et mamans de prisonniers, "La Visite de Madame Aulas au Maréchal." March 1942.

Femmes de prisonniers, Lettre da la Fédération des associations de femmes de prisonniers, "Fidèles!"

Femmes de prisonniers:

"Ceux qui sont revenus," January 1943.

"Fermeté," March 1943.

"Espérance."

"Notre Action civique."

"Fidelité II."

"Mon Amie de captivité," October 1943.

"Il y a d'autres souffrances," November 1943.

"Noël 1939 . . . Noël 1943," December 1943.

"Notre Santé," February 1944.

"Pour notre dignité, nous revendiquons."

"Espoir."

"Celle qu'il appelle maman."

"Loisirs 44," June 1944.

"Vacances quand-même," July–August 1944.

"Notre libération . . . et la leur?"

Femmes de prisonniers, Espoir. Nos. 3–7, 1945.

Femmes de prisonniers rapatriés.

Responsables, 1944–1945.

SECONDARY WORKS

Albistur, Maïté, and Daniel Armogathe. *Histoire du féminisme français du moyen âge à nos jours.* Paris: Editions des femmes, 1977.

Amouroux, Henri. *La Vie des français sous l'occupation.* Paris: Librairie Arthème Fayard, 1961.

Azéma, Jean-Pierre. *La Collaboration (1940–1944)*. Paris: Presses universitaires de France, 1975.

———. *From Munich to the Liberation, 1938–1944*. Trans. Janet Lloyd. New York: Cambridge University Press, 1984.

Bairoch, P. *La Population active et sa structure*. Vol. 1. Brussels: Editions de l'Institut de sociologie de l'Université libre de Bruxelles, 1968.

Baley, P. "Influences psychiques de la dernière guerre mondiale." *Sauvegarde* 28–29 (February–March 1949): 58–84.

Barker, A. J. *Behind Barbed Wire*. London: B. T. Batsford, 1974.

Batiot, Anne. "The Political Construction of Sexuality: Contraception and Abortion 1965–1975." In *Social Movements and Protest in France*, ed. Philip Cerny, 125–45. New York: St. Martins, 1982.

Baud, Georges, Louis Devaux, and Jean Poigny. "Mémoire complimentaire sur quelques aspects des activités du Service diplomatique des prisonniers de guerre, S.D.P.G.-D.F.B.-Mission Scapini 1940–1945." Paris: Georges Baud, 1984.

Baudot, François. "Les Prisonniers des kommandos et l'image de la France." *Revue d'histoire de la deuxième guerre mondiale* 71 (July 1968): 49–76.

Bédarida, François. *La Stratégie secrète de la drôle de guerre*. Paris: Fondation nationale des sciences politiques, 1979.

Bédarida, René. *Les Armes de l'esprit: Témoignage chrétien (1941–1944)*. Paris: Editions ouvrières, 1977.

Bellanger, Claude, and Roger Debouzy. *La Presse des barbelés*. Rabat: Editions internationales du document, 1951.

Berenson, Edward. "The Politics of Divorce in France of the Belle Epoque: The Case of Joseph and Henriette Caillaux." *American Historical Review* 93, no. 1 (February 1988): 31–55.

Bernard, Philippe, and Henri Dubief. *The Decline of the Third Republic 1914–1938*. Trans. Anthony Forster. New York: Cambridge University Press, 1985.

Bey, Douglas R., and Jean Lange. "Waiting Wives: Women Under Stress." *American Journal of Psychiatry* 131 (March 1974): 283–86.

Billig, Joseph. "Le Rôle des prisonniers de guerre dans l'économie du IIIème Reich." *Revue d'histoire de la deuxième guerre mondiale* 37 (January 1960): 53–76.

Blayo, Chantal, and Patrick Festy. "Les Divorces en France: Evolution récente et perspectives." *Population* 31, no. 3 (March–April 1976): 617–43.

Bloch, Marc. *Strange Defeat*. Trans. Gerard Hopkins. New York: Norton, 1968.

Bolle, Pierre, and Jean Godel, eds. *Spiritualité, théologie et résistance*. Grenoble: Presses universitaires de Grenoble, 1987.

Borot, François. "Classement et analyse des Dossiers de l'O.F.I. contenus à la B.D.I.C. Etude sur l'information et la censure pendant l'occupation (1940–

1944)." Master's thesis in contemporary history, Université de Paris X. Nanterre, 1976.

Boudot, François. "Le Retour des prisonniers de guerre." *La Libération de la France*. Paris: Centre national de la recherche scientifique, 1976.

Bourderon, Roger. "Le Régime de Vichy était-il fasciste?" *Revue d'histoire de la deuxième guerre mondiale* 23, no. 91 (1973): 23–45.

Bovet, Lucien. *Les Aspects psychiatriques de la délinquance juvénile*. Geneva: Organisation mondiale de la santé, 1951.

Boxer, Marilyn J. "Socialism Faces Feminism: The Failure of Synthesis in France, 1879–1914." In *Socialist Women*, ed. Marilyn Boxer and Jean Quataert, 75–111. New York: Elsevier, 1978.

———. "When Radical and Socialist Feminism Were Joined: The Extraordinary Failure of Madeleine Pelletier." In *European Women on the Left*, ed. Jane Slaughter and Robert Kern, 50–73. Westport, Conn.: Greenwood Press, 1981.

Brauner, Alfred. *Ces Enfants ont vécu la guerre . . .* Paris: Les Editions sociales françaises, 1946.

Broszat, Martin. *The Hitler State: The Foundation and Development of the Internal Structure of the Third Reich*. Trans. John W. Hiden. New York: Longman, 1981.

Brun, Gérard. *Technocrates et technocratie en France*. Paris: Albatros, 1985.

Cairns, John C. "Along the Road Back to France, 1940." *American Historical Review* 64 (April 1959): 583–603.

Campbell, D'Ann. *Women at War with America: Private Lives in a Patriotic Era*. Cambridge: Harvard University Press, 1984.

Carré, J.-J., P. Dubois, and E. Malinvaud. *French Economic Growth*. Trans. John P. Hatfield. Stanford: Stanford University Press, 1975.

Cépède, Michel. *Agriculture et alimentation en France durant la deuxième guerre mondiale*. Paris: Génin, 1961.

Chafe, William H. *The American Woman: Her Changing Social, Economic and Political Roles 1920–1970*. New York: Oxford University Press, 1972.

Chalas, Yves. *Vichy et l'imaginaire totalitaire*. Arles: Actes sud, 1985.

Charrière, Guy, and P. Duquet. *Traitée théorique et pratique des prisonniers de guerre, déportés et travailleurs en Allemagne en droit français*. Paris: Librairie générale de droit et de jurisprudence, 1946.

Christophe, Robert. *Les Flammes du purgatoire, Histoire des prisonniers de 1940*. Paris: Editions France-Empire, 1979.

Clark, Francis I. *The Position of Women in Contemporary France*. London: P. S. King and Son, 1937.

Clark, Linda. *Schooling the Daughters of Marianne: Textbooks and the Socialization of Girls in Modern French Primary Schools*. Albany, N.Y.: State University of New York Press, 1984.

Cointet-Labrousse, Michèle. *Vichy et le fascisme*. Brussels: Editions complexe, 1987.

Collinet, Michel. *L'Ouvrier français, Essai sur la condition ouvrière 1900–1950*. Paris: Les Editions ouvrières, 1951.

Corbin, Alain. *Les Filles de noces: Misère sexuelle et prostitution aux 19e et 20e siècles*. Paris: Aubier, 1978.

Costantini, Clorinda. "La Presse féminine d'occupation, juin 1940–août 1944." Ph.D. diss., Université de droit, d'économie et de sciences politiques. Paris, 1980.

Coutau-Bégarie, Hervé, and Claude Huan. *Darlan*. Paris: Fayard, 1989.

Coutrot, Aline. "La Politique familiale." In *Le Gouvernement de Vichy*, 245–62. Paris: Fondation nationale des sciences politiques, 1972.

Cremieux, Albert, M. Schachter, and S. Cotte. *L'Enfant devenu délinquant: Etude médico-sociale et psychologique*. Marseilles: Comité de l'enfance déficiente, 1945.

Culture et liberté. Nogent-sur-Marne: Culture et liberté, 1979.

Dansette, Adrien. *Destin du catholicisme français 1926–1956*. Paris: Flammarion, 1957.

Daric, Jean. *L'Activité professionelle des femmes en France*. Institut national d'études démographiques. Travaux et documents 5. Paris: Presses universitaires de France, 1947.

Daridan, Jean. *Le Chemin de la défaite: 1938–1940*. Paris: Plon, 1980.

Darlan, Alain. *L'Amiral Darlan parle*. Paris: Amiot-Dumont, 1952.

David, René. *French Law: Its Structure, Sources, and Methodology*. Trans. Michael Kindred. Baton Rouge: Louisiana State University Press, 1972.

Defrasne, Jean. *Histoire de la collaboration*. Paris: Presses universitaires de France, 1982.

De Montclos, Xavier, et al., eds. *Eglises et chrétiens dans la deuxième guerre mondiale*. Lyons: Presses universitaires de Lyons, 1982.

Desforges, Jacques. *Le Divorce en France: Etude démographique*. Paris: Editions familiales de France, 1945.

Desmarest, Jacques. *La Politique de la main d'oeuvre en France*. Paris: Presses universitaires de France, 1946.

D'Hoop, Jean-Marie. "Prisonniers de guerre français témoins de la défait allemande (1945)." *Guerres mondiales et conflits contemporaines* 38, no. 150 (April 1988): 77–98.

———. "Propagande et attitudes politiques dans les camps de prisonniers: Le cas des oflags." *Revue d'histoire de la deuxième guerre mondiale* 122 (April 1981): 3–26.

Le Divorce en Europe occidentale. Vol. 1, *Données statistiques et juridiques*. Paris: La Documentation française, 1975.

Dixième Anniversaire du retour. Soissons: Association des combattants prisonniers de guerre de l'Aisne, 1955.

Doublet, Jacques. "Quelques reflexions sur les causes du divorce." *Population* 3 (July–September 1949): 557–58.

Doughty, Robert A. *The Seeds of Disaster: The Development of French Army Doctrine 1919–1939.* Hamden, Conn.: Archon Books, 1985.

Duquesne, Jacques. *Les Catholiques français sous l'occupation.* Paris: Grasset, 1966.

Durand, Yves. *La Captivité: Histoire des prisonniers de guerre français 1939–1945.* Paris: Fédération nationale des combattants prisonniers de guerre-combattants d'Algérie, Tunisie, Maroc, 1980.

————. *La France dans la deuxième guerre mondiale 1939–1945.* Paris: Armand Colin, 1989.

————. *Vichy, 1940–1944.* Paris: Bordas, 1972.

Duroselle, Jean-Baptiste. *L'Abîme 1939–1945.* Paris: Imprimerie nationale, 1982.

Dutailly, Henry. *Les Problèmes de l'armée de terre française (1935–1939).* Paris: Imprimerie nationale, 1980.

Dutourd, Jean. *Au bon buerre.* Paris: Gallimard, 1952.

Dyer, Colin. *Population and Society in Twentieth-Century France.* New York: Holmes and Meier, 1978.

Ferro, Marc. *Pétain.* Paris: Fayard, 1987.

Fisher, H. A. L. "The Codes." In *The Cambridge Modern History.* Vol. 9: *Napoleon.* Cambridge: Cambridge University Press, 1907.

Fishman, Sarah. "Grand Delusions: The Unintended Consequences of Vichy France's Prisoner of War Propaganda." *Journal of Contemporary History* 26 (April 1991): 229–54.

Fontaine, Arthur. *French Industry during the War.* New Haven: Yale University Press, 1926.

Fonvieille-Alquier, François. *The French and the Phoney War 1939–1940.* Trans. Edward Ashcroft. London: Tom Stacey, 1973.

Francos, Ania. *Il était des femmes dans la résistance.* Paris: Stock, 1978.

Frankenstein, Robert. *Le Prix du réarmement française, 1935–1939.* Paris: Publications de la Sorbonne, 1982.

The French Institute of Public Opinion. *Patterns of Sex and Love: A Study of the French Woman and Her Morals.* Trans. Lowell Bair. New York: Crown, 1961.

Funk, Arthur L. "Negotiating the 'deal with Darlan.'" *Journal of Contemporary History* 8, no. 2 (April 1973): 81–117.

Gaillard, Lucien. *Histoire de la guerre 1939–1945: La captivité.* Bibliothèque de travail no. 406, June 1958.

Garaud, Marcel, and Szramkiewicz, Romuald. "Women and the Family." In

Frank A. Kafker and James M. Laux, eds. *Napoleon and His Times: Selected Interpretations.* Malabar, Fla.: Krieger Publishing, 1989.

Garrett, Richard. *P.O.W.* London: David and Charles, 1981.

Gascar, Pierre. *Histoire de la captivité des français en Allemagne.* Paris: Gallimard, 1967.

Gemaehling, Paul. *La Statistique des divorces en France.* Paris: Berger-Levrault, 1947.

Gilbert, Sandra. "Soldier's Heart: Literary Men, Literary Women and the Great War." *Signs* 8, no. 3 (Spring 1983): 422–50.

Goblot, Edmond. *La Barrière et la niveau.* Paris: F. Alcan, 1925.

Goldman, Philippe. "La Propagande allemande auprès des prisonniers de guerre français à travers 'Le Trait-d'Union' 1940–1945." Master's thesis in contemporary history, University of Paris I: Sorbonne, n.d.

Gordon, Betram M. *Collaborationism in France during the Second World War.* Ithaca, N.Y.: Cornell University Press, 1980.

Le Gouvernement de Vichy 1940–1942. Paris: Fondation nationale des sciences politiques, 1972.

Goy, Joseph. "Civil Code." In *A Critical Dictionary of the French Revolution,* ed. François Furet and Mona Ozouf. Trans. Arthur Goldhammer. Cambridge: Harvard University Press, 1989.

Guélaud-Leridon, Françoise. *Recherches sur la condition féminine dans la société d'aujourd'hui.* Institut national d'études démographiques. Travaux et documents 48. Paris: Presses universitaires de France, 1967.

———. *Le Travail des femmes en France.* Institut national d'études démographiques. Travaux et documents 42. Paris: Presses universitaires de France, 1964.

Guerrand, Roger H. *La Libre Maternité 1896–1969.* Paris: Casterman, 1971.

Halimi, André. *La Délation sous l'occupation.* Paris: Editions Alain Moreau, 1983.

Hall, Richard C., and William Simmons. "The POW Wife: A Psychiatric Appraisal." *Archives of General Psychiatry* 29 (November 1973): 690–99.

Halls, W. D. *The Youth of Vichy France.* Oxford: Oxford University Press, 1981.

Hanford, Jeanette. "Some Case-Work Notes on the Impact of the War on Family Relationships." *The Social Service Review* 17, no. 3 (September 1943): 354–61.

Hartmann, Susan M. "Prescriptions for Penelope: Literature on Women's Obligations to Returning World War II Veterans." *Women's Studies* 5 (1978): 223–39.

Henige, David. *Oral Historiography.* New York: Longman, 1982.

Henry, Louis. "Mesure de la fréquence des divorces." *Population* 7, no. 2 (April–June 1952): 267–82.

Heuyer, G. *Enquête sur la délinquance juvénile. Etude de 400 dossiers.* Paris: Pour l'enfance "coupable," 1942.

———. "Psychopathologie de l'enfance victime de la guerre." *Sauvegarde* 17 (January 1948): 3–46.

Higonnet, Margaret, Jane Jenson, Sonya Michel, and Margaret Wietz, eds. *Behind the Lines: Gender and the Two World Wars.* New Haven: Yale University Press, 1987.

Hilden, Patricia. *Working Women and Socialist Politics in France 1880–1914.* Oxford: Clarendon Press, 1986.

Hill, Reubin, and Elise Boulding. *Families under Stress: Adjustment to the Crises of War Separation and Reunion.* New York: Harper Brothers, 1949.

Hirschfeld, Gerald, and Patrick Marsh, eds. *Collaboration in France.* New York: Berg, 1989.

Hoffmann, Stanley. "Aspects du régime de Vichy." *Revue française de science politique* 6, no. 1 (1956): 44–69.

———. "Collaborationism in France during World War II." *Journal of Modern History* 40, no. 3 (September 1968): 375–95.

———. "Paradoxes of the French Political Community." In *In Search of France,* ed. Stanley Hoffmann et al., 1–117. Cambridge: Harvard University Press, 1963.

Homze, Edward L. *Foreign Labor in Nazi Germany.* Princeton: Princeton University Press, 1967.

Hoopes, James. *Oral History, An Introduction for Students.* Chapel Hill, N.C.: University of North Carolina Press, 1979.

Horne, Alistair. *To Lose a Battle: France 1940.* London: Macmillan, 1969.

Hunter, Edna J. "Treating the Military Captive's Family." In *The Military Family: Dynamics and Treatment,* ed. Florence Kaslow and Richard I. Ridenour, 167–96. New York: Guilford, 1984.

Huss, Marie-Monique. "Pronatalism in the Inter-War Period in France." *Journal of Contemporary History* 25, no. 1 (January 1990): 39–68.

Hutt, Maurice, ed. *Napoleon.* Englewood Cliffs, N.J.: Prentice Hall, 1972.

Images de la France de Vichy. Paris: La Documentation française, 1988.

Institut d'histoire du temps présent. *Répertoire des archives centrales de la Jeunesse ouvrière chrétienne.* Paris: Centre national de la recherche scientifique, 1983.

Institut national des statistiques et des études économiques, *Mouvements de la population, Statistiques annuelles 1953–1954–1955.* Paris: Imprimerie nationale, 1966.

International Labour Office. *The Exploitation of Foreign Labour by Germany.* Montreal: International Labour Office, 1945.

Irvine, William D. *French Conservatism in Crisis*. Baton Rouge: Louisiana State University Press, 1979.

Isselé, Lucien. *Le Divorce, Les Causes admises, la procédure, les effets*. Paris: Editions sociales mercure, 1956.

Jäckel, Eberhard. *La France dans l'Europe de Hitler*. Paris: Fayard, 1968.

Jones, Adrian. "Illusions of Sovereignty: Business and the Organization Committees of Vichy France." *Social History* 11, no. 1 (January 1986): 1–31.

Joubrel, Henri, and Fernand Joubrel. *L'Enfance dite "coupable."* Paris: Bloud et Gay, 1946.

Joutard, Philippe. *Ces Voix qui nous viennent du passé*. Paris: Hachette, 1983.

Juillet, P., and P. Moutin. *Psychiatre militaire*. Paris: Masson, 1969.

Kafker, Frank A., and James M. Laux, eds. *Napoleon and His Times: Selected Interpretations*. Malabar, Fla.: Krieger, 1989.

Kedward, Roderick. *Occupied France: Collaboration and Resistance 1940–1944*. Oxford: University Press, 1985.

Kedward, Roderick, and Roger Austin, eds. *Vichy France and the Resistance*. London: Croom Helm, 1985.

Kitchen, Martin. *Europe between the Wars: A Political History*. N.Y.: Longman, 1988.

Knibiehler, Yvonne. *Nous, les assistantes sociales*. Paris: Aubier, 1980.

Knibiehler, Yvonne, and Catherine Fouquet. *L'Histoire des mères du moyen-age à nos jours*. Paris: Hachette, 1977.

Kuisel, Richard. *Capitalism and the State in Modern France*. Cambridge: Cambridge University Press, 1981.

Kupferman, Fred. *Pierre Laval*. Paris: Masson, 1976.

Lacan, Jacques. "La Psychiatrie anglaise et la guerre." *L'Evolution psychiatrique* 1 (1947): 293–318.

Larkin, Maurice. *France since the Popular Front*. Oxford: Clarendon Press, 1988.

LeBras, Gabriel, and Marc Ancel. *Divorce et séparation de corps dans le monde contemporain*. Vol. 1. Paris: Librairie du recueil sirey, 1952.

Leca, Dominique. *La Rupture de 1940*. Paris: Fayard, 1978.

Ledermann, Sully. "Les Divorces et les séparations de corps en France." *Population* 3, no. 2 (April–June 1948): 313–44.

Lefebvre, Georges. *Napoleon: From 18 Brumaire to Tilsit, 1799–1807*. Trans. Henry F. Stockhold. New York: Columbia University Press, 1969.

Levade, Maurice. *La Délinquance des jeunes en France 1825–1963*. Vol. 1. Paris: Editions cujas, 1972.

Levy, Claude. *Les Nouveaux Temps et l'idéologie de la collaboration*. Paris: Fondation nationale des sciences politiques, 1974.

Lewin, Christophe. *Le Retour des prisonniers de guerre français*. Paris: Publications de la Sorbonne, 1986.

Lottman, Herbert. *Pétain: Hero or Traitor, the Untold Story.* New York: Morrow, 1985.

McCubbin, Hamilton, et al., eds. *Family Separation and Reunion: Families of Prisoners of War and Servicemen Missing in Action.* Washington, D.C.: U.S. Government Printing Office, 1974.

McCubbin, Hamilton, Edna Hunter, and Barbara Dahl. "Residuals of War: Families of Prisoners of War and Servicemen Missing in Action." *Journal of Social Issues* 31, no. 4 (1975): 95–109.

MacIntosh, Houston. "Separation Problems in Military Wives." *American Journal of Psychiatry* 125, no. 2 (August 1968): 260–65.

McLaren, Angus. *Sexuality and Social Order, The Debate over the Fertility of Women and Workers in France 1770–1920.* New York: Holmes and Meier, 1983.

McMillan, James F. *Dreyfus to De Gaulle: Politics and Society in France 1898–1969.* London: Edward Arnold, 1985.

———. *Housewife or Harlot: The Place of Women in French Society 1870–1940.* New York: St. Martin's Press, 1981.

Marrus, Michael, and Robert Paxton. *Vichy France and the Jews.* New York: Basic, 1981.

Marwick, Arthur. *War and Social Change in the Twentieth Century.* New York: St. Martin's Press, 1974.

Mason, Tim. "Women in Germany, 1920–1940: Family, Welfare, and Work." 2 parts. *History Workshop* 1 (1976): 74–113; 2 (1976): 5–32.

Matsakis, Aphrodite. *Vietnam Wives: Women and Children Surviving Life with Veterans Suffering Post Traumatic Stress Disorder.* Kensington, Md.: Woodbine House, 1988.

Mauco, Georges. "Le Centre psycho-pedagogique de l'Académie de Paris au lycée Claude-Bernard." *Sauvegarde* 15–16 (November–December 1947): 56–65.

Mayeur, Jean-Marie, and Madeleine Rebérioux. *The Third Republic from its Origins to the Great War, 1871–1914.* Trans. J. R. Foster. New York: Cambridge University Press, 1984.

Melka, Robert L. "Darlan between Britain and Germany 1940–1941." *Journal of Contemporary History* 8, no. 2 (April 1973): 57–80.

Michel, Andrée. "France." In *Women Workers in Fifteen Countries,* ed. Jennie Farley. Ithaca, N.Y.: Cornell Labor Relations Press, 1985.

Michel, Henri. *La Défaite de la France.* Paris: Presses universitaires de France, 1980.

———. *La Drôle de guerre.* Paris: Fondation nationale des sciences politiques, 1979.

———. *Pétain, Laval, Darlan, Trois politiques?* Paris: Flammarion, 1972.

Milward, Alan. *The New Order and the French Economy.* Oxford: Clarendon Press, 1970.

Milza, Pierre. *Fascismes et idéologies réactionnaires en Europe (1919–1945).* Paris: Armand Colin, 1969.

Mommsen, W. J., and L. Kettenacher, eds. *The Fascist Challenge and the Policy of Appeasement.* London: Allen and Unwin, 1983.

Moses, Claire Goldberg. *French Feminism in the Nineteenth Century.* Albany, N.Y.: State University of New York Press, 1984.

"Les Mouvements familiaux populaires et ruraux: Naissance, développement, mutations, 1939–1955." *Les Cahiers du Groupement pour la recherche sur les mouvements familiaux* 1 (August 1983).

Mysyrowicz, Ladislas L. *Autopsie d'une défaite: Origines de l'effondrement militaire français de 1940.* Lausanne: L'Age d'homme, 1973.

Neron, Guy. *L'Enfant vagabond.* Paris: Presses universitaires de France, 1952.

Nice, Stephen, Barbara McDonald, and Tom McMillan. "The Families of U.S. Navy Prisoners of War from Vietnam Five Years after Reunion." *Journal of Marriage and Family* 43, no. 2 (1981): 431–37.

Nolte, Ernst. *The Three Faces of Fascism.* New York: Holt, Rhinehart and Winston, 1966.

Offen, Karen. "Depopulation, Nationalism, and Feminism in Fin-de-Siècle France." *American Historical Review* 89, no. 3 (June 1984): 648–76.

Ollier, Nicole. *L'Exode sur les routes de l'an 40.* Paris: Laffont, 1970.

Organization of Economic Co-operation and Development. *Historical Statistics 1960–1985.* Paris: OECD, 1987.

———. *The Integration of Women into the Economy.* Paris: OECD, 1985.

Ory, Pascal. *Les Collaborateurs 1940–1945.* Paris: Seuil, 1976.

Osgood, Samuel. *The Fall of France.* Boston: Heath, 1965.

Paxton, Robert O. *Parades and Politics at Vichy: The French Officer Corps under Marshal Pétain.* Princeton: Princeton University Press, 1966.

———. *Vichy France: Old Guard and New Order, 1940–1944.* New York: Columbia University Press, 1982.

Pearlman, Chester A. "Separation Reactions of Married Women." *American Journal of Psychiatry* 126, no. 7 (January 1970): 946–50.

Pedersen, Susan. "Social Policy and the Reconstruction of the Family in Britain and France, 1900–1945." Ph.D. diss., Harvard University, 1989.

Pierrard, Pierre. *Juifs et catholiques français.* Paris: Fayard, 1970.

Pollard, Miranda. "*Femme, Famille, France*: Vichy and the Politics of Gender, 1940–1944." Ph.D. diss., Trinity College, Dublin, 1989.

Posen, Barry R. *The Sources of Military Doctrine: France, Britain, and Germany Between the World Wars.* Ithaca, N.Y.: Cornell University Press, 1984.

"La Réforme des régimes matrimoniaux." *Sondages* 29, no. 1 (1967): 9–103.

Remond, René. *La Droite en France de 1815 à nos jours*. Paris: Aubier, 1954.

Rioux, Emmannuelle. "Les Zazous, Un Phénomène socio-culturel pendant l'occupation." Master's thesis in contemporary history, University of Paris X. Nanterre, 1987.

Romi. *Maisons closes dans l'histoire, l'art, la littérature et les moeurs*. 2 vols. Paris: Editions serg, 1965.

Ronsin, Francis. *La Grève de ventres: Propagande neo-malthusienne et baisse de la natalité en France, 19e–20e siècles*. Paris: Aubier, 1980.

Rossignol, Dominique. *Vichy et les Francs-Maçons: La Liquidation des sociétés secrètes 1940–1944*. Paris: J. C. Lattès, 1981.

Rossi-Landi, Guy. *La Drôle de guerre*. Paris: Armand Colin, 1971.

Rossiter, Margaret L. *Women in the Resistance*. New York: Praeger, 1986.

Rouast, André, and Léon Bour. *Adultère, divorce et union libre*. Paris: Editions familiales de France, 1945.

Roussel, Louis. "L'Attitude de diverses générations à l'égard du mariage de la famille et du divorce en France." *Population* 26, special number (June 1971): 101–42.

———. "Les Divorces et les séparations de corps en France (1936–1967)." *Population* 25, no. 2 (March–April 1970): 275–302.

Rousso, Henry. "L'Activité industrielle en France de 1940 à 1944: Economie 'nouvelle' et occupation allemande." *Bulletin de l'Institut d'histoire du temps présent* 38 (December 1989): 25–68.

———. *La Collaboration*. Paris: Editions MA, 1987.

———. *Le Syndrome de Vichy (1944–198 . . .)*. Paris: Seuil, 1987.

Sauvy, Alfred. *Richesse et population*. 2d ed. Paris: Payot, 1944.

———. *La Vie économique des français de 1939 à 1945*. Paris: Flammarion, 1978.

Scheiber, A. *Un Fléau social. Le Problème medico-policier de la prostitution*. Paris: Librairie de Medicis, 1946.

Schuker, Stephen A. "France and the Remilitarization of the Rhineland, 1936." *French Historical Studies* 14, no. 3 (Spring 1986): 299–338.

Schwartz, Paula L. "*Partisanes* and Gender Politics in Vichy France." *French Historical Studies* 16, no. 1 (Spring 1989): 126–51.

———. "Precedents for Politics: Pre-War Activism in Women of the French Resistance." Master's thesis, Columbia University, 1981.

Segal, Julius, Edna Hunter, and Zelda Segal. "Universal Consequences of Captivity: Stress Reactions among Divergent Populations of Prisoners of War and their Families." *International Social Science Journal* 28, no. 3 (1976): 594–97.

"Seizième Rapport sur la situation démographique de la France." *Population* 42, nos. 4–5 (July–October 1987): 605–48.

Shamgar-Handelman, Lea. *Israeli War Widows: Beyond the Glory of Heroism.* South Hadley, Mass.: Bergin and Garvey, 1986.

Smith, James P., and Michael P. Ward. *Women's Wages and Work in the Twentieth Century.* Santa Monica: Rand, 1984.

Sohn, Anne-Marie. "*La Garçonne* face à l'opinion publique: Type littéraire ou type social des années 20?" *Le Mouvement social* 80 (July–September 1972): 3–27.

Sorlin, Pierre. "The Struggle for Control of French Minds." In *Film and Radio Propaganda in World War II,* ed. K. R. M. Short, 245–68. London: Croom Helm, 1983.

Soucy, Robert J. *French Fascism: The First Wave 1924–1933.* New Haven: Yale University Press, 1986.

———. "French Fascist Intellectuals in the 1930s: An Old New Left?" *French Historical Studies* 8, no. 3 (Spring 1974): 445–58.

———. "The Nature of Fascism in France." *Journal of Contemporary History* 1, no. 1 (1966): 27–56.

Sowerwine, Charles. *Sisters or Citizens? Women and Socialism in France since 1876.* Cambridge: Cambridge University Press, 1982.

Sternhell, Zeev. *La Droite révolutionnaire, 1855–1914: Les Origines françaises du fascisme.* Paris: Seuil, 1978.

———. *Ni droite ni gauche: L'Idéologie fasciste en France.* Paris: Seuil, 1983.

Strebel, Elizabeth. "Vichy Cinema and Propaganda." In *Film and Radio Propaganda in World War II,* ed. K. R. M. Short, 271–89. London: Croom Helm, 1983.

Struminger, Laura S. *Women and the Making of the Working Class: Lyon 1830–1870.* St. Albans, Vt.: Eden Press, 1978.

Sullerot, Evelyne. *Les Françaises au travail.* Paris: Hachette, 1973.

———. *Histoire et sociologie du travail féminin.* Paris: Gonthier, 1968.

———. *Pour le meilleur et sans le pire.* Paris: Fayard, 1984.

Sweets, John. *Choices in Vichy France.* New York: Oxford University Press, 1986.

Szpiner, Francis. *Une Affaire de femmes, Paris 1943, Execution d'une avorteuse.* Editions Balland, 1986.

Talmy, Robert. *Histoire du mouvement familiale en France 1896–1939.* 2 vols. Paris: L'Union nationale des caisses d'allocations familiales, 1962.

Thomas, Keith. "The Double Standard." *Journal of the History of Ideas* 20, no. 2 (April 1959): 195–216.

Tompkins, Peter. *The Murder of Admiral Darlan.* New York: Simon and Schuster, 1965.

Un de la résistance, Francis Chirat. Paris: Les Editions ouvrières, 1945.

United Nations. *Demographic Yearbook.* 10th ed. New York: UN, 1958.

———. *Demographic Yearbook (1985).* 37th ed. New York: UN, 1987.

————. *The Economic Role of Women in the ECE Region.* New York: UN, 1980.

U.S. Department of Health and Human Services. *Vital Statistics of the United States.* Vol. 3: Marriage and Divorce. Hyattsville, Maryland. 1989.

Vallot, Françoise. "Mariages et divorces à Paris: Analyse des actes de mariage de quatre cohortes." *Population* 26, special number (June 1971): 67–100.

Veillon, Dominique. *La Collaboration. Textes et débats.* Paris: Hachette, 1984.

————. *La Mode sous l'occupation.* Paris: Payot, 1990.

————. "Résister au féminin." *Pénélope* 12 (Spring 1985): 87–92.

Vidalenc, Jean. *L'Exode du mai–juin 1940.* Paris: Presses universitaires de France, 1957.

La Vie de la France sous l'occupation 1940–1944. Paris: Librairie Plon, 1957.

Vignal, Thierry. "Bibliographie analytique de la politique démographique de la France depuis 1939." Report. Institut national des techniques de la documentation, 1960.

Vittori, Jean-Pierre. *Eux, les S.T.O.* Paris: Temps actuels, 1982.

Vuillemin, Jules. *Le Problème prisonnier.* Paris: Editions du chêne, 1945.

Warner, Geoffrey. *Pierre Laval and the Eclipse of France.* London: Eyre and Spottiswoode, 1968.

Weber, Eugen. *Action française.* Stanford: Stanford University Press, 1962.

————. "Nationalism, Socialism, and National-Socialism in France." *French Historical Studies* 2, no. 3 (Spring 1962): 273–307.

Williams, John. *The Home Fronts: Britain, France, and Germany 1914–1918.* London: Constable, 1972.

Wright, Gordon. *France in Modern Times.* 3d ed. New York: Norton, 1981.

Wylie, Laurence. *Village in the Vaucluse.* 3d ed. Cambridge: Harvard University Press, 1974.

Young, Robert J. *In Command of France: French Foreign Policy and Military Planning.* Cambridge: Harvard University Press, 1978.

Zdatny, Steven M. *The Politics of Survival: Artisans in Twentieth-Century France.* New York: Oxford University Press, 1990.

Zeldin, Theodore. *France 1848–1945: Ambition and Love.* Oxford: Oxford University Press, 1979.

INTERVIEWS

Paulette Aouroux, member of the Commission nationale des Veuves, FNCPG.

Andrée Aulas, President, FAFP.

Jeanne Bajeux, president of the Service des femmes de Prisonniers, MPF.

Jules Braunshwig, former prisoner of war, past president of the Alliance israélite.

Agnès Griot, director of publications, FAFP.

Jacqueline Join-Lambert, wife of Pierre Join-Lambert of the CGPGR.

Josette Morisson, member of the Commission nationale des veuves, FNCPG.
Robert Paumier, former prisoner of war, former secretary general of FNCPG-CATM.
Jean Vedrine, former prisoner of war, original director of the Centre d'entr'aide.

Name (changed)	*Place*
Patricia Agard	La Cluse
Jacqueline and Roger Ariel	Ste. Foy-les-Lyon
Sabine Blondel	Marcheinnes
Dominique Briand	Bernaville
Arièle Chevalier	Roanne
Marie-Hélène Corbel	Paris
Evelyne Crinon	Villefranche
Fernande Damart	Bernaville
Gisèle Desbois	Paris
Anne Devron	Paris
Aline and Maurice Didier	Paris
Micheline Doisy	Paris
Elisabeth and Jean Doremus	Bernaville
Germaine and Raymond Doucet	Paris
Michelle Dupuy	Roanne
Suzette Emile	Roanne
Lucienne Fontaine	Oloron Ste. Marie
Josette Garnier	Bron
Yvette Giraud	Paris
Hélène Jamon	Paris
Annick Kasmer	Paris
Isabelle and Joseph LeRoux	Doullens
Patricia Longet	Roanne
Josette Lorin	Nanterre
Marie-Louise Mercier	Le Havre
Florence Morin	Paris
Raymonde Moulin	St. Cloud
Monique Roussel	Paris
Estelle Sergent	Paris
Anne-Marie Vacher	Montrouge

Letters and Questionnaires

Germaine Adelet	Bernaville
Sophie Aimé	Laxou
Annick Bachelet	Montpellier
Anne Barat	Quimperle

Name (changed)	*Place*
Monique Becht	Lyons
Odette Bondois	Montpellier
Nicolle Bouchard	Bernaville
Agnès Brossier	Panazol
Louise Cadieu	Le Havre
Jeanne Capel	Chateauroux
Madeleine Capot	Paris
Camille Cassan	Montpellier
Martine Celier	Bernaville
Gabrielle Coadelot	Mimbaste
Sylvie Crouet	St. Berthevin
Claudine Dages	Montpellier
Hélène Daniel	St. Yrieux-la-Perche
Isabelle Dreux	Mimbaste
Robert Farge	Nice
Odile Faverot	Lyons
Dominique Filasto	Mimbaste
Suzanne Goupillat	Polliaunay
Marthe Jolliet	Le Mans
Josiane Lafont	Sable
Huguette Lagadec	Mimbaste
Sarah and Bernard Lisik	Besançon
Martine Lombardi	Paris
Josette Lorin	Nanterre
Francine Louvet	Chatellerault
Béatrice Madier	Nanterre
Monique Madier	Jarnac
Elisabeth Manceau	Limay
Hélène Manceau	Malakoff
Joelle Meliard	Chatellerault
Catherine Michel	Laval
Agnès Minot	Mimbaste
Christianne Motte	Verfiel
Lucette Nauman	Colombes
Louise Neron	Chartres
Hélène Noiret	Connantre
Monique Peletier	Chatellerault
Anne-Marie Perrin	Malakoff
Léonie Poirier	Le Havre

Name (changed)	*Place*
Annette Regnier	Le Havre
Françoise Ruffin	Versailles
Constance Sorel	Lyons
Stéphanie Thibault	Mimbaste
Béatrice Varan	Cabannes
Gilberte Voisin	La Côte St. André